Writing Alberta

THE WEST SERIES

Aritha van Herk, Series Editor

ISSN 1922-6519 (Print) ISSN 1925-587X (Online)

This series focuses on creative non-fiction that explores our sense of place in the West - how we define ourselves as Westerners and what impact we have on the world around us. Essays, biographies, memoirs, and insights into Western Canadian life and experience are highlighted.

UNIVERSITY OF CALGARY
Press

Writing Alberta

Building on a Literary Identity

edited by
George Melnyk and
Donna Coates

THE WEST Series
ISSN 1922-6519 (Print) ISSN 1925-587X (Online)

University of Calgary Press
2500 University Drive NW
Calgary, Alberta
Canada T2N 1N4
press.ucalgary.ca

LIBRARY AND ARCHIVES CANADA CATALOGUING IN PUBLICATION

Writing Alberta : building on a literary identity / edited by George Melnyk and Donna Coates.

(The west series ; 10)
Includes bibliographical references.
Issued in print and electronic formats.
ISBN 978-1-55238-890-7 (softcover).—ISBN 978-1-55238-891-4 (open access PDF).—ISBN 978-1-55238-892-1 (PDF).—ISBN 978-1-55238-893-8 (EPUB).—ISBN 978-1-55238-894-5 (Kindle)

1. Canadian literature—Alberta—History and criticism.
I. Coates, Donna, 1944-, editor II. Melnyk, George, editor
III. Series: West series (Calgary, Alta.) ; 10

PS8131.A43W75 2017   C810.9'97123   C2017-902847-2

C2017-902848-0

The University of Calgary Press acknowledges the support of the Government of Alberta through the Alberta Media Fund for our publications. We acknowledge the financial support of the Government of Canada. We acknowledge the financial support of the Canada Council for the Arts for our publishing program.

 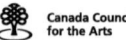 Canada Council for the Arts   Conseil des Arts du Canada

Printed and bound in Canada by Marquis
♲ This book is printed on Enviro Book 100 paper

Copyediting by Francine Michaud
Cover image *Chinook Arch*. Marion Twyman (artist), Kristina Twyman (photographer)
Cover design, page design, and typesetting by Melina Cusano

Table of Contents

Writing Alberta: Continuities, Interventions, and Lacunae

George Melnyk and Donna Coates

In 2005, art critic Mary-Beth Laviolette published *An Alberta Art Chronicle* covering the post-1970 art history of Alberta. Its length of five hundred pages suggested that there was something to say about the province's art scene. To talk about an Alberta art identity within the context of Canadian art does not seem strange or unusual. So, too, it should not seem strange to talk about an Alberta literary identity. The conversation started sixty years ago with the publication of the *Alberta Golden Jubilee Anthology* in 1955. It offered Albertans their first collection of Alberta writers and was followed in 1967 with *Chinook Arch* and *The Alberta Diamond Jubilee Anthology* in 1979. In 1986, Fred Stenson edited *Alberta Bound: Thirty Stories by Alberta Writers*, followed by Aritha van Herk's 1990 volume, *Alberta Rebound: Thirty More Stories by Alberta Writers*, and then *Boundless Alberta* in 1993. Clearly, at least as far as fiction was concerned, there was an acknowledgement that Alberta writers were producing valuable work and making a statement about the province. In 1999 a new anthology, *Threshold: An Anthology of Contemporary Writing from Alberta*, edited by Srjda Pavlovic, which included poetry, was published. Pavlovic was not afraid to use the term "Alberta literature" in his introduction. All seven volumes were statements of creativity, not critical studies. Then came George Melnyk's two-volume *Literary History of Alberta*, published in 1998-99, which argued for the distinct nature of Alberta's literary identity. It was followed by the four-hundred-page *Wild Rose Anthology of Alberta Prose* (2003), edited by George Melnyk and Tamara Palmer Seiler and, most recently,

Wild Words: Essays on Alberta Literature (2009), edited by Donna Coates and George Melnyk, which was the first collection of scholarly essays dealing specifically with Alberta writing.

Alberta writing has a distinctive literary identity, but there has been a pushback from traditional quarters tied to previous categories—Canadian Literature (1960s) and Prairie Literature (1970s). In Quebec, literature was viewed as independent of Canadian literature because of the post-1960 sovereignty movement and its distinctness within the context of a bi-national and bilingual literary identity. But what could justify a province like Alberta seeing its literary heritage as identifiable and distinct? If we examine how national literatures come to be defined, we can see that Alberta literature shares characteristics with the terms used to define a national literature without being a nation. First, Alberta literature has a *history* that is identifiable, traceable, and acknowledged. Second, its literature shares certain *thematic concerns* that link its writers. Third, its literature has a specific hierarchy of important writers and works. In short, it has a *canon*. Fourth, Alberta literature shares the limits placed on national literatures by having a political *boundary*. While these are categories normally applied to a national literature, a provincial literature can be studied much in the same way through history, authorship, literary styles, thematic concerns, and cultural identity.

The literary history of Alberta extends from the pictographs and winter counts of the First Nations, through the writing of explorers and fur traders to the fiction and non-fiction books of European settlers, and then through the emergence of the first voices of modernism through to the postmodernist experimentation and post-colonialism of the late twentieth and early twenty-first centuries. This history has a number of unifying themes: the diverse geography and landscapes of the province, the socio-economic evolution of its peoples, the quest for a sense of selfhood that distinguishes it from the rest of Canada, and the desire to be expressive of, and connected to, literary trends in the western world. The literary history and its themes are united through a literary canon, which began with William Francis Butler's 1872 non-fiction classic, *The Great Lone Land*, followed by Robert Stead's trilogy of *Prairie* novels, and Georges Bugnet's masterful *La Forêt (The Forest)*. W.O. Mitchell's much beloved *Who Has Seen the Wind* inaugurated a postwar literature that included Sheila Watson's *The Double Hook*, Robert Kroetsch's *The Studhorse Man*,

Rudy Wiebe's *The Temptations of Big Bear*, and Aritha van Herk's *Judith*. Together, these writers and their colleagues confirmed the power of Alberta writing in the second half of the twentieth century through both national and international recognition. More recently, the post-colonial sensibility has been expressed through Esi Edugyan's award-winning *Half-Blood Blues*, while the poetry of Christian Bök has challenged the boundaries of that genre. But there are complexities involved in cultural milieus that come from the overlap and interaction of cultural innovation across international boundaries. Alberta is not an isolated literary environment and never has been from the time of exploration literature.

However, there are also characteristics that reflect a specific socio-political environment. Alberta has had a non-conformist political history, with two political parties having ruled the province for a total of eighty years (Social Credit 1935-70 and Progressive Conservatives 1971-2015). This history played a role in developing the province's literary identity. For example, the first three anthologies of Alberta writing were all sponsored or funded by the Alberta government, a cultural intervention that is not the norm in English Canada. Cultural identity within a political discourse can be turned into a rhetoric of homogeneity, but the cultural material itself is diverse and offers resistance and a homogenous narrative. This is the main theme of this volume. What this volume suggests is that this homogeneity of political culture has generated counter-narratives that subvert the dominant conservative ideology that has come to characterize the province. In *Mavericks: An Incorrigible History of Alberta*, van Herk concludes: "The emblem of our province is the prickly wild rose, a hardly fenceline thorn, pretty and tough—just like Alberta" (405). The flowering pink thorn is an apt metaphor for Alberta writing.

An attempt to define an "Alberta writer" may be contentious, but identity is also an area of debate and disagreement in national literatures, especially in our postmodern, post-colonial age of major migration. When does a migrant writer's work become part of Canadian literature, especially if it deals with that writer's mother country? Place of birth is one designation; current residence is another; language is a third; and setting is a fourth. There are other possible criteria as well. In Alberta's pre-agrarian period, writers who passed through the geographic area—now designated as Alberta—but who did not live in it but wrote about it, should have their works on the territory considered part of Alberta writing, even though they may also belong to another national literature, be it British or American. Their writings contribute to both Alberta's literary identity and to the identity of their national literature. A contemporary example, discussed in this collection, is David Albahari, born in the former Yugoslavia, who came to Alberta in 1994 and departed for Serbia in 2012. He wrote his novels and short stories in Serbian, and the greater part of his writing during his Alberta years was set in Europe. Only some of his fiction was Alberta-specific. We consider those works to be part of Alberta literature, though Albahari clearly belongs to the literature of the former Yugoslavia which was his birth country that existed until the twenty-first century, in name at least, but which is now politically constructed as Serbia. Today he is regarded as a Serbian writer, since Yugoslavia no longer exists. All the writers we discuss in this volume were either born in Alberta, have lived or live in Alberta, or have written about Alberta. It is the influence of the place on their writing that matters and how that writing has contributed to articulating the province. Likewise, a writer or a work can be considered as overlapping with, and connected to, other literary identities, whether national or regional. While political scientists may be attuned to drawing boundaries, literary scholars acknowledge that drawing boundaries around identities is problematic, contested, and open to revision.

This collection highlights the continuities, the interventions, and the lacunae that make up Alberta literature from the perspective of the twenty-first century. We have chosen these three concepts and the tensions they generate because they undermine the idea of a central theme or dominant concept. It is up to the reader, as much as the editors, to determine what may or may not be present in Alberta writing. In terms of continuity, the volume provides essays on playwriting of the 1930s, while also showing the role of Alberta-themed opera from the 2000s. Or, as in the case of the essay by the novelist Katherine Govier, there is valuable information on the role of place in her writing even though she is no longer resident in Alberta. But there are also other foci at play. There is the sense of interruption or intervention that comes whenever something new erupts on the literary scene, such as work or works that jerk literature out of its complacency and its accepted pathways to push the literary agenda to a new level or in a new direction. The literary postmodernism of Robert Kroetsch that Harry Vandervlist discusses in Chapter Eight is a good example. Finally, there are lacunae and gaps in a literature that are spaces that wait to be filled, elements that have been ignored or forgotten that are resurrected and assert themselves in a way as to question all that has gone before them. Tasha Hubbard's discussion of First Nations and Métis writing brings to light sensibilities that formerly had no voice. By putting these three foci together, we believe this collection strengthens and expands our understanding of who has contributed to and what constitutes the strength of Alberta literature.

Wild Words: Essays on Alberta Literature signaled the academic recognition of a "distinct literary identity" that could be named Alberta literature, but it was not specific about the content of that distinctness (Coates and Melnyk vii). This introduction attempts to put meat on the bones of that concept while recognizing the complexity, inter-textuality, and non-generic qualities of Alberta writing. *Writing Alberta* is the next step in defining Alberta literature through scholarly analysis. The chapters are structured to emphasize the interplay of past and present in Alberta writing. This volume itself is an act of continuity (it follows on *Wild Words*) and an act of intervention (it brings something new to the study of the field), but it has its limitations because it leaves out numerous talented writers and significant works. Grounding itself in the contemporary, it seeks to connect with past manifestations of writing.

This non-chronological, non-thematic, and non-generic structure is a postmodernist response to the rationale of the first anthology, the *Alberta Golden Jubilee Anthology* (1955), whose editor W.G. Hardy, a historical novelist and classicist at the University of Alberta, stated that its goal was "to present chronologically the story of the province" (13). As a modernist of the late agrarian period, his ties were very much with a Euro-centric settler society wanting to celebrate a historical sense of itself through literature. Of the contributors to that early volume only a few remain significant—R. Ross Annett, Elsie Park Gowan, Henry Kreisel, W. O. Mitchell, and Kerry Wood. Twelve years later John Patrick Gillese edited *Chinook Arch: A Centennial Anthology of Alberta Writing* to commemorate Canada's centennial. While Hardy's volume drew one thousand submissions, Gillese's received two thousand. An increase in population could not justify such an explosion of submissions. Clearly there was something else at work. Gillese, using a rhetorical tone, states that "No people has ever become great without its own literature" (xi). With Canadian literature just beginning its age of self-consciousness, Gillese's placing Alberta squarely in the mix was a welcome move. Among the new names that appear in his anthology that are central to Alberta literature are the Franco-Albertan novelist, Georges Bugnet; the genre novelist, Marie Jakober; the Ukrainian Alberta novelist, Illia Kiriak; the Icelandic Albertan poet, Stephan G. Stephansson; and the non-fiction writer, and later Lieutenant-Governor of Alberta, Grant MacEwan.

John W. Chalmers viewed the *Alberta Diamond Jubilee Anthology* as a reflection of the energy and diversity of Alberta's literary culture. Among the surprises in his volume were the first appearance of Nellie McClung and Wilfrid Eggleston. Why such valued writers were omitted earlier is a mystery. Perhaps the requirement of the first two volumes, that work had to be submitted by the authors, was a factor. By 1979, there was a growing sense of who were important Alberta writers. The 1979 anthology can be considered a proto-literary canon, but it remained very much a populist phenomenon, as were the previous two. It created an imaginary equality (a work by W. O. Mitchell was given the same space as a work by Elsie Wilson Colby) and it heralded the voice of the known and the unknown with equal vigour. Nevertheless, until George Melnyk's two-volume *Literary History of Alberta* appeared in the late 1990s, there had been little critical work done on the subject. Today Alberta literature is no longer a young literature. It has a history and a tradition. The subtitle of this volume, "Building on a Literary Identity," acknowledges that history.

In her "Introduction" to *Wild Words*, Aritha van Herk asks "What does an Alberta writer encompass?" She concludes that "there is simply no essential set of measures that can delineate an Alberta writer" (2). She's right. It is not the goal of this volume to delineate an essential Albertanism. Instead, it purports to expose the historically contingent nature of so much of Alberta writing and to show how defining a literary identity is always a work-in-progress. This volume contains thirteen essays that range from bio-literary discussions of historical figures to critical studies of single texts. The result is not a straight line from point A to point B. Rather, it is a tenuous thread that zigzags and spirals back and forth. While we gradually move the reader from now to then, the contributors mix genres, literary styles, and also make bold comparisons. It is the sign of the maturity of a literature that it can withstand deviation and controversy. It is also the sign of a mature literature that it can challenge, deconstruct, and resist the conventional and the official. If this volume demonstrates anything, it is that Alberta writers, especially in the contemporary period, are not afraid to uncover, re-think, and re-imagine parts of Alberta history, exposing what had been lain to rest as unfinished business needing serious re-consideration. The work of Fred Stenson is a prime example.

We begin this volume with a work of creative non-fiction by the novelist Katherine Govier, in which she explores her relationship to Alberta, both personally and in her fiction. It is an acknowledgement that the writer is the primary focus of this volume and it is valuable to see how writers reflect on their own work. Born and raised in Edmonton, Govier spent her post-adolescence in central Canada, where she developed a major career as a novelist. "Where is home?" she asks, when she has spent half her life split between Alberta and Toronto. Her answer is that "home" is an interior concept that melds memory and experience into a sense of attachment, of belonging. After describing moments of remembrance from her days in Edmonton, she offers a synopsis of her writing and those of her works that were Alberta-influenced. Because she has seen Alberta from "afar" as well as lived its identity, her fiction carries the tension of her observer-participant status. Today her literary consciousness has returned to Alberta with a novel about Canmore and Banff National Park, *The Three Sisters Bar and Hotel* (2016).

The next chapter is a complex and intense discussion of First Nations writing by Tasha Hubbard. In "'My Bones Have Known this Land Long Before Alberta Was Born': Intersections in Indigenous Geography and Indigenous Creative Expression," Hubbard points out that canonical prairie literature and criticism have been shaped by colonialism "entrenched" in a white-male-settler tradition. Even though the land was occupied by thousands of Indigenous peoples and as many as thirty million buffalo, settlers regarded the land as an empty space for them to conquer. Ironically, by the 1880s, as a result of what Hubbard terms a "lethal combination of military intervention, government policy, and private enterprise," that empty space was achieved, the buffalo were extinct and the Indigenous Peoples ravaged in part through treaty promises which were ignored. Often with a comprehensive background to historic Indigenous concerns, Hubbard's essay then examines the poetry of Indigenous poets Beth Cuthand, Marilyn Dumont, and Louise Halfe, who document the legacies of being removed and dislocated from the land the Indigenous peoples shared with the buffalo. Their poems suggest that the western conceptions of land are far more complex when seen through the eyes of the Indigenous, who regard themselves to be part of an "interconnected and dynamic place filled with history and meaning." As women, they not only seek to write back to the "imposition of white male space on the land," but also through their poetry to "lament, remember, and rejuvenate the relationship between land, buffalo, and Indigenous peoples," which may also be read as "acts of resistance" against historical injustices, including genocide. Hubbard's essay stresses that Indigenous peoples and their stories of the buffalo are now a growing aspect of Indigenous literatures.

Tamara Palmer Seiler takes up the issue of historical justice or injustice in her comparative study of *Filumena*, an opera by John Estacio and John Murrell, and Betty Jane Hegerat's creative non-fiction book, *the Boy*. Both works are creative treatments of murder and the execution of those found guilty of the crimes. Seiler argues that the two works have similar "narrative strategies," since they are both hybrid art forms. The literary form is a hybrid of fiction and non-fiction, while the opera is a combination of performance and song (lyrics and music), drama and concert. Because both works are based on historical events that happened in Alberta, their Alberta authors have to retain a factual core, while meeting the demands of creativity and storytelling. Seiler's goal is to identify "the similarities between seemingly dissimilar works." The book tells the story of a family that was murdered in central Alberta in the 1950s and the young man who was executed for the crime. The opera tells the story of two Italian immigrants to the Crowsnest district of southern Alberta who were hanged for the murder of a policeman in the 1920s.

Seiler sees *Filumena* as a work of creative non-fiction. The librettist John Murrell worked with the known facts and with the prerequisites of grand opera and its tradition of tragic heroines. The result is "an accurate rendering of known facts," while creating an intense experience of the "redemptive power of the human spirit." She describes *the Boy* as a "work of historiographic metafiction," by which she means a fiction "grounded in historical, social, and political realities." Using two narratives, the author of the book offers non-fictional and fictional elements for consideration. This structure allows the author to surpass the strict limits imposed by journalistic accounts of events and personalities. Seiler points out that in both cases—the opera and the book—their narrative strategies are able to put a human face on formerly rigid categories like murderer and victim, and she concludes by noting that if all narratives are captive to conventions in storytelling, the combining of fact and fiction allows the human spirit of those involved to receive a fuller representation.

The blend of fiction and history used in the counter-narratives of Seiler's study raises the issue of the current state of critical writing and thinking in Alberta. Whenever an ideological construct comes to dominate a subject matter through state and media loyalties, anti-narratives appear that question and challenge this discourse. This has certainly been the case on environmental issues and the contribution of Alberta's energy industry to pollution and climate change. Geo Takach analyzes the work of two Calgary-based non-fiction writers on environmental issues, Chris Turner and Andrew Nikiforuk, who have developed national and international reputations. Both writers represent a reaction to the unrelenting tar sands' development of this century that propelled Alberta into the forefront of climate change, sustainability, and Aboriginal rights debates on a global scale. Takach sees the tar sands as the defining issue for Alberta. That two Alberta writers should take on this history of unrelenting energy development is a noteworthy example of the crucial role that writers play in public discourse.

Takach begins with a crash course in environmental literature and its history in the province. He then turns to Nikiforuk's work and what he terms his emphasis on "the land as a maternal shelter." He surveys each of his books, including his 2011 work on the voracious pine beetle and how global warming has contributed to its destruction of North American forests and his highly provocative 2012 book, *The Energy of Slaves: Oil and the New Servitude*, in which he draws parallels between the southern American plantation system and our own energy servitude. Takach concludes that Nikiforuk is fundamentally a moralist who "wants to scare, anger, and shame us into curing our addiction to fossil fuel." While Nikiforuk seeks to slay the beast with condemnation, Chris Turner seeks to slay it by offering alternatives.

Chris Turner burst on the national scene with his first environmental book *The Geography of Hope* (2007), which studies green innovations around the world and argues that their success (wind power) means that alternative energy sources can help us lower our carbon footprint and influence climate change through reducing greenhouse gas emissions. His second book, *The Leap: How to Survive and Thrive in the Sustainable*

Economy (2011), builds on the technological and scientific focus of the first book, with a call to re-thinking how we view economic growth and the costs of the status quo. Takach considers Turner a thinker who "wants to inspire us to leap into a brave new world of environmental sustainability." Both writers, in Takach's view, have produced a new corpus that "transcends much of the body of nature writing that preceded them in Alberta." In an environmental apocalyptic age, they have provided two contrasting approaches to fundamental change. Turner's techno-utopianism can find more traction in a corporate environment than Nikiforuk's preaching about social and environmental evil. Turner is currently writing a book about the tar sands at a time when Alberta has a new government (NDP) ready to make *some* changes to the historical narrative about wealth, jobs, and the oil patch.

While First Nations writers, environmental writers, and creative non-fiction writers spar with established narratives about events and peoples, the immigrant writer engages with Alberta at a different level. Diasporic existence is a conflicted region of the mind. A writer formed in another world, through another language, and within a different culture, must navigate the shoals of the unfamiliar, the very strange, and the confusing when arriving in Alberta. Recent examples of that navigation have been the Alberta novels of David Albahari, a Serbian writer who came to Calgary in 1994 to take up a one-year post as Distinguished Writer-in-Residence at the University of Calgary. Because of the civil war in the former Yugoslavia (1991-99), he chose to stay in Calgary after his appointment ended, and to live in Alberta as a writer. He visited his homeland annually to launch new titles because he wrote all his books in Serbian. He is a prolific novelist, short story writer, essayist, and translator who published over a dozen novels, a few short story collections, and other work during his years in Calgary. Considered a literary giant in his birth country with work translated into thirty languages, he remains relatively unknown in Alberta and throughout Canada.

Albahari published three novels that deal specifically with Alberta during the time he lived in Calgary. The first is *Snow Man* (Serbian 1995, English 2005); the second is *Bait* (Serbian 1996, English 2001); and the third is *Globetrotter* (Serbian 2001, English 2014). Melnyk's essay examines these three works and their avant-garde and postmodern writing style. Each novel appears as a surrealist narrative that is one paragraph and often told in the first person by a disembodied voice. Melnyk views Albahari's Alberta novels as a twenty-first-century continuation of the European immigrant literature that began a century earlier with writers such as Stephan G. Stephansson, Georges Bugnet, Laura Salverson, and Illa Kiriak. While the split personality that inhabits diaspora writers generates hybridity in some, in others it casts a different shadow. In Albahari's case, the unwavering commitment to writing in Serbian has created a language barrier that was only occasionally breached by translation. It also meant that Albahari had a focus on Europe, with his Alberta novels being only a minor part of his output during his time in Calgary.

Melnyk points out that Albahari's novels are defined primarily by a postmodern sensibility that sees the world as a pastiche of impressions and subjectivities. Alberta appears in these three novels as a place in which his protagonists evolve from a state of uncertainty and confusion (*Snow Man*) to a genuine identification with place (*Globetrotter*). There is a movement from an initial world of shadows and fog to a concluding world of historical light that indicates that a new world has come to be understood. Melnyk concludes that Calgary was a place of refuge for Albahari from which he could observe his European roots in a state of creative peace. His European imagination was nurtured by the province's lack of ethnic strife and bloody history. It was a space of peace from which he developed a major reputation. He returned to Serbia in 2012 when he was in his mid-sixties.

While the diasporic imagination engages with a new reality through tension and uncertainty, an imagination that feels at home in Alberta seeks to know the place through a careful study of its aura. This is the case of the poet Alice Major, who has spent many years in Edmonton. In "Science and the City: The Poetics of Alice Major's Edmonton," Neil Querengesser notes that Edmonton's first poet laureate, Alice Major (2005-07), has expressed her empathy and love for her adopted city throughout eleven books of poetry. Querengesser's essay, a penetrating and insightful study, convincingly demonstrates how Major incorporates the ideas, facts, and discourse of science into much of her work, particularly that dealing with her adopted city since the 1980s. Through a close reading of several poems that apply such perspectives as the psychological, anthropological, and geographical to the people and places of Edmonton, from the denizens of funky cafés to the bedrock of the North Saskatchewan River, Querengesser effectively complements Major's own unique and sometimes startling renditions of this rich and varied urban landscape. He further notes that Major's poetry also contains numerous allusions to literary works and their writers, which add to her creation of vivid poetic images. While Querengesser observes that Major "has the advantage of seeing this city from fresh and imaginative perspectives," his essay suggests those who read her challenging poetry (with Querengesser as an informed tour guide) will also undoubtedly find their own perspectives on this northern prairie city much enhanced.

Alberta has a murky and sometimes unsavoury past, which contemporary writers have worked hard to expose, so that the province's history has become an important element or source for writing in Alberta. In "Double Vision and *Jennie's Story*," Cynthia Zimmerman writes that *Jennie's Story* (1987), a play by Calgary-born Betty Lambert, is based on a true story about Jennie, a prairie teenager sexually abused by a priest who employed her as a domestic during the 1930s. Told she needed to have her appendix removed, Jennie was taken to Calgary for the operation. Years later, happily married but unable to conceive, Jennie discovers that she had been lied to—that she had, in fact, been legally sterilized under The Sexual Sterilization Act (Alberta 1928). Zimmerman's essay explains why, given the heart-breaking dimensions of the story, Lambert should have chosen to give the play a happy ending, a question that has puzzled many critics and reviewers. The wretched tale of *Jennie's Story*, by Betty Lambert, should be familiar to many Alberta readers, who will recall that Leilani Muir, who had been unjustly sterilized as "mentally defective" in 1959, sought legal counsel to sue the Alberta Government for wrongful sterilization. The success of that case, launched in 1995, led to the Alberta Government's apology for the forced sterilization of more than two thousand and eight hundred people, as well as the rewarding of large sums of money in damages to survivors.

It is clear from the range of work discussed to this point that Alberta's socio-economic history and its treatment of human beings and the environment falls short on a number of fronts. How a writer generates new insights from selecting historical forms of writing such as "hornbooks" is evident in Harry Vandervlist's highly imaginative and insightful comparison of Robert Kroetsch's *The Hornbooks of Rita K.*, a reflection on poetics, with the work of the American minimalist conceptual artist, James Turrell. In particular, Vandervlist examines Turrell's "Twilight Arch" installation from 1991, referenced on several occasions in *The Hornbooks*.

A hornbook was simply a piece of wood with a handle on which there was writing. In the eighteenth and nineteenth centuries, they were used to teach children when books were not available. Because Vandervlist decides that both works are "unusual," he delves into the nature of their deviation from generic norms. He sees both works as engaging with "the concepts of framing and transparency" and being self-reflective on "fundamental artistic processes," and how both attempt to transcend the "ordinary experience" of art. Vandervlist explores the convergence of two different media by searching for their commonalities. The focus of the convergence is their framing of absence and the tools each creator uses to *highlight* a presence through absence. He concludes that the main difference between Turrell's art and Kroetsch's can be understood as the former's individual-response goals, while the latter's work "retains irreducibly social elements." Vandervlist's exploration of the elemental features of both works brings a new perspective to Kroetsch's engagement with writing at a reflective point in his career. Like Seiler's comparison of creative non-fiction with an opera, Vandervlist's comparison of literature and art opens the door to trans-generic art forms and the cross-fertilization of different media. This cross-fertilization is particularly important for expanding the traditional boundaries of the written word in Alberta.

A move beyond traditional prose styles had occurred several decades earlier in the groundbreaking novel *The Double Hook* by Sheila Watson. Although the novel is not situated in Alberta (it is set in the analogous ranching country of British Columbia), it was written by a writer who devoted much of her professional academic life to the literary arts in her adopted province. Joseph Pivato's essay is a bio-critical study of the works of Sheila Watson, in which Pivato points out the modernist interests and influences which gave biblical and mythological depth to her writing. Watson's Catholicism informed her literary consciousness and was foundational to her sensibility as a writer. Pivato provides a brief overview of Watson's life but devotes most of his chapter to comments on the critical approaches to her work over the past half-century. He provides a synopsis of the thinking found in George Bowering's edited collection, *Sheila Watson and The Double Hook* (1985) and Stephen Scobie's insightful volume, *Sheila Watson and Her Works* (1984), with an emphasis on her mytho-poetic approaches. Pivato is particularly impressed with Barbara Godard's 1979 essay on language style in *The Double Hook* and discusses it at some length.

Pivato notes that interest in Watson continued into the 1990s with chapters on her work in Arnold Davidson's *Coyote Country: Fiction of the Canadian West* (1994) and Margaret Turner's *Imagining Culture: New World Narrative and the Writing of Canada* (1995). He also discusses Fred Flahiff's 2005 biography of Watson, titled *Always Someone to Kill the Doves: A Life of Sheila Watson*. The essay's bibliographic and biographical focus is not about textual analysis, but rather summarizes clearly the relationship between creativity and literary reputation as developed through critical commentaries. What Pivato makes clear is that Sheila Watson's work continues to challenge critical thinking, an indication of the importance of her writing.

The contribution of women writers to Alberta's literary identity is significant as the case of Sheila Watson indicates. In fact, the majority of the writers studied in the volume are women—women as poets, women as novelists, creative non-fiction writers, and playwrights. The originality and vitality of drama in Alberta's literary history are captured in the work of two outstanding playwrights—Gwen Pharis Ringwood and Elsie Park Gowan. Their writing, covering five decades, is discussed by Moira Day in "Gwen Pharis Ringwood and Elsie Park Gowan: Writing the Land, 1933-1979." Day observes that both playwrights moved to the "boom" province of Alberta—Gowan, from Scotland to Edmonton in 1912, and Ringwood, from Washington State to McGrath in 1913—at a time when radical change in terms of immigration, feminism, and populism were altering the nature of "the province's social, political, intellectual, and physical landscape." This stimulating environment compelled both playwrights to produce, from the 1930s to the 1970s, distinctively Canadian radio and stage plays which engaged with the land, their depiction always "complicated by the forces of industrialization, urbanization, commercialization (including logging and entertainment), and economic self-interest." Both playwrights insisted that their audiences, comprised of people who inhabited the prairies, forests, and mountains, would regard works about their own land and local issues of far more interest than imperial British plays or men's drawing-room comedies.

Day's essay provides a fascinating overview of the amazing scope and range of these authors' subjects, dramatized both on stage and radio. Gowan's documented the history of Manitoba from 1812 to 1870, including the Riel Uprising, the story of Edmonton, the impact of the fur trade and the arrival of the railway, as well as the lure of the gold rush. Ringwood, too, documented life in towns and cities such as Edson and Edmonton. Both women's dramatic works reflected the arrival of immigrant groups such as Ukrainians, Asians, and Africans to the prairies; both playwrights often incorporated aboriginal characters into their early works. But in spite of their prodigious output, at the end of their lives—Ringwood died in 1984 and Gowan in 1999—both were disappointed that they had not created a climate in which it was possible to be "female, Canadian, western Canadian, and a playwright without contradiction or inequity." Nevertheless, Day argues that these courageous playwrights' efforts to write the land—to "make place"—paved the way for the burgeoning of western Canadian theatre.

When historians study the work of other historians, they quickly develop the context and limitations of this work. Doug Francis has provided an essay on Alberta historiography that surveys a century of historical writing in Alberta. In general he finds Alberta history "a rich harvest of books and articles." What he provides is a historiography of six "survey histories of the province" and what they tell us about the evolution of historical interpretation over ninety years. The first work is Archibald MacRae's *History of the Province of Alberta* (1912), which was followed a dozen years later by John Blue's *Alberta: Past and Present: Historical and Biographical.* These preliminary surveys had to wait for fifty years before the next book appeared—James G. MacGregor's *History of Alberta* (1972). The early volumes were biographical in nature, with a focus on prominent figures from the early years. According to Francis, even MacGregor's volume was "highly anecdotal." It was not until 1990, with the publication of Howard and Tamara Palmer's *Alberta: A New History*, that we finally had a history informed by academic standards. A decade later, there was a return to popular history of the sort written by MacGregor, but with a decidedly postmodern sensibility with the appearance of Aritha van Herk's entertaining *Mavericks: An Incorrigible History of Alberta* (2001). When Alberta celebrated its centenary a few years later, a number of academics marked the event with a collective history titled *Alberta Formed, Alberta Transformed* (2006).

Francis concludes that each work is "unique in its approach and emphasis." He views the writing of provincial history as a challenge in which the historian argues for the distinct nature of the province, while placing its evolution in "a larger history, be it regional, national, continental or global." With so few general surveys of Alberta history during the past century, there continues to be a need for future historians to rise to face the challenge.

The genre of fiction continues to dominate the articulation of an Alberta identity. Of contemporary writers who have made Alberta a focus for their fiction, Fred Stenson has moved to prominence. Like other writers studied in this volume, he has used Alberta history as a foundation. In "Fin de Siècle Lunacy in Fred Stenson's *The Great Karoo*," Donna Coates points out that this is the first novel to fictionalize Canadian participation in the South African War (1899-1902), even though Stenson's characters step straight out of history. In his attempt to explore issues of national identity at the outbreak of war, Stenson asks why Albertans were "different" and "what right they had to be different," which are the questions Coates also attempts to answer in her essay. She observes that regional variation in the composition of the reputedly better-educated eastern Canadian Dragoons and the working-class western cowboys who comprised the Canadian Mounted Rifle (CMR) troops played a role. But like Joseph Boyden's First World War novel *Three Day Road* (2005), *The Great Karoo* draws attention to the previously neglected contributions of Métis soldiers who become superb scouts, trackers, and snipers during these conflicts. Stenson's novel also stresses the vital role that horses played in the war, and again points out that the men from Western Canada were much more knowledgeable about their selection of horses and how to help them survive the war than the British. While the CMR officers may not have decided the course of the war, they proved that, having stemmed from a non-militaristic, non-violent country where deference to rank and hierarchy played no role, when given a chance to lead, were intelligent and compassionate men who cared about their subordinates. Ultimately, Coates argues that Stenson's novel ought to be required reading for those contemplating how positive interactions between superiors and their subalterns might be stimulated, and moreover how men in command should react under the appalling conditions of war.

The period that Stenson uses for his fictional account (the South African War) was also the period in which eastern European settlers began their great trek to Western Canada by ship and train. Jars Balan's account of the work of Nestor Dmytrow, a Ukrainian clergyman who visited

Alberta at the turn of the twentieth century, reflects a vision of Alberta framed by foreign experience like that of David Albahari a century later. Dmytrow began by penning a journalistic account of his travels to the early Ukrainian settlements in Alberta (1897) for a Ukrainian-language newspaper in Pennsylvania. The articles were collected into a fifty-six-page book and sold to its readers. Dmytrow also provided pieces of short fiction to the same journal as an alternative way of describing what he saw and heard. His was the first piece of literary prose in the Ukrainian language written in Canada that was published. Balan provides a biography of the writer and quotes extensively from his reports. He also describes Dmytrow's longer prose fiction, including a novel about the immigrant experience. Balan assesses the clergyman's writing as an "entertaining" and "fascinating record" of the agrarian settlement period.

The continuities, interventions, and lacunae that this volume articulates are a contemporary reading of Alberta writing. This reading indicates that Alberta is not a monolithic sensibility. It takes into account the anomalies of Alberta identity, such as Edmonton and Calgary having as their current mayors two of the most progressive figures in Canadian politics, or the surprise election of the provincial New Democratic Party led by Rachel Notley in 2015 after eighty years of conservative government. Clearly Alberta is a multi-cultural, multi-racial, and diverse province. Its two urban centres are the foci of new populations and new thinking. The scholarly criticism presented here suggests that Alberta writing is rich enough and deep enough for fruitful academic research. This research shows that Alberta writing has a self-consciousness that is not afraid to challenge official discourse about problematic events and institutions in its past. By reflecting on the failures, wrongdoing, and oppression found in the past, contemporary Alberta writing moves beyond nostalgia and self-congratulation to a tone of vigorous investigative courage. It would not be a stretch to say that Alberta writing has come of age in the period from 1970 to 2015, and that this maturity is a phenomenon that scholars need to continue investigating.

Works Cited

Bugnet, Georges. *The Forest*. Translated by Dave Carpenter, Harvest House, 1976.

Butler, William Francis. *The Great Lone Land: A Narrative of Travel and Adventure in the North-West of America*. Sampson Low, 1872.

Chalmers, John W., editor. *The Alberta Diamond Jubilee Anthology: A Collection from Alberta's Best Writers*. Hurtig, 1979.

Coates, Donna, and George Melnyk, editors. *Wild Words: Essays on Alberta Literature*. Athabasca UP, 2009.

Edugyan, Esi. *Half-Blood Blues*. Serpent's Tail, 2011.

Gillese, John Patrick, editor. *Chinook Arch: A Centennial Anthology of Alberta Writing*. Government of Alberta, 1967.

Hardy, W.G., editor. *The Alberta Golden Jubilee Anthology*. McClelland & Stewart, 1955.

Kroetsch, Robert, *The Studhorse Man*. Macmillan, 1969.

Laviolette, Mary-Beth. *An Alberta Art Chronicle*. Altitude Publishing, 2005.

Mitchell, W.O. *Who Has Seen the Wind*. Macmillan, 1947.

Stenson, Fred, editor. *Alberta Bound: Thirty Stories by Alberta Writers*. NeWest Press, 1986.

Van Herk, Aritha, editor. *Alberta Rebound: Thirty More Stories by Alberta Writers*. NeWest Press, 1990.

———, editor. *Boundless Alberta*. NeWest Press, 1990.

———, *Judith*. McClelland & Stewart, 1978.

———, *Mavericks: An Incorrigible History of Alberta*. Viking, 2001.

———, "Wrestling Impossibilities: Wild Words in Alberta." Introduction. *Wild Words: Essays on Alberta Literature*, edited by Donna Coates and George Melnyk, Athabasca UP, 2009, pp. 1-10.

Watson, Sheila. *The Double Hook*. McClelland & Stewart, 1959.

Wiebe, Rudy. *The Temptations of Big Bear*. McClelland & Stewart, 1976.

My Alberta *Home*

Katherine Govier

I am in front of the MacDonald Hotel on Jasper Avenue in Edmonton. It is November. At four o'clock in the afternoon daylight is gone. An icy, transparent curlicue of wind attacks my ankles, raising a thin layer of snow from the pavement. The whole earth whitens. *Home.* I know the place. But I've been gone a long time. And the place doesn't know me.

I've stood on this corner hundreds of times. Every Tuesday, Thursday, and Saturday, after ballet class, I waited for the Number 1 bus to take me down 101st Street Hill, across the toe-tickling metal struts of the Low Level Bridge and up the hill to Garneau. I stamp my feet: can I force recognition into this recalcitrant, frozen bit of earth? There is no signal, no spark of love for the returning native.

Earlier that afternoon I had taken the "Redway"—a covered pedestrian walk—through downtown. I recognized it all and I didn't recognize a thing. Some worm had been at work, the worm of franchising, of homogenization, of forgetfulness. As I walked, one story above the ground, I felt inordinate sadness, even grief. Why are we so separated from the past? The city as I knew it is erased, plastered over, driven down under a new layer of settlement. Where will my memories go? Where will anyone's?

Even the Bay, the Hudson's Bay Company, whose fort this was over two hundred years ago, is gone from Jasper Avenue. Surrendered once along with Rupert's Land, surrendered again to The Gap. We bought lavender at Christmas here; we sat in the basement "Town Square" with the ersatz English village painted on its walls. There was a proverb on the menu: Man Cannot Live by Bread Alone. I thought then it was an admonition to try the soup or the meatloaf. I'm much wiser now.

The MacDonald Hotel, at least, with its chateau-inspired turrets, and the addition beside it, always known as "the box it came in," still perches above the North Saskatchewan River valley. My windows look southward: in the waning light the river is as ever, a wide green muscle studded with grey ice. The old Riverdale flat houses have been razed for modern townhouses; I can still glimpse the set of wooden steps my friends and I climbed. And over the valley the same huge sky presides: a layer of rose at the horizon above which is a cuttlebone of charcoal, then green, then peacock, then a glorious budgerigar blue stripe rising to the clear, deep, royal blue overhead. It darkens by the moment.

Home. Its dimensions are impressed on our minds for life. All my childhood versions of far and long and high, of danger, of cold, of shame, or wonder were formed around this valley. If you missed the bus and had to walk from the South Side to the North, that was far. You might take the High Level Bridge, a two-tiered strap across from bank to bank, hundreds of metres high above the water. And it was just what I said: high. The last year I lived in Edmonton, a boy named Murray Siegel and I walked over the High Level on the railroad track. I know, mad. There were only the wooden ties and two iron rails and no place to go if the train came roaring through, as trains more frequently did then. But it was spring and the snow was melting after the longest cold snap on record: forty days of twenty below Fahrenheit weather. The radio stations were giving out certificates saying "I survived." I already knew I was leaving Edmonton. And Alberta.

I turn from the window. The city has fallen into darkness and I am somehow relieved. All over town my points of contact are disappointing me: Old Government House, the gravel pit, the Normal School, Tipton Park, the South Side Swimming pool. The city has gone to enormous lengths to consume itself and the past. I dine in a darkened bar with a kind of "international nowhere" in its DNA. What did I expect? Did I hope to find that some shadow self has been here all along holding my place? That out of loyalty to me, change had been held off? No, not here. Progress, the future, innovation, growth, expansion, all these are held dear in Alberta. This is the West, land of the tomorrow tamers. Perhaps my error is to imagine that in revisiting the place I can revisit the time. I ask myself, in a life nearly split in half between Alberta and Toronto, where is home? And realize maybe it is nowhere at all.

As casually as, in 1971, I drove away eastward in a red Ford Econoline van, I came back. After thirty years in Toronto I began spending months every year in Alberta, in Canmore. I visit my parents and my sisters. Sometimes I meet old friends, like the night I was sitting on the verandah of Tapas, the Spanish restaurant in town, and a man walked in on crutches, after a hip transplant. I immediately recognized him as Steve, last seen in Grade Six at Windsor Park School.

Back when I was growing up in Edmonton in the fifties and sixties, we used to say it was the largest city of any size this far north, rivaled only by Moscow. Then I had never been to Moscow. Now I have. Frankly, there's no comparison. In Moscow one feels the huge and vengeful empire that grew, fell, was rebuilt, crumbled again, and groans with agony; that the ground is soaked in blood; that people have been crushed into it by furious tyrants; that hinterlands press on it. In Edmonton we bobbed on the surface. The North Saskatchewan took several absent-minded turns in its great gouged valley and left our rapidly assembled city exposed as if on a platter through frigid winters and short, brilliant summers. The landscape was of telephone poles, rapid-growing poplar trees which shed fluff every spring, and frame houses in subdivisions. Edmonton was far from everywhere. Before email, the internet, skype, and all, geography counted. Distance counted. To get to Calgary, Banff, Vancouver, or Montana we drove for hours on dead straight roads that never faltered in their rush over the horizon.

The house where I lived from the age of two was a big, square, two-story in a neighbourhood that wrapped around the western edge of the university overtop the river valley. My father designed it. Our house was one of the first to go up, while the other crescents were still mudholes. We played in a little wild sunken grove where there was a spring. At the end of the street was the steep toboggan train called Lolly Bacon where my sister gouged her leg straight through to the bone.

The planes of the house were flat, the roof was flat, and the second floor was a smaller box set on top of the first. We had an attached garage where I was occasionally sent to eat my dinner if I couldn't stop giggling, and a square sundeck where one night Dad got us out of bed to see Sputnik. Sometimes we slept out on that deck. From my bedroom window I could see across the park to my friend Beth's house, and try to send her Morse code signals with my light. I lay in bed thinking that the car lights that traveled across my ceiling were German soldiers marching below.

Until I left home for university I lived in spaces my father designed: thrifty, sensible modernist spaces with tidy storage, arborite counter tops, and adequate electrical outlets, heated by natural gas. He designed our priorities too. We had and we did what was necessary, what was useful, and what made sense (to him.) We three girls adored the laundry chute down which we threw clothes from our bedroom closet, which opened up by the washing machines near the kitchen. For birthday parties my mother would turn it into a fishing pond—we'd drop down a line and she'd catch it below and tie on a gift which we then pulled up. But the house was unsentimental. Little was around that spoke of history, what came before. A couple of beautiful old Japanese dolls that my grandfather had bought while he was trading silks in the thirties fascinated me. There were other touches of magic: ballet and books.

At six on summer mornings I would cut across the street to the Gainer's house. Mrs. Gainer would be gardening or washing her car. After I helped, I was rewarded with bacon, sausages, and maple syrup for breakfast. Mrs. Gainer also gave me a book of poetry—*A Child's Garden of Verses* by Robert Louis Stevenson. There was a lot of gardening. It was the urban equivalent of breaking the land. A city had to have green lawns and flower gardens so we brought in topsoil and planted grass seed, hedged and trimmed, and put in snapdragons. On Arbour Day we planted saplings because a city, even one on the northern edge of the plains, had to have tree-lined streets.

My job was to dump the grass clippings. I pushed the full wheelbarrow to the edge of Lolly Bacon. One day, there, I had a moment of vertigo when the illusion of a modern city wavered. I had only gone a hundred steps to the end of our street but I could see deep forest and wide river, bounded by quicksand. I saw that we were "in the middle of nowhere" as the saying went. Nothing lay between us and the four points of the compass. It frightened me. I remember having that feeling one other time. It was winter: Dad had made a rink in our backyard. I skated in circles under a thin moon. In the lit kitchen window I saw my mother at the counter making dinner. I had a looming, falling sensation: I was suspended over great empty spaces. I felt alone: the world was far away. If my mother's lit face went away, I was gone.

Perhaps she felt it too. The men were involved with drilling and rigs, and classrooms of engineers and formulas. My mother did her best to fill our life with art. My sister took music, I took dance. We went to every theatre presentation we could. Mum took us to the library every week and we read what Canadian books there were. The novels set in the prairies involved weather-beaten farmhouses and howling coyotes, or small towns where everyone knew your business. But I was a city girl. Anne of Green Gables and her village charmers did not speak to me. I did love the animal books—Farley Mowat's *The Dog Who Wouldn't Be* and *Silver Chief, Dog of the North*. But my imagination was caught by English novels, and as soon as I could write my name in cursive to get a library card allowing me upstairs to the adult section, French ones too, like *Les Misérables*, which I read too young and which made me vow never to steal a loaf of bread.

As I went through school the empty stretches of Alberta began to fill up. We fished and skied and walked on the river banks and discovered the beauty of the place. I read the Janey Canuck books of Emily Murphy. I knew writers—I passed Sheila Watson's house on the way to school and later took a course from her at the University of Alberta. Elsie Park Gowan examined me for my Writer's badge in Brownies. W.O Mitchell played badminton with my mother. A colleague of Dad's was R.B. Millar, a biologist who studied trout and who wrote a book called *A Cool Curving World*. I remember him sitting out in our garden after a barbecue, his forehead absolutely black with mosquitoes. I begged him to swat them. "I've eaten my fill," he said. "Let them eat theirs." Into our backyard, too, came international students, from Turkey and Pakistan and China, with their stories and their families.

When I graduated from university I moved to Toronto because I wanted to publish, and that's what people did then, who wanted to publish. There was culture shock being in "the East"—my clever graduate student friends and I found the culture derivative, too dependent on New York, and wrongheaded in the idea it held of Alberta. "The Texas of Canada?" Was that my home? I didn't think so. Before my first novel came out I lived in London, England, but I was too attached to be an exile. I loved the language as the English spoke it and wrote it. I felt the absence of native people in Britain and understood that despite the nostalgia it raised in me, for the world of nursery rhymes and English lit, it was not my home and that we, in Canada, were colonizers. When I lived in Washington DC I grew more and more resolutely Canadian. I then settled in Toronto where I raised my children, always making sure they came to Alberta at Christmas and in the summer, in hopes that they might become, in part, westerners. And when I began to write, it was the spaces and the sounds and the look of the place, and the people and their ways, that came to my mind, and to my heart.

It was the newness of Alberta that had discouraged me, as a young woman who wanted to write, the insistence on industry, the thin cultural soil. I didn't want to be a pioneer. I knew about pioneers: my grandfather and his general stores in small prairie towns, falling prey to bad crops and finally to the car, which carried his customers to bigger towns. My mother taught Canadian fiction to scores and scores of Calgary women, outside of universities which at that time didn't want much to do with books written by the locals. She had defended her friend W.O. Mitchell to an American academic at the University of Calgary, who called him "a sort of Canadian Amos and Andy." I admired the first, but I did not want it. I wanted to exist in a milieu where stories and dance and history were deep and well-established. And I have enjoyed those places, but Alberta remains my home.

I have discovered by now that we are all pioneers in the writing business in Canada: it is still new and tentative, and on thin ice. The stories that were not yet written when I was a child are being written now. It has been a short flowering—forty years and not much more. Long may it continue, but, in the recent struggles in the business of books and bookselling, there are no guarantees.

In 1979 I published my first novel, *Random Descent,* describing the experience of moving West, picking up and moving again, until finally you had to go back East or fall off the edge. *Going Through the Motions* followed, set in Toronto. Then came the short story collection *Fables of Brunswick Avenue,* chronicling the struggles of young artists who have moved to the centre of the city (Toronto again!) to make their way in the world.

Then, in 1985, I published *Between Men,* a novel set in Calgary and dealing with a historical murder, Calgary's first, of a young Cree woman in a hotel on Stephen Avenue. In it I set a pattern for novels to come: I worked in archives and libraries to research a real moment in history and wrote a contemporary novel that explicated the past. My journeying between East and West now became journeying between past and present as I followed that novel with more stories, *The Immaculate Conception Photography Gallery*, and then spent five years writing *Angel Walk*.

In *Angel Walk,* published in 1996, I revisited family history, this time tracing my father's family in Parry Sound on the shores of Georgian Bay, and the role of that town—Nobel, Ontario—in producing explosives for the world wars. I continued also my interest in artists as central figures in fiction. The artist in this case was Cory Ditchburn, a war photographer who looks back on her adventures in Belgium in the Second World War, from the "Safe Harbour" of a cottage on Georgian Bay.

At this point, restless, I began to look at the wider world. Not many Canadian writers did that at the time: we had lots to write about at home. But I had said a great deal about what I knew. It was what I didn't know that drew me. I wrote *The Truth Teller* about a small private school for misfit kids and their encounter with Greek mythology. And then I chanced upon the Toronto Public Library's John James Audubon prints from his elephant-portfolio *Birds of America*. These brilliantly coloured, stagey, timeless aquatint engravings astounded me. I discovered that Audubon spent a little-known summer in Labrador searching for the great seabirds and discovering that loss of habitat was leading to their disappearance. That became the novel *Creation*, which was published in the United States and Canada and became a New York Times Notable Book.

It also started me on a journey through nineteenth-century printmaker Audubon to the nineteenth- and early twentieth-century pearl traders, and to that other astounding printmaker, the Japanese Hokusai, almost Audubon's exact contemporary, and like the French-American, a man who introduced his contemporaries to the wonders of a natural world they would never otherwise see. The trio of novels—*Creation, Three Views of Crystal Water,* and *The Ghost Brush*—occupied a decade of my life, from 2002 to 2012. It was terrific fun to travel to private homes in Holland, to visit tiny collections of *ukiyo-e* in rural Japan with a translator, to meet with curators at the Metropolitan Museum in New York. I became a reporter and a detective. My credo was that I would find out as much as I could from the historical record, and then armed and convinced about what had happened in "the gaps," I would speculate. It was a method I learned writing *Between Men* while using the Calgary Public Library.

And now, I have returned to Alberta with *The Three Sisters Bar and Hotel*, a novel about the family of a packtrain outfitter in the early years of

Banff National Park. A mystery surrounds the disappearance of a scientific expedition he guided, a mystery that involves his daughter and eventually his grandchildren. It centres around a homecoming. I must say, using the Whyte Museum in Banff was that for me. I speak the language. My main characters shout from every shelf to be put on the page. Half the time I've met the people they're based on, or their descendants.

I wonder if it matters if you are an Alberta writer or an Ontario writer. It matters that the stories are told, and that those tellings are not lost. The stories are everywhere and always growing; they are begging to be told, actually. What I have come to understand about my Alberta childhood and family is how very lucky I am to have been born in this place to people who adopted Alberta. Because my parents, and their generation, were immigrants themselves, although it was never spoken of that way. My mother's parents had migrated as adults from England to Vancouver, and she had come to Alberta as a bride in 1940, to mud streets. My father's family, we have recently discovered, dates back to the Pilgrim Fathers, but his mother too had been nearly an adult when she found herself set down outside of Moose Jaw beside the CPR tracks. They made every effort to come to terms with the enormous scale of the province, its rawness, and the mingling of cultures. From my parents and their generation I learned to appreciate not only the physical grandeur of the mountains and foothills, but the intellectual wonder of books and ideas.

When I published my first novel, there was a newspaper headline: "She's not called Margaret and she's not from a small town." People have found it difficult to classify me as a writer: I don't do the expected thing or take the expected turn. But a closer look finds traces of my past in everything I do: I first encountered the culture of Japan in that Edmonton neighbourhood, when a student came to board with us. I first learned about Audubon in the South Side Library in Strathcona.

When I dream about the house my father built us in Windsor Park, I dream about newfound rooms. I discover an entire wing or a new basement; my god! it has been there empty and unnoticed until this very moment. In my dream I take one step around a corner on the familiar linoleum into an enormous new territory, great reaches of domestic space, gleaming wood floors fit for a ballroom, huge sunlit windows. It is all there, in the place where I have always been—although inexplicably I had not seen it before.

These are wonderful dreams. Discovering great reaches through old door-ways gives me a kind of peaceful elation.

I believe we all harbour a knowledge of brilliant, untouched worlds within our real spaces. Last night it was the basement, in fact the furnace room. It was very tidy with old shoes, hats, photograph albums, books, skates, camping supplies—all clearly labeled in large wooden crates. I wandered farther and found two closets. I've always loved closets—they hold whatever evidence of the past has survived. The doors were shut and it was dark inside. I'll have to get in there soon.

2

"My Bones Have Known this Land Long Before Alberta Was Born": Intersections in Indigenous Geography and Indigenous Creative Expression

Tasha Hubbard

Alberta, born as a province in 1905, shares a literary history with the other two prairie provinces, all underscored by their agrarian roots. However, Melnyk and Coates elaborate on Alberta's contemporary evolution in the "Introduction" to the first collection of *Wild Words*: "With a population in 2008 that was almost triple each of the other provinces and with an oil and gas economy (extraction, processing, and transportation) that was booming, Alberta evolved into a different kind of entity" (ix). Alberta's literature, influenced by its diversified economy and impressive geography, may have moved away from agrarian narratives, but what underscores those narratives never completely disappears. In her introduction to *Wild Words*, Aritha van Herk claims that "Our writing cannot help but be influenced, positively or adversely, by this spectacular space and our specular gaze" (2). In this vein, the land is an object of admiration, a mirror for reflection, and usually, a fodder for the economy.

However, if we consider Alberta's literary history, as well as just how that land was settled in the first place, we need to return to the genre of prairie literature. Jenny Kerber, in *Writing in the Dust*, reminds readers that we must employ a historical consciousness of the legacies that form the foundation of the writing: "In the prairie region, those cultural and environmental legacies have been profoundly shaped by colonialism—a fact that becomes clear when one considers how much of the canonical literature and criticism about prairie landscape or nature-related writing has been entrenched in a white male settler tradition" (16). Within a settler understanding, the land is an empty space to be filled, altered, and conquered, thereby contributing to the agrarian myth. As Shirley McDonald spoke about at the 2012 Association of Literature, Environment and Culture in Canada Conference, the agrarian myth is a self-legitimizing discourse brought about through settler labour. The hard-work pioneer narratives seek to calcify a claim to the land.

Despite the narrative of empty space, the territory of what is now known as Alberta already had long-standing occupants, namely Indigenous peoples and buffalo, who were seen as obstacles to the primary settlement goals of farming and ranching. Patrick Brantlinger describes this process as follows: "The creation first of the new white colony in the wilderness and then of the new nation-state demands the vanishing of the primeval others who cannot become or supposedly refuse to be part of its future" (190). The use of the term "wilderness" needs to be unpacked to reveal the underlying assumptions that place Indigenous peoples and buffalo on the deficient (and therefore inevitably extinct) end of a dichotomy of wilderness versus civilization, with civilization and domestic animals emerging victorious. The buffalo, conservatively estimated to be thirty million strong at the time of contact, were removed through a lethal combination of military intervention, government policy, and private enterprise and Indigenous peoples' lives were subsequently devastated. By the 1880s the buffalo was eradicated, and the "empty space" was realized.

Furthermore, wilderness discourse, according to Jodi Adamson, "fails to account for what happens to indigenous peoples after they are removed" (16). An examination of the numbered Treaty history of Alberta sheds light on the attempts by Indigenous peoples to continue to survive on their homelands. The lands of the buffalo range within the province of Alberta are the sites of Treaties 6 and 7, concluded in 1876 and 1877 respectively, the first with the Cree and their allies and the second with the Blackfoot and their allies. Indigenous peoples wished to participate in the new economy and requested support to do so in exchange for sharing the land to the depth of a plow with the newcomers. However, they did not forget the buffalo and asked for protection of the few that were left as part of the Treaty negotiations. They were not successful. The collective authors of a publication discussing the oral history of Treaty 7 maintain that, "[a] significant number of Cree leaders, including Big Bear, Piapot, and Little Pine, who were committed both to the goal of preserving the buffalo and to making the transition to agriculture, did not sign the treaty because they doubted that the government would honour the treaty agreements" (Treaty 7 Elders et al. 221). They were correct. The Indian Act was passed in 1876 and effectively regulated the non-participation of Indigenous peoples in the new settler economy, despite promises in the Treaties. Oral history of Treaty 7 reveals the Treaty Elders' understanding that the buffalo were purposely slaughtered in order to facilitate Indigenous people's removal. Tom Yellowhorn is quoted as saying "the two governments agreed to try to kill off all the buffalo" so that Indian people would no longer have a livelihood (101).

Despite being physically and metaphorically erased from the land, Indigenous peoples and their stories of the buffalo are both remembered and resurgent in Indigenous literatures. It is my hope that anyone who participates in what van Herk calls a specular gazing exercise sees Indigenous literatures, some of which existed long before Alberta came to be, reflected back at them. George Melnyk, in *The Literary History of Alberta*, argues for the inclusion of petroglyphs and pictographs, such as Writing-On-Stone, within the category of Alberta literature, contending that, "Placing Alberta's literary origins outside the history and traditions of English language and literature is not an act of cultural appropriation but a recognition of the cultural diversity this land has spawned" (8). I agree, and yet would go a step beyond the concept of "culture" and say that these sites, stories, and songs of the people form the foundation of Blackfoot, Tsuu T'ina, Nakota, Cree, and Dene nations.

The late Narcisse Blood taught me about the Blackfoot word "manotoya," meaning "they got here yesterday," which refers to the waves of settlers who came to this land. Indigenous literature has a history and origin that vastly predate provincial boundaries and narratives. "My bones have known this land long before Alberta was born" says Emma LaRoque. The title line is taken from the Cree-Métis scholar and poet's monograph *When the Other is Me: Native Resistance Discourse 1850-1990*. She reminds us that Indigenous creative expression can be understood in the following way:

[I]t is about a whole way of perceiving, practicing, and connecting land, knowledge, skill, and spirituality, and human-nature relationships from our land-based cosmologies. If "cultural difference" has any meaning, it lies here. But now it is a difference that has obviously been compounded by dispossession and repeated geographical and cultural dislocations. Even so, land remains central to Aboriginal ethos, even to those who are distanced from it. (136)

I wish to examine the poetry of several Indigenous women who have ties to Alberta and who write about their own histories they share with buffalo: a legacy of being cleared and dislocated from the land. I am interested in the potential of applying an emerging Indigenous geography to several of their poems that lament, remember, and rejuvenate the relationship between land, buffalo, and Indigenous peoples. Beth Cuthand, Marilyn Dumont, and Louise Halfe are grounded in their respective land-based cosmologies and are affected by physical and psychic dislocation from the land. Their work reflects what Donelle Dreese describes as a "reterritorialization," or the retrieval of a sense of place as integral to rebuilding an identity impacted by colonial constructions of land and people (17), which includes the imposition of patriarchy on both. I wish to include gender as part of this decolonizing discussion. Feminist geographer Doreen Massey explains the gendering of space and place in this way: "From the symbolic meaning of spaces/places and the clearly gendered messages which they transmit, to straightforward exclusion by violence, spaces and places are not only themselves gendered but, in their being so, they both reflect and affect the ways in which gender is constructed and understood" (179). Thus, the work of these women answers back to the imposition of white male space on the land, which is both embedded and legitimized in western-based geographies.

Western geographies empty place of Indigenous peoples and their stories, replacing them with alternative stories, such as the agrarian myth (and more current narratives), revealing what Oakes and Price describe as the intricate relationship between the making of place and the making of meaning (254). Indigenous geographies make a concentrated effort to decolonize a discipline of study that has a long history as a colonizing tool. Integral to the geography, or literally "place" writing, is mapping, a practice that can claim space as part of an imperialist agenda. Physical mapping in the colonial tradition seeks to claim, freeze, and calcify place as domain for white males. In contrast, mapping within Indigenous geographies seeks to be inclusive and reflective of those who share the land—both human and non-human, male and female. Indigenous geographies function similar to the ways post-colonial geographies function. Bill Ashcroft describes the latter as "interpolat[ing] the discipline, employing some conventional practices and technologies and yet injecting them with non-Western ways of conceiving space (perhaps even ways that are totally incommensurable with Western conceptions)" (151). These non-western conceptions of space come out of the Indigenous cosmologies that LaRoque referred to earlier.

A geography invested in western space conceptions is primarily interested in the physical surface (or depths in the case of resource extraction) of the land and borders. However, Indigenous geographies are not bound by the same limits. In "Resisting Exile in the "Land of the Free": Indigenous Groundwork at Colonial Intersections," Anthony Tyeeme Clark and Malea Powell push beyond the boundaries usually set by western geography: "We think of the physical landscapes and Indigenous geographies as they connect and constitute the world above, below, and on the earth as a series of mutually constitutive and interdependent relations" (10). These relations constitute more than human relations but also correspond to an understanding of kinship to water, animals, and other beings who live on the land. Understanding peoplehood to be inclusive of other beings besides humans automatically shifts the relationship to the world around us to one of respect. Kainai writer Betty Bastien explains kinship in this way: "The natural world with its various resources are [sic] experienced as interrelated in a manner that respects all its beings—whether the wide-open grass plains for the buffalo or other four-legged animals, or forested hills for shelter, or timbered river valleys for winter camps, or roots, berries, and plants" (12). What Bastien describes is knowledge of the way in which each living being is important and has a role. According to Vine Deloria Jr., "everything in the natural world has relationships with every other thing and the total set of relationships makes up the natural world as we experience it" (34).

People and the landscape do not exist in individual stasis bound by arbitrary distinctions and boundaries; rather, people understand themselves to be within an interconnected and dynamic place filled with history and meaning. According to Margaret Kovach, "Place links present with past and our personal self with kinship groups. What we know flows through us from the 'echo of generations,' and our knowledges cannot be universalized because they arise from our experience with our places" (61). What echoes through countless generations is not a romanticized concept, but a very real influence for Indigenous writers and for their readers too, if they are willing to listen.

The land and an Indigenous understanding of the complexities of our connection to the land profoundly influence the creative expression from those writers who seek to repair or rejuvenate a relationship temporarily damaged by colonization. Halfe, Dumont, and Cuthand use poetry as their main vehicle of expression. Robert Warrior, a leading Indigenous critic, discusses the ways in which Indigenous writers have adopted, adapted, and used poetry as a form of resistance against European systems: "Poetry has provided a vehicle for such resistance because of the way it can unsettle prevailing ideologies and give voice to what is not being spoken within a culture" (117). Thus the land and its inhabitants become central again to Indigenous peoples after decades of dislocation and disassociation.

Dean Rader, in *Engaged Resistance*, suggests Indigenous poetry pushes back against western poetic forms that are about "demarcation, borders, and boundaries" (128). Using the language of geography, Rader's discussion opens up a dialogue on how Indigenous poetry can function as "compositional resistance" to the borders and boundaries on the page, and I would argue, on the land itself. Indigenous poets' work seeks to overturn *terra nullius* and other mythologies, or what Andrews calls "the very basis upon which dominant narratives of discovery and nation-building were constructed" (141). Critiquing and questioning dominant national myths eventually create space for an Indigenous poetics to reflect Indigenous conceptions of self, nation, land, and relations. Rader discusses Navajo poet Lucy Tapahonso and the ways in which she "elicits an utterly original perception of how a geographic space becomes part and parcel of the language spoken within it and the people who live on it" (139). While Rader is discussing Tapahonso's specific Navajo poetic sensibilities, there are commonalities with the way plains Indigenous poetics are influenced by the geographic space of the prairies. Cree scholar Neal McLeod defines "Cree space" as a "metaphorical way of describing the narratives, the land, and all the things that allow the nehiyawak to express themselves in relation to their ancestors" (86). Cuthand, Dumont, and Halfe's Indigenous poetics respond to dominant narratives with voices that went unheard at the time of nation (or province) building, and replace them with narratives grounded in Indigenous belief systems.

Beth Cuthand, Cree, grew up both in Saskatchewan and the Kainai First Nation, Alberta. According to Renate Eigenbrod, Cuthand's poem, "Four Songs for the Fifth Generation," spans "four generations of a Cree family," wherein "the speaker for the first generation laments the vanishing of the buffalo who once gave life to her children" (128). In Cuthand's poem, the buffalo is placed in relationship with both the people and the land they inhabit:

> They were our life the life
>   of the prairies
> We loved them
>   And they loved us. (63)

The break in the line between "our life" and "the life" focuses the connection from a subjective viewpoint from the speaker as Indigenous person, to a more general importance to the land itself. By describing them as "the life of the prairies," Cuthand positions the buffalo as central to the health of the land, which acknowledges their status of a keystone species that profoundly influences the well-being of other species, both plant and animal. As "the" life of the prairies, the buffalo signals a thriving and healthy ecosystem. Furthermore, Cuthand's speaker establishes the bond between Indigenous peoples and the buffalo, which affirms the kinship that existed between the buffalo in Cree and Blackfoot cosmology.

The next three lines of the poem establish the way in which the buffalo were part of the land itself. The sheer volume of their numbers, almost unimaginable today, transforms them into a part of the landscape itself:

> Sometimes   they were so many
> they flowed   like a river
> over the hills   into the valleys. (63)

Each line has a similarly placed break, which may suggest the fragmentation that is to be their fate, as the next lines show that their numbers disappeared: "they are gone." Ultimately, the speaker tells us of the buffalo's transformation into "ghosts" as a result of their slaughter.

According to Eigenbrod, in the rest of the poem, now that the buffalo are gone, Cuthand "describes the history of her family… as a process of moving freely, like the buffalo, to fighting 'for a place in the neighbourhood'" (128). They must do so while suffering the trauma of the loss of their relations, which functions as a legacy for each subsequent generation. In the poem, the brother struggles with the impacts of loss and dislocation: "he had a rage/ that wouldn't go out" (68). The speaker speaks of her inability to live fully, describing a process of withdrawal: "I just retreated,/ and retreated/ until I couldn't/ find myself" (68). The trauma that they are living with is a direct result of the severing of the buffalo and the people's connection with the land. Pueblo scholar Gregory Cajete explains the connection in this way: "Inner kinship with the Earth is an ancient and natural extension of the human psyche and its severance can lead to a deep split in the consciousness of the individual and the group, in addition to social and psychological problems that can ultimately be healed only through reestablishing meaningful ties" (188). Kinship bonds are bonds that are not meant to be broken, and when they sustain damage, it takes many years to repair them.

Dislocation and disruption of kinship relationships are also at the core of Marilyn Dumont's poem, "Les Animaux." Dumont is a Métis writer who grew up near Red Deer, Alberta and currently lives in Edmonton. She recently said in an interview with Maja Pasovic that she is moving into a new direction in her writing: "At this stage in my life, I feel compelled to write about the history of the Métis to bring awareness to the injustices and the contributions of the Métis in Canada. What I write, will not please a large part of the public, but a few will support my findings" (Pasovic and Dumont). In "Les Animaux," Dumont, like Cuthand, laments the loss of the buffalo. However, Dumont's poem is from the perspective of Gabriel Dumont, the Métis leader. The speaker calls him "Uncle," following the kinship practices where older male relatives are included in that term out of respect. Furthermore, like Cuthand, Dumont positions Indigenous peoples and the buffalo within a kinship relationship:

> the brothers have left us   they have moved to another
> plain.

She, too, uses spacing to force the reader to pause and consider the connection of family with the buffalo, before moving into the spatial loss described by "another plain." This technique is reminiscent of oral tradition where Indigenous peoples, unable to fathom that the seemingly limitless buffalo could be reduced to a handful, instead thought the buffalo had moved into a different space: "their great size is swallowed by the bigger prairie / prairie that once seemed like it couldn't hold all." The land was seemingly overfilled with buffalo at one time, and now the emptiness looms over everyone.

The speaker's conception of the land and buffalo's interconnectivity is disrupted by the loss, resulting in silencing of what was once a symphony of life: "gone, and now the prairie is mute." By combining the loss of the buffalo with a silencing of the land, Dumont mixes French and English languages with Cree cosmology, creating what Renate Eigenbrod and Jennifer Andrews describe as "a eulogy not only for the buffalo herds displaced by the settlers—'the new herds'—but also for the potential loss of a linguistic and aesthetic heritage that uniquely combines French and English along with Cree." The poem is reminiscent of elegy. Brantlinger tells us that the proleptic elegies that mourned the vanishing Indian and even the buffalo can be understood as a "nation-founding genre" (3), and thus, according to Rader, Dumont's appropriation of this poetic form is an example of the ways Indigenous poets appropriate western forms: "Incorporating aspects of the sonnet, Western rhyme schemes, or the elegy can be seen as a form of counting poetic coup, a symbolic but telling manifestation of triumph" (145). By composing an elegy of the loss of the buffalo, Dumont is pushing her readers to understand the depth of the loss experienced by her ancestors.

The loss is personalized and internalized when Dumont's speaker tells us that with the loss of the buffalo, "something in us goes too." Dumont names the loss without being specific as to what exactly the loss entails with the use of "something." Returning to Dreese's concept of reterritorialization, we can understand this process as "the claiming of space for oneself and an understanding of the place's history, its physical constituents, and one's own psychological reaction to these aspects" (115). The speaker is acknowledging the buffalo's rightful place on the land by highlighting what happens when it is gone. Adrian Stimson, a Blackfoot artist from Siksika, does similar work in his *Reherd*, where he invites observers to paint small stone buffalo and then place them on an enlarged (and empty) map of Alberta, simultaneously reminding people of the buffalo's absence while metaphorically restoring them to the land where they belong. Both of these creative works point to the injustice of the colonial exercise of removal of species and peoples who were deemed unfit in the settler project.

Dumont speaks to her motivation for writing poems like "Les Animaux" as follows: "I recognize that I write about historical injustices not just for myself, but for generations that came before me and those that come after me" (Pasovic and Dumont). By speaking in the voice of an ancestor who was directly affected by the loss, Dumont brings the past into the light of the present. She also reminds those of us living in the present that there is something integral missing from the land, perhaps a fact we have not considered before. According to LaRoque, Indigenous writers like Dumont "not only retrieve our histories and experiences, a process that is both necessary and painful, but they also collect and thread together our scattered parts and so nurture our spirits and rebuild our cultures" ("Reflections" 152). While the rebuilding occurs outside of Dumont's poem, the injustices and the loss are acknowledged.

Louise Halfe's book-length poem *Blue Marrow* also acknowledges historical injustices, with the understanding that this acknowledgement is a necessary part of recovery of Indigenous ways of knowing. Halfe was born on the Saddle Lake First Nation and went to residential school at Blue Quills in St. Paul. In an article co-written with archaeologist Ernie Walker, Halfe explains her process and the ways in which language becomes a metonym for colonial struggle: "Through dreams, ceremony, and the recollection of memory, my community continues to battle the rift between our Native tongue and the foreigner's language. … There are times when community would rather express itself in the safety of the drum, song, and dance, its skeletal wounds often too penetrating" (Walker and Halfe 6). The wounds may be penetrating, but Halfe does not shy away from exposing the wounds themselves, or what caused them. LaRoque says Halfe's poetry "takes us to the marrow of shadows and light that humans are—she lifts the rocks and makes us look at what is under there" ("Reflections" 169). By lifting the rocks that scatter across the prairie (and Alberta) landscape like a literary archaeologist, Halfe reveals a history of death that is the underbelly of settlement, a history that many would prefer to remain covered.

Halfe's speaker begins by invoking her many Grandmothers, women who were not named by colonial history and who are her ancestors, waiting to be called. She names each Grandmother and invites her to be a part of this ceremony of revelation and recovery of stories. Azalea Barrieses and Susan Gingell, in "Listening to Bones that Sing: Orality, Spirituality, and Female Kinship in Louise Halfe's *Blue Marrow*," determine that the focus on female kin "animates the retrieval of female stories from the colonially imposed silence, thus recuperating Cree women's power as the life-giving force acknowledged in her people's oral creation stories and other forms of oral history …" (70). Halfe repopulates the literary landscape with these women's stories and voices in order to tell us how colonization shaped the land once buffalo and other peoples had been erased and silenced.

The primary speaker is identified as the "Keeper of Stories" and is bestowed the responsibility of both telling and caring for these women's narratives. Jenny Kerber reminds us that "[o]ne cannot be a good caretaker of the stories of the ancestors without also being a good caretaker of the land from which they come" (136), and this includes listening to the voices from the non-human beings. A ceremony begins where voices that have been silenced are asked to speak: "Voices / filled with bird calls, snorting buffalo, kicking bears, mountain goats" (Halfe 17). The animals and birds from all directions and from different lands come together to be heard once again. It is a painful process, because the stories that need to be told are stories of genocide, theft, and erasure. However, the speaker ends the passage with instructions to the rest of us: "Listen to the bones" (18).

As we listen to what the bones of both humans and animals have to say, the bones release a litany of historic injustices against women's bodies and subsequently, against Indigenous peoples as whole, ending with the following:

> The land weeps. I am choking, choking.
> The buffalo are a mountain of bones.
> My son is shot for killing their cow. (19)

The land is a witness to the atrocities that come with colonization and grieves alongside the people. The buffalo, once relatives and livelihood tied together to sustain life, transform the land with their death, as their bones create new silhouettes on the landscape. Halfe's Grandmothers also reveal the ways in which the buffalo's death resulted in starvation for the people. In their hunger and desperation to keep their children from dying, men would shoot the animals that had replaced the buffalo. This would result in persecution from the settlers, who saw this as a transgression of property and yet ignored Indigenous peoples' desperate bid to stay alive. These are the stories embedded in the bones of both human and animal people.

Kerber refers to the prairie as being a "graveyard of story" within *Blue Marrow*. However, while the stories have been covered up, they are not dead. Halfe finds the stories embedded in the land, both original and altered, and, as LaRoque referred to earlier, lifts and shifts the rocks, earth, and, yes, gravestones. There has been the death of people, the buffalo, and other beings. However, their stories remain a part of the landscape and point to a possibility of the land's inhabitants "entering into a new kind of environmental relationship—one that, instead of burying and ignoring the bones of those who have trod the prairie landscape before us, names and honours them as seeds of knowledge about how to construct more sustainable relations between prairie people and prairie place" (Kerber 136).

Indigenous women's poetry is inevitably a site of reterritorialization, as it marries the land with the survival of Indigenous women and the spirits of the stories long suppressed. While Dumont's poem's elegiac leanings open up a deep earth wound so it does not fester, Cuthand's and Halfe's provide guidance to move towards healing through ceremony. As Kainai scholar Leroy Little Bear explains:

> Our stories arise out of the land. Our ceremonies occur because of the interrelational network that occurred all over our land. Our way of mapping our territory is through our stories. There is a story about every place. There are songs about each place. There are ceremonies that occur about those places. The songs, the stories, these ceremonies are our map. (19)

Cuthand's chorus provides the reader with such a map, and it is repeated throughout the poem, ultimately becoming the final lines:

> Drums, chants, and rattles
> pounded earth and
>   heartbeats
>   heartbeats. (63)

Eigenbrod suggests that the chorus "does not really conclude the poem but, rather, creates a new beginning: the song of the future generations" (129). The fifth song belongs to the next generation, the future. The pounded earth under the buffalo herd's hooves is still animated with their spirits, even if the buffalo are no longer able to nourish the people with their bodies. Indigenous philosopher George Tinker describes it this way: "Like humans, each buffalo has its own life spirit—that is, a spirit that is given to it at the moment of its conception. That spirit is indestructible and, as with any species, including humans, survives even the physical death of the animal" (116). The heartbeats, repeated twice, remind us that life has continued on the land through ceremony.

Similarly, Halfe evokes the renewal through her mention of the Ghost Dance at the end of the passage:

> I will not lose my Pipe.
> This holy war I stitch to my dress.
> This Skull Dance, this Ghost Dance. (21)

The Ghost Dance, begun in the 1880s in the United States as a response to the devastation wrought by colonization, was performed to return life to the way it was before contact, including the return of the buffalo, so life would be renewed. The Keeper of Stories remembers its intent. By stating she will not lose her pipe, she is claiming a ground of battle in order to fight for the stories and the peoples' future on the lands they know as home.

The stories held within the poetry of Cuthand, Dumont, and Halfe are brought to the page in an effort to bring healing to a people and a land that have been under assault for the past two centuries. As Warren Cariou states, "If they heal, it is through bearing witness, speaking the truth of their pain, their people's pain, and the legacy of violence that underlies the history of prairie settlement" (732). The violence left little untouched, and certain species such as the buffalo are only beginning to recover. By engaging with this kind of work, Albertans and Canadians in general can contribute by ending the denial and the silencing of these narratives. And by listening to the messages embedded in the work, readers may also gain insight into how life can continue on this land in sustainable ways through the honouring of kinship roles and responsibilities. The poetry of these three women draw in the teachings that have survived in order to give space to grieve, remember, and honour those who lost their lives, but whose spirits have survived to provide guidance. Indigenous geographies, rather than functioning like a closed categorization, can be used to view the ways in which Indigenous poetic voices, despite violence and silencing, express how the land and its inhabitants continue to live in kinship with one another.

Works Cited

Adamson, Joni. *American Indian Literature, Environmental Justice, and Ecocriticism: The Middle Place.* U of Arizona P, 2001.

Andrews, Jennifer. *In the Belly of a Laughing God: Humour and Irony in Native Women's Poetry.* U of Toronto P, 2011.

Ashcroft, Bill. *Postcolonial Transformation.* Routledge, 2001.

Barrieses, Azalea, and Susan Gingell. "Listening to Bones that Sing: Orality, Spirituality, and Female Kinship in Louise Halfe's Blue Marrow." *Studies in American Indian Literatures*, vol. 23, no. 3, 2011, pp. 69-93.

Bastien, Betty. *Blackfoot Ways of Knowing: The Worldview of the Siksikaitsitapi.* U of Calgary P, 2004.

Brantlinger, Patrick. *Dark Vanishings: Discourse on the Extinction of Primitive Races, 1800-1930.* Cornell UP, 2003.

Cajete, Gregory. *Native Science: Natural Laws of Interdependence.* Clear Light Publishers, 2000.

Cariou, Warren. "Haunted Prairie: Aboriginal 'Ghosts' and the Spectres of Settlement." *University of Toronto Quarterly*, vol. 75, no. 2, 2006, pp. 727-34.

Clark, D. Anthony Tyeeme, and Malea Powell. "Resisting Exile in the "Land of the Free": Indigenous Groundwork at Colonial Intersections." *American Indian Quarterly*, vol. 32, n. 1, 2008, pp. 1-15.

Cuthand, Beth. "Four Songs for the Fifth Generation." *Voices in the Waterfall.* Theytus Books, 1992.

Deloria, Vine Jr. "Relativity, Relatedness, and Reality." *Spirit and Reason: The Vine Deloria Jr. Reader,* edited by Barbara Deloria et al., Fulcrum Publishing, 1999, pp. 32-39.

Dreese, Donelle N. *Ecocriticism: Creating Self and Place in Environmental and American Indian Literatures.* Peter Lang, 2002.

Dumont, Marilyn. "Les Animaux." *Studies in Canadian Literature. Études en littérature canadienne*, vol. 31, no. 1, 2006.

Eigenbrod, Renate. *Travelling Knowledges: Positioning the Im/Migrant Reader of Aboriginal Literatures in Canada*. U of Manitoba P, 2005.

Eigenbrod, Renate, and Jennifer Andrews. "Introduction: From Conference to Special Issue: Selected Articles on "The Love of Words"." *Studies in Canadian Literature. Études en littérature canadienne*, vol. 31, no. 1, 2006.

Halfe, Louise. *Blue Marrow*. Coteau Books, 2004.

Kerber, Jenny. *Writing in Dust: Reading the Prairie Environmentally*. Wilfred Laurier U P, 2010.

Kovach, Margaret. *Indigenous Methodologies: Characteristics, Conversations, and Contexts*. U of Toronto P, 2009.

LaRoque, Emma. "Reflections on Cultural Continuity through Aboriginal Women's Writings." *Restoring the Balance: First Nations Women, Community, and Culture*, edited by Gail Guthrie Valaskakis et al., U of Manitoba P, 2009, pp. 149-74.

———. *When the Other is Me: Native Resistance Discourse 1850-1990*. U of Manitoba P, 2010.

Little Bear, Leroy. "Aboriginal Relationships to the Land and Resources," *Sacred Lands: Aboriginal World Views, Claims, and Conflicts*, edited by Jill Oakes et al., Canadian Circumpolar Institute, 1998, pp. 15-20.

Massey, Doreen. *Space, Place and Gender*. U of Minnesota P, 1994.

McLeod, Neal. *Cree Narrative Memory: From Treaties to Contemporary Times*. Purich, 2007.

McDonald, Shirley. "Imagining the Canadian Agrarian Landscape: Prairie Settler Life Writing as Colonial Discourse." Paper presented at the Association of Literature, Environment, and Culture in Canada Conference, University of British Columbia's Okanagan campus, BC, 8 Aug. 2012.

Melnyk, George. *The Literary History of Alberta: Volume One. From Writing-on-Stone to World War Two*. U of Alberta P, 1998.

Melnyk, George, and Donna Coates. Preface. *Wild Words: Essays on Alberta Literature*, edited by George Melynk and Donna Coates, Alberta U P, 2009, pp. vii-xi.

Oakes, Timothy S., and Patricia Lynn Price. *The Cultural Geography Reader*. Routledge, 2008.

Pasovic, Maja, and Marilyn Dumont. "Interview with Marilyn Dumont." *Luvah: Journal of the Creative Imagination*, vols. 1-2, no. 1, 2012.

Rader, Dean. *Engaged Resistance*. U of Texas Press, 2011.

Smith, Linda Tuhiwai. *Decolonizing Methodologies: Research and Indigenous Peoples*. Zed Books, 1999.

Tinker, George. "The Stones Shall Cry Out: Consciousness, Rocks, and Indians." *Wicazo Sa Review*, vol. 19, no. 2, 2004, pp. 105-25.

Treaty 7 Elders, et al. *The True Spirit and Original Intent of Treaty 7*. McGill-Queen's U P, 1996.

Van Herk, Aritha. "Wrestling Impossibilities: Wild Words in Alberta." Introduction. Melnyk and Coates, pp. 1-10.

Walker, Ernest G., and Louise B. Halfe. "Stored in the Honeycomb Heart of Memory: The Role of Oral Tradition and Archaeology in Cultural Survival." *Structurist*, vols. 37-38, 1997-98, pp. 4-11.

Warrior, Robert. *Tribal Secrets: Recovering American Indian Intellectual Traditions*. U of Minnesota P, 1995.

3

Strategies for Storying the Terrible Truth in John Estacio's and John Murrell's *Filumena* and Betty Jane Hegerat's *the Boy*

Tamara Palmer Seiler

Most people are shocked and repelled by horrific crimes such as murder. Many are also attracted to accounts of such events: various genres of crime fiction and drama, for example, are perennial favorites, and information about actual crimes is a valuable commodity for news media. However, writing about violent crime, whether fictional or actual, poses a number of challenges such as finding the right balance between circumspection and sensationalism. Moreover, chronicling actual crimes can lead both writers and readers into dark and complex places where determining and then telling "the truth" can be daunting. Two such events in Alberta's social/ legal history have garnered particular attention: the murder in the Crowsnest Pass, in September 1922, of Alberta Provincial Police Constable, Steve Lawson, and the subsequent trial, conviction, and execution of Emilio Picariello and Florence (Filumena) Lassandro; and the murder in Stettler in June 1959 of seven members of the Cook family and the subsequent trials, convictions, and execution of Robert Raymond Cook, son, stepson, and half-brother of the respective victims.

My purpose here is to discuss the narrative strategies employed in recent representations of each of these events—the opera *Filumena* (2003) by John Estacio and John Murrell, and the creative non-fiction book *the Boy* (2011) by Betty Jane Hegerat. Because *Filumena* is a grand opera, while *the*

Boy is a work of creative non-fiction, they are quite different artistic forms; however, I believe these two genres (and the particular texts I consider here) are sufficiently similar as verbal expressions to warrant comparison. After all, hybridity is a defining feature of both grand opera and creative non-fiction. As well, since these particular texts are based on actual events, their authors faced a number of similar challenges in constructing them and arguably employed some similar strategies in doing so. Since the authors in both cases live in Calgary, there is the added feature of Albertans commenting on Alberta stories. My modest goal here is neither to be exhaustive nor definitive with regard to either of these works or the events they chronicle; rather, I hope to highlight some of the challenges involved in writing about such charged historical events and thus the similarities between seemingly dissimilar works that take on this task, while illuminating, however dimly and briefly, some dark corners of Alberta's past.

Who, What, When, and Where

Aside from being crimes that happened in Alberta, the Lawson murder and the Cook murders would seem at first glance to have little in common; they took place almost forty years apart in very different regions and circumstances. However, in both cases, the "truth" about what actually happened was, and has remained, to varying degrees, contested (Lee 48; Pecover xxi; Hegerat, *the Boy* 76). Moreover, it is this element of uncertainty that fascinates and creates points of entry for revisiting each story while, at the same time, creating particular challenges and pitfalls for those who take up the task of doing so.

As mentioned, these crimes took place in very different settings. The Crowsnest Pass, in the southwestern corner of Alberta, was one of the province's major mining areas, consisting of a series of small towns. Like other mining communities in the province, "The Pass" attracted immigrant workers from central, eastern, and southern Europe, as well as Great Britain, and it was characterized by a marked degree of social stratification, with an ethnic pecking order that mirrored the one enshrined in Canada's immigration policy of the period (Palmer and Palmer, *Peoples* 250; Wood 24, 39). The social cleavages and tensions following the First World War, together with the existence at the time of prohibition (enacted in Alberta in

1916 partly in response to fears among the Protestant elite about the negative social impact of immigrants), were fundamental aspects of the context in which the Lawson murder and the subsequent trial and conviction of Picariello and Lassandro took place. So too were jurisdictional conflicts among various provincial governments and the federal government. These conflicts complicated law enforcement, leading the RCMP to cancel their police contract with the Alberta government, which was then forced to create the Alberta Provincial Police. This organization had limited resources, and business for rum-runners flourished. Unsurprisingly, then, when the new UFA government (United Farmers of Alberta) came to power in 1921, one of the thorniest issues it faced was prohibition—a situation that very likely contributed to the fate of Picariello and Lassandro (Palmer and Palmer, *Alberta* 176, 213).[1]

In contrast, the Cook murders occurred in a less turbulent time and place. Stettler was a community much more congruent with Alberta's dominant image at the time as a "breadbasket to the nation."[2] Stettler had been settled primarily by people from western and northern Europe, and while there was considerable ethnic diversity in the area, for the majority of the region's residents, the forces of assimilation had been at work for decades. This, along with the expanding economy and the popularity of the Social Credit government of the day, made the setting for the Cook family murders a much less tense and divided community than the Crowsnest Pass had been in the early 1920s. While ethnicity was apparently not a factor in the trials and subsequent conviction of Robert Raymond Cook, as it almost certainly was in those of Picariello and Lassandro, Cook's fate, like theirs, was affected by politics: Cook's effort to have his sentence commuted was ill-timed since it came in the wake of considerable furor over a recent and very controversial commutation. Prime Minister John Diefenbaker, usually sympathetic to avoiding the death penalty, likely felt it was politically impossible to commute Cook's sentence at this particular time (Pecover 425-29).

The accused in these two cases had little in common. Born in Capriglia (Avellino) Italy in 1879, Emilio Picariello had immigrated to Canada in the late nineteenth century. He married Marianna Maria Marrucci (also an Italian immigrant) in 1904, and the couple eventually had seven children (Lee 56; Floren 40). They moved to Fernie BC in 1911, where Emilio worked for (and eventually managed) a number of enterprises catering primarily to the Italian community in the area. Over the years, he became "… the Padrino of the Pass and as the 'Padrino' character, he had all the good as well as the bad traits: liberally open handed, highly enterprising, daringly adventurous, and disrespectful of the law" (Lee 48). Known as "Emperor Pick," he was powerful and well liked within the local immigrant community. Prohibition provided new business opportunities, and Picariello was able to make substantial profits running liquor from British Columbia into Alberta and Montana, which was also "dry." Less is known about Filumena Costanzo. She was born in Italy in 1900 and immigrated with her family to Fernie BC when she was nine, marrying Italian immigrant Carlo Sanfidele/Charles Lassandro in an arranged marriage when she was only fifteen. Charles, twenty years her senior, was recruited to run booze by Picariello, who regarded the couple as useful cover for his smuggling operations; however, Filumena soon became estranged from Charles, and just where her true affections lay has been a matter for much speculation (Lee 49). What is certain is that both Emilio Picariello and Filumena Lassandro stood trial in Calgary in the late Fall of 1922 for Constable Lawson's murder, a crime they allegedly committed on 21 September 1922. They were found guilty, despite scanty evidence, and they were both hanged on 2 May 1923 for first-degree murder at the Alberta Provincial Jail in Fort Saskatchewan, northeast of Edmonton.

This sad story was ancient history when Robert Raymond Cook was executed by hanging at the same Provincial Jail on 14 November 1960. However, as it turned out, Filumena Lassandro and Robert Raymond Cook would share the oddly parallel distinction of being the last woman and the last man to be hanged in Alberta, both in their early twenties at the time of their deaths. As with Lassandro, it is difficult if not impossible to be certain that Cook was guilty of the horrific crimes of which he was convicted; indeed, Jack Pecover's extensive research indicates that there were sufficient gaps and problems with the evidence presented at both of his trials to warrant a reasonable doubt. What is certain is that seven members of Cook's family were brutally murdered sometime on the night of 24-25 June 1959. Their bodies were discovered several days after the murders, concealed in a grease pit in the garage adjacent to the family's home. Cook, who had been apprehended earlier on a charge of false pretenses for using his father's identification to purchase a car in Edmonton, claimed complete surprise when the bodies—and the scene of horrendous violence in the house—were discovered. He was tried twice (the second trial ordered because of an error on the part of the judge in the first) and convicted both times. He lost an appeal to the Supreme Court of Canada and an eleventh hour attempt to have the sentence commuted, and went to his death still insisting that he was innocent.[3]

Filumena: Grand Opera as (Historical) Creative Non-fiction

Though some might regard opera as an unlikely vehicle for chronicling western Canadian history, both librettist John Murrell and composer John Estacio set out expressly to highlight this often overlooked region and its people (Calgary Opera 19). As well as being known for his plays about western Canadian history, Murrell is known for his plays about women and for bringing to his work a revisionist sensibility, including a desire to revisit the past with a view to offering a more inclusive version of the historical truth (Melnyk 228). One of his earliest works, *Power in the Blood* (1975), is about a woman evangelist and his well-known play *Memoir* (1978) explores the life of Sarah Bernhardt. Set in Calgary, *Waiting for the Parade* (1980) depicts the experiences of five women during the Second World War, and *The Faraway Nearby* (1995) focuses on American artist of the southwest, Georgia O'Keefe. As George Melnyk points out, Murrell has been particularly interested in the challenges faced by "women triumphant rather than women as victims" (101). In *Filumena*, however, he turns his attention to someone who was arguably the quintessential female victim. Murrell has explained in several contexts that he had always wanted to write a libretto, and the Picariello/Lassandro case seemed to provide the perfect material for such a project. When he approached Calgary Opera with the idea, John Estacio (composer in residence at the time) was "immediately transfixed," seeing in this piece of southern Alberta history not only the very stuff of great opera, but also "a true Canadian story with immigrants as the central characters" (Calgary Opera 19). As a new Canadian whose parents had emigrated from Portugal, Estacio was particularly drawn to an opportunity to highlight immigrants, people whose stories are often forgotten.[4]

Thus in *Filumena*, Murrell and Estacio aimed to bring history to life in a way that seems wholly compatible with the definition of creative non-fiction (CNF) offered recently by Charles Foran. Foran argues that "the emphasis in creative nonfiction is on the use of inventive and dramatic techniques to support fact-based narratives." However, Foran cautions, this emphasis does not give writers of creative non-fiction *carte blanche* as if they were writing fiction. "Rather, it gives them a similar toolbox to enrich and enliven their presentation of the facts. Using such tools, the CNF writer seeks to achieve, in the words of author Tom Wolfe, 'a larger truth than is possible through the mere compilation of verifiable facts or direct quotation.'" Drawing on such a "toolbox," what strategies do Murrell and Estacio employ in their effort to turn the story of Filumena/Lassandro into compelling theatre while, at the same time, not violating the requirement for accuracy that necessarily accompanies the use of sensitive historical material?

Perhaps the most obvious strategy is their choice of genre: casting the story as an opera enables them to tap into the narrative conventions of the genre as well as the enormous emotive power of music. Clearly, drawing on historical material involving high profile and/or sensational personalities is an established operatic tradition, as exemplified by such works as Handel's *Giulio Cesare* (1724), Mozart's *La Clemenza di Tito* (1791), Donizetti's *Maria Stuarda* (1835), and Verdi's *Simon Bocanegra* (1857; revised 1881). The tradition continues in such contemporary works as *Nixon in China* (1987), by John Adams and Alice Goodman, and *Dead Man Walking* (2000), by Jake Heggie and Terrence McNally, to say nothing of such popular musicals as *Evita* (1978) by Andrew Lloyd Webber and Tim Rice. Moreover, tragic death is often a central feature of these narratives, and the grand gestures of Grand Opera seem well-suited to capturing characters and events that are almost larger-than-life. According to Murrell, "one of the most difficult things in the world is to make the spoken word sing and soar. It tends to waddle, or at best, to strut." Noting that while words are superb for capturing the struggles of daily life, Murrell insists that it is music, not words, that enables one to express "pure meaning," and thus "to convey … what is beyond words." When they are attached to music, "words fly … when they need to, they swoop, or they alight and grow still for a breath-taking pause, or they plunge from a great height, only to soar again" (Calgary Opera 19). Clearly, Murrell's characterization of the key figures in this historical drama—Filumena Lassandro, Emilio Picariello, Charlie Lassandro, Stefano Picariello, Maria Picariello,

McAlpine, Constable Lawson, and Mamma Costanzo—is heavily dependent upon and enormously enriched by the musical score through which they, in large measure, make themselves known to the audience. Perhaps paradoxically, the musical dimension adds heft and weight—a kind of additional materiality—to these historical characters about whom so little is actually known. Estacio's musical score is eclectic, drawing on the traditions of serious or tragic "grand" opera as well as on those of the lighter operetta, with its vernacular dialogue and elements of humour (DeLong, "Filumena's Tragedy" C8). The spare, yet highly nuanced score, builds "on a pair of five-note motifs, which mutate in shape and purpose throughout," as, for example, with the recurring waltz that evokes both tenderness and foreboding, depending on context and inflection, and the recurring "There will be a storm" motif (Everett-Green R3).

In addition to this rich musical vocabulary, the stark realism and elemental natural beauty of the sparse set—stylized (blue) Rocky Mountains in the background and plain wooden structures in the foreground, structures that at once evoke both an old-world village and a frontier mining town wordlessly—point to the sharp contrasts within the complex social world the historical figures/characters inhabit. In concert with these non-verbal modes of expression, Murrell's libretto, which is one-third Italian and two-thirds English, further emphasizes the often-competing narratives that defined the world of the Italian immigrants living in "The Pass" in the early decades of the twentieth century.[5] An amalgamation of several powerful modes of representation at once—drama, poetry, music, and visual art—the operatic genre enables a rich and nuanced yet economical treatment of setting, character, and theme. Thus aided by multi-dimensional modes of expression, Murrell as librettist is able to say a great deal about the Crowsnest community—about his characters and their relationship to each other—through a seemingly simple libretto. Moreover, while a grand opera traditionally contains five acts, *Filumena* contains only two—a compression that builds momentum and a relentless sense of inexorability. That Estacio's score, which music critic Robert Everett-Green has referred to as at once "bold and ingratiating," is highly melodic, in the tradition of Verdi and Puccini, lends even more emotive power to Murrell's treatment of these characters, as of course, do the dramatic and musical skills of the various performers (R3).

The opera opens with townsfolk gathered outdoors to celebrate the wedding of Filumena to Charlie Lassandro. This scene introduces the main characters and forces that will collide to create the tragedy that unfolds in the scenes that follow.[6] The deceptively simple, often repeated, phrase, "in English only," symbolizes the efforts of Emilio Picariello to promote the acceptance of the Italian community he leads and the power-relations that define that community, pressured from without to assimilate and from within by divisive dynamics of generation and gender. Similarly, the dual names of key characters—Stefano/Steven and Filumena/Florence—embody the painful struggle over identity often central to immigrant experience. Charlie, already dissatisfied with his wife, berates her for speaking Italian with her mother, as well as for not seeming to be sufficiently happy on their wedding day. "You embarrass me and I don't like to be shamed," he tells her angrily. Foreshadowing her fate, Charlie, after handing her a bouquet of white lilies (flowers symbolic of innocence and purity and also associated with death), accuses her of looking "like an old lady at a funeral."[7] Filumena's struggle to be true to herself within a straightened world is artfully expressed in a melodic aria where she promises "inside my heart … I will keep my own name." When an expansive Picariello arrives with his wife Maria and eldest son Stefano, he salutes the young couple, asking Stefano to sing an old-country love song in their honor. Reluctant, Stefano nevertheless complies, transfixing the assembly, particularly Filumena, with a delicate aria whose key motifs recur at crucial moments throughout the opera, capturing the tenderness of young love. However, the moment is soured by Charlie's jealousy and the arrival of Constable Lawson. By the scene's end, Filumena and Picariello have become sympathetic characters, misunderstood by smaller-minded people in the community.

Scene Two moves us ahead several years to Picariello's Alberta Hotel in Blairmore, where Florence and Charlie have joined Picariello's household. The growing affinity between "Emperor Pick" and Filumena is apparent in his sympathetic and protective responses to her disapproval of "the business," and to Charlie's attempts to control her. Picariello confides in her his dreams for the community's future, dreams he believes she shares. In the meantime, she and Stefano are increasingly attracted to one another. Picariello asks Filumena to help in "the business" by acting as a decoy. She and Stefano are to pose as "a young couple in love" in order to convey liquor across the border, the idea being that as such a couple, they won't attract police attention. She agrees, though Constable Lawson's sudden arrival and his stern warning to "Pick" to "get out of the business" lend a note of foreboding.

Sharp, ironic contrasts between the characters' lived realities and their dreams also pervade scenes Three and Four. Scene Three takes place in early summer in an idyllic alpine meadow where Stefano and Filumena share a picnic as they wait to play their parts as decoys. Predictably, the pretense of being "a young couple in love" is too much for them; they kiss and acknowledge their feelings for one another. They are interrupted by the arrival of Pick and Charlie, who transfer the load of illegal liquor to their car. Scene Four returns us to Blairmore a few months later, and to Pick's campaign for election to the Town Council. Juxtaposed with the enthusiastic cheering of his supporters outside, the sharply contrasting scene inside the hotel kitchen is one of rising tension between Stefano, Filumena, and Charlie, since the latter has discovered the nature of the relationship between his wife and the boss's son. Later, Charlie confronts Picariello with "the truth." The scene ends ominously with Charlie meeting Constable Lawson surreptitiously in the hotel while the others are outside with the campaign crowd. The gulf between grim reality and the dream of a better life grows.

The Second Act begins on the fated 21 September 1922. Filumena, awaiting Stefano alone in the hotel kitchen, notes that a storm is approaching. Charlie arrives with news that Steve has gone on what Pick, having been elected to the Town Council, has termed a "last haul." Since Steve has not returned, a worried Maria immediately summons Picariello from a council meeting. When the straight-talking McAlpine arrives looking disheveled and upset and reveals that Constable Lawson pursued him and Steve, that shots were fired, and that "Steve was hit real bad," Picariello swears revenge. Grabbing Filumena, he heads for the police barracks. In the next scene, Picariello and Filumena arrive at Lawson's home. The homely set and the presence of Lawson's young family as he steps out onto a wooden porch suggest Lawson's vulnerability, evoking some sympathy for this public servant who, in his frequent "pestering" of Picariello, is merely doing his job.

Murrell's libretto does not offer a straightforward representation of the killing of Lawson. Picariello is armed and also thrusts a pistol into Filumena's hands as he accuses Lawson of murdering his son. The three struggle, Filumena's efforts seemingly aimed at restraining the men. When a shot is fired, Lawson drops to the ground. Who fired the fatal shot is unclear. In Scene Three, the widow and children follow the coffin through the streets, trailed by the townspeople, who, as a traditional chorus, voice the concerns of the wider community as they speculate about what happened and vow revenge on the perpetrators.

Scene Four, set in a Calgary jail cell in November of 1922, reveals the full horror of Filumena's situation. She learns just how alone she is when Stefano and Maria visit and implore her to assume responsibility for Lawson's death. After all, they argue, since Pick is a man with a wife and children, his life must be spared, and besides, since she is a woman, she is unlikely to be hanged "by a jury of upstanding Canadians." He, on the other hand, surely will be if he is found responsible. "I know what the truth has to be," sings Stefano soulfully. As well as indicting Canadian justice, this scene serves to ennoble the character of Filumena. Although disappointed and saddened by Stefano's actions, she resists the temptations of righteous anger. Instead, she tells him sadly, "You are a son any father would be proud of." And, although she doesn't agree to do as Stefano and Maria have asked, neither does she refuse.

The final scene reveals that all of Stefano's entreaties and Filumena's anguish were ultimately for naught. Both Picariello and Filumena have been convicted and sentenced to hang. As they await execution, the bleakness of the setting contrasts poignantly with the liveliness of the opera's opening scene. This contrast and the arias that the doomed characters sing, revealing their innermost thoughts, combine to evoke empathy for both, but also deep admiration for Filumena. As guards prepare to escort him to the gallows, a distraught Picariello expresses horror at losing his family and his dreams for a better life. In contrast, Filumena, now a full-blown tragic heroine, is dignified and transcendent as she prepares calmly for her death.

In this scene, and throughout *Filumena*, Murrell and Estacio negotiate the complex conventions of grand opera to tap into the healing powers of tragedy. As Murrell notes, "the greatest artists of opera and theatre have relentlessly been drawn to the tragic ... because they know that suffering ... has the power ... not just to heal us of our pain at the fates of these ... characters but to heal us of the pain of our own fates." (Calgary Opera 19). As Murrell goes on to explain, the "gimmick" of tragedy is that it transports us to heights of existence that enable us to put the inevitable depths into perspective, and then to persevere in the face of it. In turning the relatively scant facts about the lives of Emilio Picariello and Filumena Lassandro and their role in the murder of Constable Lawson into such a story—and one that aims to represent the experience of immigrants more generally—Murrell and Estacio have been able, indeed compelled, to move away from the dark moment of "truth." Their telling does not linger on what happened on Lawson's front porch on 21 September 1922, but rather on the hopes and dreams of the two principal characters, as revealed in memorable and expressive arias and duets. As Murrell explains, "Filumena soars upward, beyond blame and self-pity, up to a height where she can begin to perceive and to embrace a truth which is both bright and dark, both deep and high" (Calgary Opera 19). Thus one might say that while Murrell and Estacio have not in any way violated the "rules" of creative non-fiction that require an accurate rendering of known facts, they have succeeded in offering up a "larger truth" than would have been possible had they relied solely on the facts; moreover, they have done so by using the expansive, multi-faceted genre of grand opera to produce a representation of the "terrible truth" that deflects attention from the gritty, but elusive "facts" surrounding the murder of Constable Steve Lawson, focusing instead on the longings and redemptive powers of the human spirit in the face of insurmountable odds.[8]

the Boy: Metafiction as (Historical) Creative Non-fiction

A former social worker, Calgary writer Betty Jane Hegerat had written two novels—*Running Toward Home* (2006), which tells the story of a troubled foster child, and *Delivery* (2009), which explores a complicated mother-daughter relationship—and a book of short stories, *A Crack in the Wall* (2008), which examines the meaning of home through the experiences of a disparate group of characters, when she took on the complex writing project that ultimately became *the Boy* (2011). Although this hybridic work represents a departure for Hegerat in terms of its form, like her previous books, it is set in Alberta and reflects her continuing interest in families and the complex dynamics that hold them together and/or tear them apart.

In *the Boy*, Hegerat seemingly takes quite a different approach to "telling the terrible truth" than that taken by Murrell and Estacio in *Filumena*. While *the Boy* defies easy classification, it can be seen, at least in part, as a work of historiographic metafiction; however, since *the Boy* is quite clearly divided into two distinct narratives, one that is fictional and one that is not, less than half of the work (eleven of twenty-eight chapters) is unproblematically encompassed within a definition that sees historiographic metafiction as "*fiction* that is intensely, self-reflexively art, but also grounded in historical, social, and political realities" (Hutcheon 13). Nevertheless, the non-fictional half (all of the seventeen chapters entitled "Roads Back") is so self-consciously intertwined with the fictional (the chapters entitled "The Boy"), that separating them is impossible. Moreover, the juxtaposition of these two narratives is the author's fundamental strategy in her effort to make some sense of the Cook family murders. What she sees as the question at the core of that story, however, is not "who did it"—the question that Jack Pecover explores so thoroughly in *The Work of Justice*—but rather, "why?" As she explains, "… it wasn't the details of the murder case or Cook's trials and execution that I was examining, but what went before. It was the family I was interested in" (Hegerat, *the Boy* 108).

The other closely related question that draws Hegerat to the Cook family story is one that haunts her from the years she spent as a social worker, as well as from her experience as a mother: "How does someone learn to love someone else's child?" (15). This question focuses attention on Robert Raymond Cook's stepmother, Daisy: as Hegerat's main fictional character, Louise, puts it in one of the conversations between her and the author that occur (usually at the ends of chapters) throughout the book, "We care about Daisy" (61). The affinities among these three women—the author, her fictional character Louise, and the long-deceased Daisy Cook—are central to the various linkages among the fictional and non-fictional narratives.

The Boy is, then, a work of creative non-fiction that draws heavily on metafictional strategies to bring the past to life as well as to illuminate what *might* happen in human relationships. For example, one of Hegerat's main strategies is to create a complex symbiotic relationship between the book's fictional and non-fictional elements, both of which are infused with her own story—as a writer/researcher struggling with her current project, and also as someone of a certain age who grew up in central Alberta and who remembers the Cook murders from her childhood. Thus the book comprises three interrelated narratives, but their juxtaposition is often uneasy, as when the fictional Louise asks, *"And what about the Cooks?,"* Hegerat answers almost angrily that she is "not writing a story about bludgeoning and hanging" (38), and as early as the end of Chapter Four, the author insists that her research into the Cook murders (primarily reading) is now sufficient: "Surely I could leave the Cook family to their rest" (43). But this turns out not to be the case, and Hegerat takes her quest a step further by looking for individuals who might have known the family. When one of her interviewees is curious about her interest in the topic, Hegerat confides in her readers that she was "tempted" to say that she too was surprised by her interest, and that she even shares the revulsion of one of her friends who told her she would never buy the book when it's finished. Somewhat defensively, Hegerat explains to the curious interviewee that her research into the murders is primarily in the service of her fiction:

> I told Marion Anderson that my quest was really on behalf of a character in a story I was writing. I remembered the murders from my own eleven-year-old perspective, but another story, a piece of fiction seemed to be demanding that I try to find the family in this crime. (67)

Prior to articulating this strategy, however, Hegerat explains that she has actually tried to keep the two stories separate; however, the psychological impossibility of doing so and, indeed, the strategic utility of not doing so become increasingly apparent both to writer and reader as the seemingly bifurcated project evolves.

Of course to call the book bifurcated falls short of doing justice to its structure since, as noted above, as well as comprising fiction (the eleven chapters devoted to "The Boy") and non-fiction (the seventeen chapters devoted to "Roads Back"), it also encompasses an ongoing conversation between the author and her main fictional character. This conversation (set off in the text by indentation and, for Louise's voice, italics) is a kind of third section of the work. It is also a major metafictional tool for highlighting the complicated and sometimes troubled relationship between authors and their subjects, as well as the constructed and somewhat arbitrary nature of narrative. Perhaps most importantly, these conversations between the author and her character (along with the ongoing resonances between the fictional and non-fictional narratives) blur the lines between fact and fiction, forcing readers to consider how difficult it is to be sure about what really happened in the past, to ascertain the whole truth. As Louise puts it, *"Doesn't Daisy feel like fiction too? All of this gets a little blurry sometimes doesn't it?"* (65).

Appropriately, then, the book begins with a fictional chapter, "The Boy (June 1994)". The setting (Edmonton) and situation are presented via the point of view of Louise Kernan. That Louise is not an altogether reliable narrator is another important part of the author's strategy of highlighting the difficulty of ascertaining the truth. An unmarried school teacher in her late thirties, Louise is at a bar with colleagues, supposedly celebrating the end of the school year, though she is not really having a good time, admitting (to readers) that she "hates" these events. However, it is here that she meets Jake Peters, "a man at the next table who seems as much an outlier to his party as she is to hers" (9). They eventually leave the party and over a snack at a nearby Tim Hortons, start to get acquainted. A car salesman who remembers selling a car to Louise several years before, Jake is a widower with a twelve-year-old son, Danny. Jake insists that Danny is "good at heart and smart too, just not real motivated when it comes to school, and … a bit rambunctious." For her part, Louise knows "from that one sentence" that "Daniel is a problem at school" (12). Despite this potential "red flag," Louise, who "imagines herself married, raising a family"(10) but who has had no luck with relationships, is pleasantly surprised when Jake asks to see her again, and the chapter ends with their making a date to see a movie together.

This first chapter, having set the stage for the fictional narrative, is followed by a non-fictional one in which the author confesses that she is frustrated with her work. She is struggling to envision the fiction she is trying to write with the clarity that will enable her to get on with the task. At first her problem seems to be a block in her usual creative process, whereby, if she listens carefully, her characters speak to her, enabling the story to "find its way onto the page." This time, though, her main character is not cooperating: "Instead of telling me the story herself, she seemed to expect me to tell her what would happen next" (14). But as she contemplates this problem, Hegerat begins to realize that the situation is actually more complex, and that "behind the image of Louise in my mind, there was sometimes a dark shadow, something she couldn't see, and I didn't want to illuminate" (14). Searching for, and yet at times trying to, escape from this dark shadow is yet another strategy Hegerat uses to link the fictional and non-fictional narratives, and in particular to insert her own story within both. Thus, in this second "Roads Back" chapter, not only do readers encounter for the first time the conversations between Hegerat and Louise that highlight the "constructedness" of the story, but they also begin to get to know the writer/narrator. Virtually a character in her own story, she is haunted by the tragedies of the human condition that she has witnessed as a social worker and, like any parent, worries about her own children. She is also currently feeling haunted by something horrific that happened in her childhood, something that seems to creep unbidden into her mind as she tries to write or go about her daily life.

For example, a trip from Calgary to Longview for dinner with friends evokes unpleasant memories for her. As she "stared across the street at a clapboard house," one that is eerily similar to the Cook house in Stettler, as per the photograph (Plate 6) and the written description in Pecover's book (103-04), she fantasizes about buying such a house in a small town and redecorating it in 1950s style as a weekend retreat. But her fantasy soon turns frightening as she begins to see ghosts: "a woman on the porch, children gambling across the patch of packed dirt at the side of the house. A man … watching from a shadowy garage set diagonally on the end of the property" (17). Louise's question (*"Is it my house you're imagining?"*) and her plea (*"Don't move me into that sad place"*) leave the author shaken, and her fantasy about the garage and "the smell of grease" triggers an even more disturbing memory:

> I closed my eyes and I was eleven years old, reading a copy of the *Edmonton Journal* my mother had hidden under a stack of *Star Weekly Weekend* magazines because she did not want me to know the gruesome details of a nearby crime. Reading about the bodies hidden under layers of greasy rags and cardboard. (18)

Asking her husband and friends if any of them remember the Cook murders from their childhood years, the story of a "whole family bludgeoned to death" conjures yet another dark memory for her, that of the impact on her as a child of the word "bludgeoned," a "word that was new to my vocabulary when I was eleven years old. I remembered sitting on the back step, my mouth full of that blunt, ugly word." Pictures also flood her memory—images of "a small clapboard bungalow, a flashy convertible, a madman rampaging through the countryside. The eldest son of the murdered family" (18).

These memories, and Louise's question—"*The son? The son murdered the family?*"—propel the author forward in her effort to tell Louise's (fictional) story and to re-visit the long-ago tragedy of the Cook family. Her fictional project and her personal quest to determine the "why" of the Cook tragedy, as well as to unmask the shadows in her own mind, become intertwined, providing the structural framework as well as the thematic heart of *the Boy*. Hegerat gives voice to the reader's ambivalence about the book's disturbing subject, and raises uncomfortable questions about how to deal, both individually and collectively, with real-life horror. Should we learn all we can about actual, horrific events, or avert our eyes?

Hegerat's strategy of not only interweaving the fictional and the historical, but of also entangling her own story within both strands draws readers into a complex meta narrative that is not easily put aside and into a world of questions about what happened and why, what can happen and why, and the personal and collective relevance of raising and attempting to answer such questions. By the end of the second chapter, the author's musings have brought her to where she needs to be to truly begin her quest for answers. While she feels emboldened, she knows it will not be easy:

> Louise was right. When I sat at the computer that morning, I finally acknowledged that her story wasn't just about family dynamics, a rebellious teenaged stepson, a crisis, a resolution. There was a reason for my recall of the Cook story. Write boldly. Hadn't I given that advice to other writers? If the writing frightens you, you're finally getting somewhere? (21)

Throughout *the Boy*, juxtaposing and interweaving the fictional, the non-fictional, and the personal continue to be the author's primary strategy for attempting to answer the questions at the centre of each of the book's narratives. She links the settings, characters, and plots in all three strands in inventive ways that enrich the book's separate parts and their interconnected sum. For example, the small and medium sized towns of central Alberta provide the backdrop to Louise's story, to the Cook story, and to the author's story and the similarities vis-à-vis the setting that reverberate across the narratives highlight the importance of place as a factor in the development of all three. All three narratives involve a move that impacts the "characters" profoundly. After Louise and Jake Peters marry, they move from Edmonton to his hometown of Valmer, since Jake is convinced that Danny's troubles are in large part a product of his not having the family and communal supports that a small town offers, though the move does not have the desired ameliorative effects on the increasingly alienated and troubled youngster. Similarly, as Hegerat tells us in "Roads Back," the Cook family moved from Hanna to Stettler after Ray Cook married Daisy Gasper, a move that his son Robert resented. The author also tells us that she experienced a move as a child, from New Serepta, where her parents ran a small café, to Camrose. The effect of this reiteration of place is to intensify the reader's awareness of the book's central Alberta setting. In transforming that setting from "prairie wholesome" to something closer to "prairie gothic," Hegerat creates the possibility of a compelling, if unsettling, answer to Northrop Frye's famous query: "Where is here?" In so doing, she transforms a landscape that for some may have barely registered as a place at all, real or imagined, into one that commands attention.

Certain other motifs reverberate through all three narratives, heightening suspense and intensifying the complexity of the quest for answers at the heart of each. Such motifs frequently serve as links between chapters, and thus between the fictional and non-fictional strands of the book, as when the author refers to Daisy Cook's teaching experience and her first pregnancy near the end of a "Roads Back" chapter, and begins the following "The Boy" chapter with a focus on Louise's teaching experience and pregnancy. The following fictional chapter begins with the birth of Louise and Jake's son Jonathon, clearly suggesting the possibility of parallel trajectories. As well, subtle similarities link the fictional characters to the historical ones: Ray Cook was reportedly very indulgent of Robert, as is Jake of Danny; Robert Cook was viewed by most who knew him as a skillful (and inveterate) liar, as is young Danny. Another pervasive motif is the car: automobiles figure prominently in all three narratives. In the fictional narrative, Jake Peters is a car salesman, and his son Danny not only burns down the neighbour's garage, but also has a penchant for stealing vehicles.

Ray Cook was a mechanic who passed on his passion for fixing, acquiring, and driving cars to his son Robert, whose main activity as a petty criminal was stealing cars. Researching the Cook murders requires Hegerat to make a number of road trips from her home in Calgary. Her car as well as the various others that appear in *the Boy*—perhaps none more than the Impala convertible that Robert Cook was driving when he was picked up for questioning on false pretense charges just prior to the discovery of the murders—not only links the fictional and non-fictional narratives, but also symbolizes the restless and ongoing quest for an elusive truth.

These interconnected metafictional strategies enable Hegerat to bring the Cook story to life to a degree that would be impossible had she limited her scope to offering a purely factual rendering of that story alone. For example, the details she provides from her own experiences growing up in the time and place of the Cook murders seep into the historical narrative indirectly. Memories of her mother mopping and waxing the floor of their family restaurant every Saturday night, "the smell of Johnson's paste wax that clumped in our throats late into the evening," and the sound of "the rustle of sheets of newspaper spread over the thick wax until it dried" (33) not only add the rich sensory details that draw readers into her personal story, but also lend a startling immediacy and poignancy to the Cook narrative. This is especially the case when she draws on these details to imagine the Cook's home and the family's interaction on the afternoon and evening of 24 June 1959, when all of the family members, except Robert who had only just returned after being released from the Prince Albert penitentiary the day before, were brutally murdered. She also remembers how, for much of that summer when she was eleven, she and a friend "trudged back and forth" between their two houses, "whispering about murder, about brothers and boys," and how their "wandering" back and forth came to a quick end when Robert Raymond Cook broke out of Ponoka. "My mother didn't need to place restrictions. Rose and I imagined a murderer, one with particular interest in children, hiding behind every tree. ... Even though he was captured three days later, ... it seemed as though our summer-time freedom was irrevocably lost" (37).

While the fictional and personal strands of the book lend concreteness and immediacy to the historical Cook narrative, the fictional narrative draws emotional intensity and suspense from the author's quest for answers about the Cook murders. What really happened and why? Was

Robert Raymond Cook guilty of the crimes for which he was twice tried and ultimately executed? As Hegerat shares stories about her various research trips to interview informants in central Alberta (e.g., the man who had been the best friend of the oldest of the murdered Cook children; the only one of the defense lawyers still alive; a woman who had worked in the Ponoka Mental hospital when Robert Raymond Cook had been incarcerated there briefly prior to escaping; Jack Pecover, author of *The Work of Justice*) and to visit salient sites (e.g., the Hanna graveyard where the murdered members of the Cook family are buried; the Stettler archives where the artifacts related to the two trials are stored; the Fort Saskatchewan Provincial Jail where Cook was hanged), not only does the landscape that Cook himself had traveled so many years before begin to emerge as a ghostly backdrop to the present, but also suspense grows as the case becomes ever more, not less, complicated—suspense that spills over into the book's fictional stream as we wonder just how the historical and the fictional are related.

Thus, while the fiction creates an imaginative vehicle for getting inside the Cook household indirectly, the horrific facts of the Cook story—however much the guilt or innocence of Robert Cook is still a moot point—caste a dark shadow over the fiction. What is Danny really capable of? Will Louise's story be similar to Daisy's? Moreover, Hegerat intensifies this spillover effect in a number of ways, as, for example, when she alerts the reader that she has plans for Louise—plans that she has no intention of sharing with her character. "I had now decided on a twist of plot for her story that I did not want to divulge until the words were on the page. I wanted the reins in my own hands" (153).

Perhaps the most powerful tool Hegerat employs to connect the fictional and non-fictional narratives is intertextuality. Early on, she tells her readers about the three books that she discovered on the Cook case: Frank W. Anderson's *The Robert Cook Murder Case*, 2008, Alan Hustak's *They were Hanged*, 1987, and Jack Pecover's *The Work of Justice*, 1996 (39). Hegerat refers to and quotes substantially from Pecover throughout *the Boy*, including lengthy quotes of letters (to his parents, his lawyers) written by Cook himself. Indeed, Pecover arguably becomes a character in *the Boy*, and Hegerat admits that his "exhaustive exploration of the Cook murders had become my textbook" (224). Hegerat even arranges to meet with the retired lawyer-turned-author, reporting on her impressions of him and their conversation, the latter further confirming her sense that "he himself had considerable doubt" that Cook was guilty (225). Pecover extends Hegerat a vote of confidence via a letter to her several weeks later, after he has read one of her novels—a gift she gave to him at their meeting: "He had read my novel and said that he believed Cook had now 'fallen into good and eminently competent hands,' which I welcome." However, her admission that his confidence feels "misplaced," that she fears she will "end up with even more questions than Pecover" highlights, once again, the difficulty of determining the truth, even after doing exhaustive research (229). Similarly, Hegerat's reference to Anne Marie McDonald's *The Way the Crow Flies* (2003), a fictionalized version of the infamous Steven Truscott murder case, reinforces the notion that truth is difficult to determine, and that justice may well miscarry.[9] This reference to the murder of a young girl also underscores the power of lingering childhood fears, intensifying the sense of foreboding that suffuses each of *the Boy's* narrative strands: "Once again, I was eleven years old, imagining a girl just my age riding into a summer afternoon on her bike, and never coming home again" (42).

However, the author's boldest, most powerful intertextual references weave the Cook murders directly into *the Boy's* fictional narrative. Shortly after Jake, Louise, and Danny move to Valmer where they purchase a "charming" older home (once an Anglican parsonage), Louise, while unpacking an old box of Brenda's things, discovers a "yellowed scrapbook" filled with newspaper clippings—a series of *Edmonton Sun* articles from 1984 revisiting the Cook murders.

> What kind of morbid interest possessed Brenda to keep these clippings? People she knew? But 1959? The articles were written twenty-five years after the crime and must have been in Brenda's keeping and then in Jake's for the next ten years … She will ask Jake about this. (70)

Louise later learns from her sister-in-law, Phyllis, that Brenda knew Robert Cook. According to Phyllis, Brenda "met him once at a party when she was in high school, and she never got over the whole bloody deal" (177). When Jake later tells Louise to throw out the scrapbook, she instead stores it (secretly) in the basement. While Louise understandably queries the author about her decision to place the Cook story so directly into the fictional narrative (*Whoa! … what are those newspaper clippings doing in my story?*) and the author replies that she too is "still amazed that I placed them there" (74), this strategy, like the other metafictional devices Hegerat employs, complicates and intensifies *the Boy's* interrelated narrative strands and, of course, the underlying quest for "truth." Clearly, the presence of the real story within the fictional one serves to foreground the role of the stepmother in both, as is particularly apparent when Louise returns to the scrapbook some time later and discovers the headline: "*Place Usurped by Hated Stepmother, Spoiled Son Turns to Crime*" (96). Hegerat's question—"How does someone learn to love someone else's child?"—has clearly become Louise's question as she finds herself a loving mother to her own two children and increasingly alienated from and fearful of Danny.

While the dissenting opinions about Cook's guilt leave her with some "doubts about the conviction" (171), Louise nevertheless lies awake at night, "thinking about Daisy Cook …" (174), and admits to Phyllis that she is afraid of Daniel (177). Louise tries to resist her darkest fears about Danny, telling herself that he is, after all, her beloved husband's son, "a boy she's known since he was twelve years old, the brother of her own children," and further insisting that Danny "is not Robert Raymond Cook" and "she is not Daisy Cook. There is no connection. None" (201). Nevertheless, that she keeps Brenda's scrapbook, against Jake's will, not only underscores Louise's lingering doubts, but perhaps also the author's own uncertainty about how the story/ies should/would/did end. This dramatic interpenetration of the two narratives not only builds suspense in both, but also, once again, foregrounds the difficulty of answering the fundamental questions (what happened and why) in either historical narratives or fictional ones.

The author admits defeat with regard to the historical narrative, confessing that she is not able to "imagine Daisy's ending … what happened in the white bungalow on 25 June 1959." Louise, resentful, challenges her: "*Why don't you just write the story and cut mine loose?*" When the author counters that she can't because no one really knows what happened, Louise asserts: "*You're a writer. Make it up.*" The author refuses, noting that anything less than the truth "dishonors these people" (202). Louise, then, takes up the challenge of entering the Cook home on that June evening, saying she has dreamed a number of details, which she skillfully provides. But she too must stop, unable or unwilling to take the narrative any further than when Ray and Bobby enter the living room together. As Hegerat has confided, "The problem with the Cook Story was that the people in it were real. The ending was written, and there was no redemption" (188).

Conclusion

In both *Filumena* and *the Boy* it is not primarily the historical narrative that offers redemption, but the fictional one. Murrell makes little attempt to focus the audience's attention on the facts of the Lawson murder case, to use their scantiness, or the clearly biased context in which the trial took place to redeem his central character; rather, it is a fictional strategy—the narrative arc of the tragic heroine of grand opera—that enables Murrell to end his story of the terrible truth on a high note, and his female heroine (like Verdi's Violetta or Puccini's Mimi) to triumph in spite of the forces of fate that would make her a helpless victim. Similarly, it is not in "The Roads Back" but in "The Boy" that Hegerat offers the reassurance that readers crave. Here the author is in control, and while cruelty, death, and sorrow inhabit the fictional world she creates, their order of magnitude is considerably less than the complex imperatives of fate and/or history that shaped the real-life Cook tragedy. In the fictional story, though his father dies, Daniel struggles toward a better life as he and Louise begin the process of reconciliation; here, in this fictional telling of the "truth," readers can find the modicum of hope and happiness they long for.

And yet, the non-fictional narratives are nevertheless very important parts of both *Filumena* and *the Boy*; indeed, in each, the fictive elements in many ways serve the historical narrative, constituting (along with the strategies that link the two) the "inventive and dramatic techniques to support fact-based narratives" that Charles Foran pinpoints as the defining feature of creative non-fiction. Moreover, while history—the stories of the real Filumena and of the real Robert Raymond Cook—may offer precious little in the way of clarity, justice, or happy endings, they do serve as compelling cautionary tales. As historically-based narratives, both works offer readers a great deal to ponder about causes and effects, innocence and culpability, as they consider how the "real story" might have been different, better. Thus one might say that in skillfully wrought, historically based creative non-fiction about tragic events, narrative itself ultimately triumphs, allowing readers the best of two quite palatable and more or less compatible stories: a fact-based story that enables them to look backward from a vantage point that offers the insights and self-satisfactions of hindsight, and a fictional one that enables them to look forward to a world where their best intentions define them and their finest dreams ultimately prevail.

One might say that each of these multi-faceted texts, in its own way, highlights the degree to which all writing, be it fiction or non-fiction (for example, journalism, history, autobiography, fiction, poetry, operatic libretti), is the construction of a particular, limited sensibility and further, a construction that is inseparable from the literary conventions that make expression and interpretation possible. In producing such works, these Alberta writers have illuminated the difficulty of the quest for truth; in drawing inspiration for their narratives from Alberta's history, enlarging and complicating the corpus of stories that construct Alberta in the minds of an increasing number of diverse readers, they might also be seen as bearing testimony to Robert Kroetsch's famous assertion that "the fiction makes us real," while artfully inviting us to appreciate the fineness of the line between what is real and what is imagined.

NOTES

1   John Brownlee, the Attorney General in the UFA government (and later Premier), attended the Picariello/Lassandro trial daily throughout its duration, providing concrete evidence of the UFA government's resolve to crush rum-running.

2   Interestingly, the heart-shaped logo on the Website maintained by the Town of Stettler (www.stettler.net/default.cfm) proclaims the city to be "the heart of Alberta." Currently boasting close to six thousand inhabitants, Stettler was home to approximately five thousand in 1959 when the Cook murders took place. Highlighting the theme that all is not always as it may seem on the surface, Jack Pecover, in *The Work of Justice: The Trials of Robert Raymond Cook: The Story of the Last Man Hanged in Alberta* (1996), points out that this logo carries an element of irony for those old enough to remember a time (now fading) when, due to its being the site of two mass murders in addition to those of the Cook family, Stettler "... had come as close as anything Alberta has to offer to being a heart of darkness" (102).

3   As Pecover points out in *The Work of Justice*, while Cook was actually charged and convicted of only his father's murder, "... in a loose and non-technical sense, he was convicted as well of the murder of all the remaining members of his family ..." (xx).

4   Estacio also discusses why being the son of immigrants drew him to this project in the third disc (Estacio and Murrell). John Murrell's comments on various aspects of the opera are also included on this disc. See also Hays.

5   According to Kelly Robinson, director and choreographer of the 2003 Calgary production (as well as several subsequent productions), this balance is meant to reflect Picariello's insistence that members of the Crowsnest Italian community use English as much as possible (qtd. in Remington A3).

6   Not surprisingly, soprano Laura Whalen felt a weight of responsibility in playing Filumena, the historical character so central to the opera, some of whose relatives were present on the opening night. As she put it, "I feel an enormous responsibility. It's really important to me that I play her honestly, that I remember that she was living here, in this province" (Remington A3).

7   All quotes from the opera's libretto are taken from a live recording of the Edmonton Opera Production of *Filumena* on 9 March 2006, which appears on Disc 1 of a three-disc set produced by Filu Productions in 2007.

8   It seems important to note that while Estacio and Murrell present Filumena Lassandro and Emilio Picariello—and the Crowsnest Italian community more generally—in a favorable light, in choosing this particular Italian immigrant story, they could be accused of pandering to stereotypes. Many Italians resent the way they are represented in popular culture, particularly the seemingly endless focus on an Italian as mobster, and many might well be less than pleased by yet another representation with such a focus. See, for example, L'Orfano (5-11); Scambray (2-13).

9   The intertextuality here, as elsewhere in the book, extends to the internet. In this instance, the author searches online for information to refresh her memory of the Truscott case, learning that the fourteen-year-old Truscott, who had been sentenced to hang just two days before Cook was sentenced, ultimately had his sentence commuted. Truscott, like Cook, always maintained his innocence, and in 2007, he was proved innocent and released.

WORKS CITED

Blakey, Bob. "Opera: Only Woman ever Hanged in Alberta." *Calgary Herald*, Sunday, 26 Jan., 2003, p. A7.

———. "Opera Stirs Memories of Murder." *Calgary Herald*, Friday, 31 Jan. 2003, pp. A1, A8.

Calgary Opera. *Calgary Opera Program: 2002-2003 Season: Winter Edition.*

DeLong, Kenneth. "Filumena is Back in all her Glory." *Calgary Herald*, Friday, 8 Aug. 2003, p. E2.

———. "Filumena's Tragedy Finds its Voice." *Calgary Herald*, Monday, 3 Feb. 2003, pp. C8, C10.

Estacio, John, composer, and John Murrell, librettist. *Filumena.* 9 Mar. 2006. Live Recording of the Edmonton Opera Production, Filu Productions, 2007, disc 1.

Everett-Green, Robert. "Filumena Sways the Jury." *The Globe and Mail*, Monday, 3 Feb. 2003, p. R3.

Floren, Erik. "Emperor Pick was our Capone." *Alberta Centennial 1905-2005. The Calgary Sun*, Thursday, 1 Sept. 2005, p. 40.

Foran, Charles. "What is 'Creative Non-fiction'?" 2009, Keynote Speech to the Creative Fiction Collective. http://www.creativenonfictioncollective. com/defining-cnf/. Accessed 17 January 2013.

Hays, Matthew. "The New Ethnic Blockbuster." *The Globe and Mail*, Saturday, 6 Sept. 2003, p. R8.

Hegerat, Betty Jane. *The Boy*. Oolichan Books, 2011.

———. *A Crack in the Wall*. Oolichan Books, 2008.

———. *Delivery*. Oolichan Books, 2009.

———. *Running Toward Home*. NeWest Press, 2006.

Hutcheon, Linda. *The Canadian Postmodern: A Study of Contemporary English-Canadian Fiction*. Oxford UP, 1988.

Lee, Valeria Sestieri. "Italians and the Law in Alberta." *Italian Canadiana*, vol. 15, 2001, pp. 47-60.

L'Orfano, Francesca. "Mainstream Media and the Godfather Legacy." *Accenti*, vol. 1, no. 1, Mar.-Apr. 2003, pp. 5-11.

"The Making of Filumena." *Filumena*. Filu Productions, 2007, 3 discs.

Melnyk, George. *The Literary History of Alberta. Volume Two: From the End of the War to the End of the Century*. U of Alberta P, 1999.

Palmer, Howard, and Tamara Palmer, *Alberta: A New History*. Hurtig, 1990.

———. *Peoples of Alberta: Portraits in Cultural Diversity*. Western Producer Prairie Books, 1985.

Pecover, Jack. *The Work of Justice: The Trials of Robert Raymond Cook: The Story of the Last Man Hanged in Alberta*. Wolf Willow Press, 1996.

Remington, Robert. "1923 Alberta Execution Inspires New Opera." *National Post*, Thursday, 30 Jan. 2003, p. A3.

Scambray, Ken. "Italian Americans and Italian American Cultural Power." *Accenti*, vol. 1, no.1, Mar.-Apr. 2003, pp. 12-13.

Wood, Patrica K. *Nationalism from the Margins: Italians in Alberta and British Columbia*. McGill-Queen's UP, 2002.

Alberta's Environmental Janus:
Andrew Nikiforuk and Chris Turner

Geo Takach

If environmentalism is the defining issue of our age, then environmental writing offers fertile insights into the practices, values, and future of a people. As "Canada's Energy Province" ("Oil and gas"), Alberta has historically been a proud poster-child for the petroleum age. The province offers an insightful case study in two respects: first, as a bellwether in the evolving discursive clash between the insatiable need for economic growth mandated by globalized capitalism and its increasingly unsustainable ecological costs, and second, as an exemplar of how that clash is understood and expressed.

The polarized discourse around the environment and the economy finds an acme in the bituminous ("tar"/"oil") sands, a resource concentrated in the province's vast northeast that constitutes the world's third-largest recoverable source of oil ("Oil Sands"), and what has been called the world's largest industrial project (Leahy). This polarity echoes the Roman god Janus, depicted as two-headed and facing in opposite directions, and said to govern life's changes, including transitions between dichotomies such as past and future and, most pertinently here, between competing visions (Ouzounian). This essay takes up the Janus model in focusing on Andrew Nikiforuk and Chris Turner, two leading Albertan environmental writers with distinct approaches to defining and surviving our petroleum age. In highlighting these authors' environmentally-themed books, this work seeks to situate them in relation to Alberta's tradition of environmental writing, aspects of its provincial character, and the polarized discourse around economy and environment both within the province and beyond. Specifically, this chapter argues that Nikiforuk and Turner are motivationally allied but rhetorically opposed exponents of two divergent attitudes characterizing Alberta's provincial history, namely an austere biblical morality and a sunny technological utopianism.

Environmental Literature

Environmental literature—defined here as writing on themes or issues relating to our physical (and particularly natural) surroundings—has deep roots. From distant accounts such as Ovid's plea for vegetarianism two thousand years ago and Georgius Agricola's defence of mining in 1556 (Wall) to more recent, popular texts such as *Silent Spring* (Carson) and *An Inconvenient Truth* (Gore), writing has depicted, reflected, and even shaped our habitats and our world. After millennia of development culminating in the Industrial Revolution, the Romantic tradition in literature and other forms of art emerged in the eighteenth century in opposition to the dominant, master narrative of progress. The Romantics viewed the earth as worthy of sanctification rather than just human exploitation, and their work is exemplified by writers such as William Wordsworth (1770–1850), Ralph Waldo Emerson (1803–82), and Henry David Thoreau (1817–62). More recently, the Romantic end of the spectrum has been extended to more ecocentric perspectives by writers such as Arne Naess (1912–2009), Françoise d'Eaubonne (1920–2005), David Suzuki (b. 1936), Vandana Shiva (b. 1952), and Bill McKibben (b. 1960). Aspects of this polarity between anthropocentric and ecocentric views reverberate in Alberta's literature as much as its politics.

In his landmark study of Alberta's literary history, George Melnyk notes the eminence of nature writing in the province, tracing its lineage from Aboriginal etchings on stone and accounts from fur-traders and explorers through to the postwar work of authors such as Andy Russell (1915–2005) and Sid Marty (b. 1944), followed by books on local flora and fauna, and a flurry of tourist guidebooks, many trumpeting the Rocky Mountains. Yet despite the popularity of these works (Hardy's *A Natural History of Alberta* is said to have sold seventy-three thousand copies), Melnyk positions Albertan non-fiction since the Second World War—an era coincident with the fateful oil strike at Leduc in 1947 that inaugurated Alberta's modern age—as "circumscribed by the singular nature of politics in the province and by the public's devotion to the economic imperative of the energy and natural resource extraction industries" (2: 135). Indeed, income from non-renewable resource royalties accounted for 29% of the provincial government's revenue from 2002–03 to 2013–14 ("Background-er"), while oil has played a significant role in shaping Alberta's identity (Shrivastava and Stefanick; Takach).

Today, environmental issues increasingly populate the discourse around the province. Alberta has long been renowned for its magnificent scenery, depictions of which have beckoned to settlers and tourists since the late nineteenth century. However, in recent years, the province has also become an environmental pariah, with the management of its bituminous sands attracting mounting international wrath, protest, and ridicule (see Pratt; Sands and Brooymans; McFarlane; Takach, *Tar Wars*). Elements of this struggle and efforts to cope with it environmentally, socially, econom-ically, and culturally are reflected in a battery of recent books, mostly writ-ten by authors from beyond the province.[1] This is the climate in which the two writers studied here ply their trade.

Andrew Nikiforuk (b. 1955) and Chris Turner (b. 1973) share some key biographical details. Both live in Calgary, Alberta's largest city and the acknowledged centre of Canada's oil industry. Both are serious journalists who have been published in well-established magazines and metropolitan daily newspapers in Canada, and who have authored popular, critically acclaimed books. Both have earned several national magazine awards for their writing. Both have expressed deep concerns about the path pursued by provincial and federal governments in their headlong rush to double down on fossil-fuel extraction despite overwhelming evidence suggesting its non-sustainability. This has pushed both authors well beyond tradition-al Romantic notions of idealizing and sanctifying nature, and brought them into conflict with deeply entrenched political and economic forces committed to the status quo. In spite of these similarities, the two part ways in classical Janus fashion.

Andrew Nikiforuk and the Moral Quest

Nikiforuk's first environmental book is *Saboteurs: Wiebo Ludwig's War Against Big Oil* (2002). Reading like a political thriller, it chronicles the saga of a socially conservative church leader who came to Alberta's Peace River region with his family and a few followers from Ontario, only to experience oil company drilling, a sour-gas accident causing his wife's miscarriage, diverse acts of resistance and vandalism against the industry, an RCMP investigation, five criminal convictions against Ludwig, and the shooting death of a teenager on a predawn joyride past the family property. In introducing his account, Nikiforuk begins:

> For nearly 100 years Canadians have trekked to the Mighty Peace to cut trees, grow wheat or remake a life. When a farm goes broke, a marriage goes sour, or the law comes knocking, the Peace can be counted on to embrace you like an all-forgiving mother. That's what Wiebo Ludwig was looking for in the summer of 1985: a respite from the storms of life. (*Saboteurs* 1–2)

In personifying the land as a maternal shelter, Nikiforuk invites our sympathy with a latter-day settler following a deeply entrenched narrative of westward migration by people seeking a better life, away from the corruption and foul air of cities, repression and poverty of foreign regimes, and all number of evils unleashed by humanity on itself and its habitats. This narrative has played a fundamental role in the settlement of the West. It has resonated particularly profoundly in Alberta, a place with an agrarian and strongly Christian "pioneer" heritage which continues to brand itself as a bastion of individual freedom, with minimal "interference" from government by way of regulations and taxes—or, its critics charge, even by way of adequate public service in essential areas such as social services and environmental protection (Takach, *Real Alberta*). This rejection of state regulation reminds us that beyond the sensationalistic headlines and details of Ludwig's personal struggle looms the larger war that humans continue to wage on the earth's natural systems in the name of progress. While hardly lionizing Ludwig, Nikiforuk's depiction, dedicated as it is "To all downwinders"— citizens directly harmed by the ecological impacts of industrialization—engenders sympathy for Ludwig's cause, if not his religious convictions or his methods. It also raises unsettling concerns about how our governments, industries, and enforcement systems are running roughshod over public and environmental health in the name of private profit.

A more explicit environmentalism appears in Nikiforuk's next book, *Pandemonium: Bird Flu, Mad Cow Disease, and Other Biological Plagues of the 21st Century* (2006). Here he follows his earlier homage to pestilence, *The Fourth Horseman: A Short History of Epidemics, Plagues, Famine, and Other Scourges* (1992, rev. 1996), to turn a writerly microscope on how human health and habitat are under siege from avian flu, livestock diseases, SARS, blights, cholera, anthrax, and other biological terrors. These are presented not as natural phenomena, but the result of globalization and its dependence on the monocultural production and movement of agricultural and other goods as quickly, plentifully, and cheaply as possible. He paints a devastating picture of sloppy practices (both individual and institutional) and underfunded public-health systems that both exacerbate the spread of epidemics and leave us at the latter's mercy. Also indicted are the media's tendencies to cover pandemics only during their occurrence—and even then, melodramatically and perfunctorily—rather than to more methodically root out and attempt to neutralize their causes.

The book culminates in predicting a pandemic that will rock the global economy with sweeping force and cost countless lives. Nikiforuk brings our survival down "to family and community, the only first responders that have ever mattered in history," rather than to public preparedness plans, noting further that "Rural communities that still value self-reliance and neighborliness will pass through the ordeal with greater dignity than urban monocultures of wealth or poverty" (*Pandomium* 263). Nikiforuk tries to end his apocalyptic vision on an optimistic note:

> Long after the monotony of deprivation and separation, the survivors of the Great Mortality will kiss their loved ones each night and hold on tight. Then they will light candles, true plague of light, and pray for deliverance from more invaders. The humbled will be thankful, as Albert Camus once was, for what pandemics have always taught those receptive to biological instruction: "There are more things to admire in men than to despise." (265)

Nikiforuk closes with an ecologically oriented "canticle for local living" that encourages humility in the tradition of St. Francis (268). Here he cites the state motto of Hawaii ("The life of the land is perpetuated in right-eousness") and calls for us to consume less than we can imagine. He in-cludes as an appendix a British list of fourteen steps to reduce the risk of a hospital infection. This approach seems archetypically biblical, foretelling catastrophe and promoting its alleviation through prayer and good be-haviour. As in *Saboteurs*, the book invokes a Christian approach (albeit in narration rather than in a protagonist) and raises larger questions around how industrialization and neoliberalism are destroying the simpler life that humanity has led for all but a miniscule and relatively recent fraction of our history.

More down to earth (at least literally) is *Tar Sands: Dirty Oil and the Future of the Continent* (2010). Nikiforuk asserts himself as arguably Al-berta's pre-eminent critic of our societal petroleum addiction in general and its largest manifestation in particular. The book opens with a "dec-laration of a political emergency" (Nikiforuk, *Tar Sands* 1), cataloguing with caustic succinctness the madness of accelerating the liquidation of the sands without either a plan or a regard for the massive ecological, eco-nomic, social, political, and democratic costs. Besides consuming gargan-tuan quantities of non-renewable natural gas and irreplaceable fresh water (which is drained into toxic tailings "ponds" as large as lakes), destroying vast amounts of virgin boreal forest, flora, and fauna habitats, endangering various species, tarring Canada's international reputation as an obstacle to action on climate change, sentencing us to servitude to the US (our largest energy market, by far), and other apparently unsavoury consequences, the resource's mismanagement by the provincial and federal governments is seen as compromising both governments' responsiveness to their citizens. Here Nikiforuk cites Friedman's First Law of Petropolitics, linking rising oil prices to reduced democracy, as governments more dependent on rev-enue from petroleum rather than from taxation are less prone to listening and accounting to their citizens. He concludes with an Alcoholics-An-onymous style twelve-step program "for energy sanity" (200), which in-cludes a cap of two million barrels per day that has since been surpassed.

Three important contributions of *Tar Sands* to environmental writing in Alberta (and beyond) relate to our agency, both individually and collect-ively, in addressing the diverse and complex challenges of our addiction to oil. The first is showing that the multitude and the depth of damaging impacts of the bituminous-sands project are not separate from the rest of the province (and country), even if the site is geographically remote from all of Canada's larger population centres, with the exception of Edmonton. From the health of Aboriginal communities to the freedom of their community doctor to raise it as a concern, among many other examples, the book illustrates the risks of maintaining a business-as-usual attitude in starkly concrete terms. Second, the book exposes the ruinously false division and the forced polarity between economic development and environmental protection. Clearly, the latter is a prerequisite for the former, as there can be no long-term growth if its foundation destroys what we need to live: clean air and water, and a balance of the planet's natural ecosystems and among its non-human inhabitants. A third, important contribution of the book frames these environmental concerns as *moral* issues, embracing our duties to the casualties of the status quo: the earth's ecosystems, future generations, and all forms of life.

In his next eco-book, *Empire of the Beetle: How Human Folly and a Tiny Bug Are Killing North America's Great Forests* (2011), Nikiforuk blends themes from *Pandemonium* and *Tar Sands* by tying the meteoric proliferation of an apparently natural pestilence—the voracious pine beetle—to anthropogenic global warming and human mismanagement and arrogance. He explains how since the 1980s, the insect, smaller than a grain of rice but travelling in swarms physically larger than schools of killer whales, has devoured thirty billion conifers from Alaska to New Mexico, a swath of devastation said to be unmatched since the deforestations by European peasants from the eleventh to the thirteenth centuries. Among the environmental lessons that this history-changing event teaches us, he suggests, are that the human love of stability can be trumped by nature's volatility; that big things, the root of our social and political miseries, always fail, while smaller things adapt and survive; and that aging forests, which he likens to what he sees as our corrupt and failing banking systems and resource industries, actually require razing (by fire in the case of forests) and reconstituting to survive (the fire helps germinate seeds from the old trees). Again, the primary lesson is that the archetypically biblical moral that our human failings—in this case, selfishness, avarice, and systemic violation of the Golden Rule of doing unto others as we would have others do unto us (Matthew 7:12)—all lead to our destruction.

In *The Energy of Slaves: Oil and the New Servitude* (2012), Nikiforuk approaches the economic and environmental costs of our petroleum-based lifestyles from a historical perspective, following the critical path of the great Canadian economic historian, Harold Innis (1894–1952). Starting with the observation that the abolition of slavery in North America occurred around the dawn of the age of fossil-fuel production, Nikiforuk suggests that this abolition may have resulted from economics as well as morality since both were about harnessing energy to do our work for us. He likens our profligate use of energy in all aspects of our lives to the exploitation of slaves by nineteenth-century plantation owners. In measuring the physical work required to meet our needs, he suggests that each resident of the developed world today consumes the energy equivalent available to a Roman patrician with almost one hundred slaves. This, he argues, has shackled people to machines and mechanical thinking, which has increased our material well-being, but not our happiness.

Citing the depletion of half of the world's oil and the illusion of endless economic growth based on fossil-fuel consumption, Nikiforuk builds on his Christian-influenced moral undertones in *Saboteurs*, *Pandemonium*, and *Tar Sands* to call for a substantial reduction in our use of oil. He finds our energy servitude "debilitating," concludes that "our health, our freedom, and our humanity depend on a moral reassessment of mastery and slavery in all energy relationships" and calls for "a radical decentralization and delocalizing of energy spending combined with a systematic reduction of the number of inanimate slaves in our household and places of work" (*Energy of Slaves* 227). A notable departure in this work is his focus on the US; Alberta is scarcely mentioned, and even then mostly derisively as anti-democratic in its subservience to a petro-economy.

Finally, Nikiforuk's latest book at this writing, *Slick Water: Fracking and One Insider's Stand Against the World's Most Powerful Industry* (2015), chronicles the epic personal and legal struggle of a solitary Albertan, Jessica Ernst, against an energy colossus, Encana, the provincial government, and its industry-funded energy "regulator" after her groundwater was contaminated by the environmentally devastating practice of hydraulic fracturing ("fracking"). In portraying Ernst as courageous and complicated, and government and industry as fraudulent and corrupt, Nikiforuk depicts a quintessential clash of good versus evil—Davida versus Goliath—positioning Ernst's "ordeal" as "a troubling and important window on a brutal North American drama" (*Slick Water* 312). Adopting an overtly political stance, he declares, first, his motivation for writing the book (as opposed to merely a magazine article) as potentially offering "some measure of real justice" (312), and second, his donation of 15% of his royalties from the book towards Ernst's legal fees in her suit against Encana, the Alberta government, and the Energy Resources Conservation Board.

The sweeping narrative opens with a detailed account of a natural-gas explosion that caused "raining fire" over a quarter-mile retail area in Los Angeles. In keeping with his characteristically rigorous research, Nikiforuk provides a statistical account of the volume and the actual and potential devastation of fracking, and its ability to upset the earth's natural rhythms and equilibrium. His conclusion includes an invocation of the Christian philosopher, Jacques Ellul, in citing the ongoing threat to democracy and the social order by technology unleashed by powerful forces in furtherance of their own financial self-interest, as opposed to the greater good of the commonwealth. These apocalyptic visions are in keeping with the biblical moralism underlying his environmental volumes.

Chris Turner and the Technology of Hope

While not as numerous as Nikiforuk's book-length output, Chris Turner's environmental tomes have also distinguished themselves for their breadth of perspective, depth of investigative research, and iconoclasm. Like Nikiforuk, Turner brings a critical eye to the petroleum age, although he acts on it quite differently. He emphasizes not the cataclysmic retribution attendant on humanity's long-term destruction of the earth's natural systems, but the exciting potential for saving it, relying on the very innovation and ingenuity that fuelled the Industrial Revolution and the dizzying technological advances marking society today. In this, he echoes Alberta's self-proclaimed can-do entrepreneurialism, said to be a legacy of the same pioneering spirit from which Nikiforuk draws his biblical inspiration (Sharpe; Takach, *Real Alberta*).

Turner's first environmental book, *The Geography of Hope: A Tour of the World We Need* (2007), begins with the premise that environmentalism has failed to live up to its initial, hopeful promise, and collapsed under the weight of a mammoth mission to solve anthropogenic climate change, becoming not a "We-shall-overcome" rallying cry, but a corporate buzz-word. He recounts his own summer job as a student canvassing for Green-peace, when he came to despair at his own doom-saying rhetoric, and subsequently, the myopic, respective foci of governments and businesses on election cycles and bottom lines, which he felt would never solve any-thing. Taking his lead from a 2004-speech by Adam Werbach, an Amer-ican advocate for sustainability who declared environmentalism dead and rechanneled his outlook from apocalyptic to constructive, Turner drops the gauntlet for his readers thusly:

> To look back, perhaps half a century from now, to say to our children—to our grandchildren—that we took all this on, thought and thought, worked our asses off, tried and failed and tried again, and finally got this wonderful new contrap-tion moving down a clear path toward the sustainable city on a hill—what could be better, more worthwhile, more flat-out balls-to-the-wall exhilarating than to be part of that?
>
> What else are you working on right now? What great proj-ect that would rest upon your soul like the many bars of ribbon on a war hero's chest? What's that you would point to, and look your grandkids in the eye and say, "Now that was worth the fight"? I know how I'd answer this one: There's nothing else.
>
> Only this:
>
> To be part of the generation that beat climate change.
> (Turner, *Geography of Hope* 9)

Turner asserts that we already have the knowledge and the technology to solve the problem of carbon and climate change, and that our paralysis comes down to a tragic lack of will. From there, he embarks on an inter-continental investigation titularly billed as "a tour of the world we need." He introduces us to functioning models of sustainable power (the Danish island of Samsø; Gut Ankelohe, Germany), transport (Singapore, Port-land), housing (Freiburg, Bangkok), design (St. Louis; Hyderabad, India), and metropoli (Malmö; Aurora, Colorado). Samsø exemplifies finding solutions not through sweeping global movements, international treaties, or government policies, but simply by thinking and acting locally: one local explains how the island switched to nearly completely renewable sources of electricity through a grassroots movement of neighbours meeting at inns, one local champion, one house, one village at a time. Here Turner wryly notes that the total cost of that transformation, $125 million, was about half of the production budget of a Hollywood climate-change disaster flick, *The Day After Tomorrow* (Emmerich). He positions sustainability as a paradigm shift in the way in which we run our societies, but one that is both economically feasible and non-ideological. He also foresees a sustainability revolution happening much as the Internet plowed aside older, more cumbersome, slower, and inferior telecommunications infrastructure. He closes with a repeated allusion to the biblical notion of a "shining city on the hill" from Jesus' Sermon on the Mount (Matthew 5:14), where hope for the future becomes reality and ultimately takes comfort in the knowledge that his infant daughter has already glimpsed the dawn of a world far brighter than the darkening failures of the petroleum age.

Turner's second environmental book, *The Leap: How to Survive and Thrive in the Sustainable Economy* (2011), picks up from his first work to envision a new Industrial Revolution or operating system for the world, a cognitive leap through which civilization can advance to an economy powered by renewable energy sources rather than continue the decline that inevitably follows a dependency on fossil fuels. He points to three colossal failures under the status quo: the collapse of market fundamentalism, exemplified in the economic crash of 2008; the illogic of a system premised on unlimited growth on a planet with finite natural resources; and the breakdown in the infrastructure on which everything depends—the earth—indicated by anthropogenic climate change. He observes that grandiose schemes and technologies (for instance, geo-engineering attempts to mitigate some of that change through large-scale intervention in the climate, such as sequestering carbon) prove that it is not lack of imagination that holds us back, but our disproportionate preoccupation with ways to keep following a failed path. He challenges the myth of the rational actor, the premise of both our economic system and the Enlightenment philosophy, that we know what is best for ourselves and therefore make the best choices. Citing a few recent, catastrophic ecological statistics, Turner responds, "Like hell we do" (*The Leap* 82).

Turner fixes the primary barrier to a successful "leap" as our natural bias to the status quo, born of a fear of loss which makes us "much more deeply invested in where we are than in where we might be able to go" (87).

Such a leap requires considering the *actual* costs of our energy economy, such as its effects on our air, water, wildlife, and landscape, and making decisions based on what we value. Today, he says, the vast bulk of the cost (the value) of electricity production lies in extracting, refining, and distributing coal without accounting for the real costs, while factoring in government subsidies and other biases included to keep coal-fired electricity cheap in many places. Turner sees more value in renewable sources of power, where the fuel is free, limitless, and non-polluting, and our electricity costs, after installing wind turbines or solar panels, are limited to maintaining and repairing them. Thus, the system's focus moves from extraction and refining to manufacturing and installation, bringing tremendous economic opportunities in addition to energy autonomy and sustainability. Turner views the leaders of this leap as entrepreneurs, inventors, and municipal politicians, much as purveyors of petroleum pushed that innovation a century ago. As in his first book, the move to sustainability is accompanied by examples of advances in urban design and transportation, which he illustrates here with Copenhagen's pedestrian-friendly downtown, widespread solar panels in rural India, and rapid public transit in Bogotá. Again, his core message boils down to our choosing between "a leap of blind faith in a twisted model of business as usual and a reasoned Great Leap Sideways" (343).

Turner's third related book, *The War on Science: Muzzled Scientists and Wilful Blindness in Stephen Harper's Canada* (2013), documents what he argues, with ample supporting evidence: the former federal government was not only suspending its public duty to protect the environment in favour of facilitating further private profit by energy corporations, but also the ability of its own scientists to discuss their work. He views this as part of a larger subordination of scientific research to political imperatives, subverting not only Canada's foundational ethics of exploration, scientific achievement, and environmental contributions, but also a centuries-old tradition privileging reason which dates back to the Enlightenment. This is the same tradition he asserts in *The Leap* that we have violated with our swath of environmental destruction. While far from a jeremiad, it is an angrier work than its predecessors. The book's dedication to the campaign team behind the author's failed bid for a seat in a federal by-election in the year preceding its publication suggests a possible correlation to that unhappy result.[2]

Alberta's Environmental Janus

In considering these eight works by Turner and Nikiforuk, one finds a striking contrast. Nikiforuk seems to want to scare, anger, and shame us into curing our addiction to fossil fuels, which he believes can only beget deeper folly, servitude, pandemonium, filth, pestilence, and extinction. He sees the way out as making sweeping changes to government policies and consuming less as individuals, as outlined in his twelve-point plan closing *Tar Sands*. While occasionally resorting deftly to irony and sarcasm to make his point, the overarching sense projected is of earnest, biblical moralizing. On the other hand, Turner wants to inspire us to leap into a brave new world of environmental sustainability, one local solution at a time, and shows us how change is already underway around the globe. These approaches constitute a divergence that would do Janus proud. Yet, fundamentally, the two authors do not disagree, and their approaches can be seen as complementary, the yin and the yang of environmental writing in Alberta. Nikiforuk praised Turner's *The Leap* in a national newspaper review ("One Giant Cognitive Leap" R18), an extract of which appears on that book's front cover. In writing on the Anthropocene era—a term recently popularized in recognition of humanity's profoundly harming the earth's air, water, flora, fauna, and more (Stromberg)—both authors provide an essential service: Nikiforuk underlines the gravitas and horrific consequences of our addiction to fossil fuels, while Turner offers hope and points the way to recovering from it. In doing so, they echo two divergent attributes etched deeply into Albertans' collective psyche: on the one hand, a fundamentalist, moralistic linking of one's life's work to one's heavenly reward (and its converse, divine retribution for falling short), and on the other hand, an unshakable faith in the human capacity to dream up and realize solutions to the problems of the world, whether of our own making or not.

Alberta's oil-based economy and specifically what has been called the world's largest industrial project have pushed the province into the maelstrom of environmental debate. The eight books by Andrew Nikiforuk and Chris Turner highlighted here place Albertan writing at the forefront of that discourse. Their work is important not only because it addresses what may well be the greatest challenge to our survival that we have ever visited on ourselves, other life on earth, and the planet itself. Nor is their work important solely because it addresses the petroleum age with expansive vision, extensive research, and insightful analysis. Perhaps even more compelling is how their writing defies powerful forces both within and beyond a province that boasts a fierce political and economic monoculture in which its citizens seem to have been largely muted by affluence. With decades of nation-leading economic activity ("Backgrounder"), rare changes in government (despite the stunning election of the NDP in 2015),[3] record-low electoral turnouts, and a tradition of marginalizing, if not squashing, political dissent, Alberta has become fecund ground for a neoliberal, colonialist, uber-Darwinist ethic. This ethic is born of the longstanding and deeply entrenched master narrative of progress, enriching the privileged at the expense of the earth's natural systems and residents. Perhaps most importantly, their writing re-exposes the polarity between economic development and ecological sustainability as fundamentally false. In fact, even framing those values as polarities may be seen as an ideological tactic, because we should treat our planetary and collective survival as being in everyone's best interest, not as some kind of political compromise. Both authors illustrate the true costs of continuing our present course and different ways to survive it, although Turner's work focuses more on how to move towards sustainability in tandem with economic growth. In this way, their work transcends much of the body of nature writing that preceded them in Alberta in its scope, dissension, and intended impact.

The aforementioned works have been well received as a whole. *Tar Sands* and *The Geography of Hope* are billed as national bestsellers and have generated significant critical acclaim. For example, *The Literary Review of Canada* called *Tar Sands* even-handed, novel in showing the project's effects on real people, and emotionally powerful on both the local and global levels (Heintzman), while *Canadian Geographic* concluded of *The Leap* that "[i]ts wide dissemination would do us all a favour" (de Villiers 77). Nikiforuk won a Governor General's Award for Non-Fiction in 2002 for *Saboteurs* and the Rachel Carson Environment Book Award from the US-based Society of Environmental Journalists in 2009 for *Tar Sands*. *The Geography of Hope* was a finalist for the Governor General's Award for Non-Fiction, among other nods. Turner's *War on Science* drew minor criticism that it could have been more deeply researched, which the otherwise approving reviewer attributed to a need to publish the book in time to affect critical debates around controversial proposed pipeline projects

(Warner). Both authors' work can be found in libraries across Canada and in the US, and both men travel the speaker's circuit with their environmental tomes. For better or worse, their arguments have helped to turn the spotlight on Alberta in the greater context of rising global concern around anthropocentric climate change. This could fuel further grassroots concerns expressed in avenues ranging from individual posts to the New York Library's website (Walker) to advocacy campaigns against BP's involvement in the sands ("Dirty Diplomacy")—concerns that one day may culminate in global pressure sufficient to help curb the virtually unchecked development of the resource and its devastating results, economic downturns notwithstanding.

This question of impact is central, as both writers' work pleads for decisive and immediate action. In his literary history of the province, Melnyk concludes that writing which dissents from economic imperatives around oil extraction "has had little tangible effect" (2: 136). While presenting divergent outlooks on our potential future—environmental Armageddon and a "geography of hope," respectively—Nikiforuk and Turner concur emphatically that business-as-usual is not only unacceptable, but ecological suicide on a massive scale. In inviting us to make a Great Leap to sustainability, Turner echoes Pascal's Wager, articulated in the seventeenth century when skepticism challenged traditional religious views of natural law: Pascal held that rational people should live as if there *is* a supreme being, even if we can never know it, as we lose nothing if we are wrong and the world improves by the goodness of our actions. Transposed to the Anthropocene, this advice augurs for a clear, fail-safe, and moral alternative to perpetuating even the chance of the horrors depicted so powerfully by Nikiforuk.

Critiquing present practices of extraction, denial, and deceit while presenting progressive alternatives from *within* the province even more courageously plants small but powerful seeds of perspective, conscience, and hope for those who believe that the planet, all of its current occupants, and those who survive our stewardship deserve infinitely better. At its absolute core, this is what good writing must do: offer ideas that can inspire ameliorating action. Channeling Janus, Nikiforuk and Turner's work engenders both a deep, dark shame and a precious ray of hope.

Notes

The author heartily thanks the Social Sciences and Humanities Research Council of Canada and the University of Calgary for funding the portion of this research completed during his doctoral studies at that fine institution, and the co-editors of this volume and the reviewer of this article for their time, effort, and contributions.

1   Sample titles include *Stupid To the Last Drop: How Alberta is Bringing Environmental Armageddon to Canada (And Doesn't Seem to Care)* (Marsden); *Tar Sands Showdown: Canada and the Politics of Oil in an Age of Climate Change* (Clarke); *Journey to the Tar Sands* (Murphy et al.); *The Canadian Oil Sands: Energy Security vs. Climate Change* (Levi); *Black Bonanza: Canada's Oil Sands and the Race to Secure North America's Energy Future* (Sweeny); *The Heart of the Monster: Why the Pacific Northwest and Northern Rockies Must Not Become An ExxonMobil Conduit to the Alberta Tar Sands* (Bass and Duncan); *Ethical Oil: The Case for Alberta's Oil Sands* (Levant); *Little Black Lies: Corporate and Political Spin in the Global War for Oil* (Gailus); *The Pipeline and the Paradigm: Keystone XL, Tar Sands, and the Battle to Defuse the Carbon Bomb* (Avery); *After the Sands: Energy and Ecological Security for Canadians* (Laxer); *Tar Wars: Oil, Environment and Alberta's Identity* (Takach); and *Scripting Environmental Communication: Oil, Democracy and the Sands of Time and Space* (Takach).

2   In 2012, Turner literally put his money where his pen was by running as a Green Party candidate in a federal by-election. Alas, residents of Calgary Centre were unwilling to express sufficient support for his ideas: he finished third with 25% of the vote, splitting opposition support with a Liberal candidate (who got 32%) and losing to a Conservative who strategically avoided several campaign debates, but still netted 36% of the vote. Even worse for proponents of change (if not democracy), just 29% of registered voters in the riding made what seems to be, at least in Canada's oil province, a "Great Leap" to the polls ("History of Ridings").

3   From an environmentalist perspective, Alberta's 2015 provincial election, while exterminating the national record, forty-four-year dynasty of the Conservatives, is hardly a panacea. Despite the new NDP government's stunningly prompt completion of a climate strategy long promised, but never delivered by its predecessors, greenhouse-gas (GHG) emissions from the bituminous ("tar"/"oil") sands are still expected to double to about one hundred and fifteen megatons from 2010 to 2030, during which time the megaproject's share of Canada's GHG emissions is also expected to double, from 7% to 14% ("Oilsands' Share").

Works Cited

Avery, Samuel. *The Pipeline and the Paradigm: Keystone XL, Tar Sands, and the Battle to Defuse the Carbon Bomb*. Ruka Press, 2013.

"Backgrounder on Alberta's Fiscal Situation." Government of Alberta, 15 Jan. 2015, www.finance.alberta.ca/publications/fiscal/spotlights/2015-0115-Backgrounder-on-Alberta-Fiscal-Situation.pdf. Accessed 20 Nov. 2016.

Bass, Rick, and David James Duncan. *The Heart of the Monster: Why the Pacific Northwest and Northern Rockies Must Not Become An ExxonMobil Conduit to the Alberta Tar Sands*. All Against the Haul, 2010.

Carson, Rachel. *Silent Spring*. Houghton Mifflin, 1962.

Clarke, Tony. *Tar Sands Showdown: Canada and the Politics of Oil in an Age of Climate Change*. Lorimer, 2008.

de Villiers, Marq. "Might As Well Jump." *Canadian Geographic*, vol. 131, no. 5, Oct. 2011, p. 77.

"Dirty Diplomacy: Tar Sands Lobbying and the Fuel Quality Directive." UK Tar Sands Network, 2013, www.no-tar-sands.org/campaigns/ dirty-diplomacy-tar-sands-lobbying-and-the-fuel-quality-directive. Accessed 20 Nov. 2016.

Emmerich, Roland, director. *The Day After Tomorrow*. 20th Century Fox, 2004.

Fekete, Jason. "Oilsands' Share of National Emissions Set to Double between 2010 and 2030." *Ottawa Citizen*, 29 Jan. 2016, news.nationalpost. com/2012/02/10/stephen-harper-pushes-for-responsible-oil-and-gas-trade-in-china-speech. Accessed 7 Mar. 2016.

Gailus, Jeff. *Little Black Lies: Corporate and Political Spin in the Global War for Oil*. Rocky Mountain Books, 2012.

Gore, Al. *An Inconvenient Truth: The Planetary Emergence of Global Warming and What We Can Do About it*. Rodale, 2006.

Hardy, W.G., editor. *Alberta: A Natural History*. Alberta Education, 1979.

Heintzman, Andrew. "Bitumen: Boon or Blight?" *Literary Review of Canada*, vol. 17, no. 3, Apr. 2009, pp. 23–24.

"History of Ridings Since 1867: Calgary Centre, Alberta (2004–)." Parliament of Canada, 26 Nov. 2012, www.lop.parl. gc.ca/About/Parliament/FederalRidingsHistory/hfer. asp?Language=E&Search=Det&rid=1429&Include=. Accessed 20 Nov. 2016.

Laxer, Gordon. *After the Sands: Energy and Ecological Security for Canadians*. Douglas & Macintyre, 2015.

Leahy, Stephen. "Oil Sands: Burning Energy to Produce It." *Resilience*, 27 July 2006, www.resilience.org/stories/2006-07-27/oil-sands-burning-energy-produce-it. Accessed 20 Nov. 2016.

Levant, Ezra. *Ethical Oil: The Case for Canada's Oilsands*. McClelland & Stewart, 2010.

Levi, Michael A. *The Canadian Oil Sands: Energy Security vs. Climate Change*. Council on Foreign Relations, 2009.

Marsden, William. *Stupid To the Last Drop: How Alberta is Bringing Environmental Armageddon to Canada (And Doesn't Seem to Care)*. Knopf, 2007.

McFarlane, Andy. "Climate Camp Targets BP Oil Plan." *BBC News*, 1 Sept. 2009, news.bbc.co.uk/2/hi/uk_news/8232522.stm. Accessed 20 Nov. 2016.

Melnyk, George. *The Literary History of Alberta*. 2 vols. U of Alberta P, 1998-99.

Murphy, Tim, et al. *Journey to the Tar Sands*. Lorimer, 2008.

Nikiforuk, Andrew. *Empire of the Beetle: How Human Folly and a Tiny Bug Are Killing North America's Great Forests*. Greystone Books, 2011.

———. *The Energy of Slaves: Oil and the New Servitude*. Greystone Books, 2012.

———. *The Fourth Horseman: A Short History of Epidemics, Plagues, Famine, and Other Scourges*. 1992. Rev. ed. Penguin, 1996.

———. "One Giant Cognitive Leap for Mankind." *Globe and Mail*, 11 Nov. 2011, p. R18.

———. *Pandemonium: Bird Flu, Mad Cow Disease, and Other Biological Plagues of the 21st Century*. Viking, 2006.

———. *Saboteurs: Wiebo Ludwig's War Against Big Oil*. Macfarlane, Walter and Ross, 2002.

———. *Slick Water: Fracking and One Insider's Stand Against the World's Most Powerful Industry*. Greystone Books, 2015.

———. *Tar Sands: Dirty Oil and the Future of the Continent*. Greystone Books, 2010.

"Oil and Gas." Government of Alberta, 21 June 2016, www.albertacanada.com/business/industries/oil-and-gas.aspx. Accessed 20 Nov. 2016.

Ouzounian, Alice. "Exploring the Mystery of Janus the God of Gateways," www.plotinus.com/janus_copy2.htm. Accessed 20 Nov. 2016.

Pascal, Blaise. *Pensées*. 1669. Edited and translated by Roger Ariew. Hackett, 2005.

Pratt, Sheila. "Eyes of the World are Watching Alberta." *Edmonton Journal*, 3 Oct. 2010, p. A1.

Sands, Andrea, and Hanneke Brooymans. "Rude Message Awaits Renner; Sarcastic Newspaper Ad Slams Alberta's Environment Minister over Pollution." *Edmonton Journal*, 6 Dec. 2010, p. A1.

Sharpe, Sydney, editor. *Alberta: A State of Mind*. Key Porter, 2005.

Shrivastava, Meenal, and Lorna Stefanick, editors. *Alberta Oil and the Decline of Democracy in Canada*. Athabasca UP, 2015.

Stromberg, Joseph. "What is the Anthropocene and Are We in It?" *Smithsonian*, Jan. 2013, www.smithsonianmag.com/science-nature/what-is-the-anthropocene-and-are-we-in-it-164801414. Accessed 20 Nov. 2016.

Sweeny, Alastair. *Black Bonanza: Alberta's Oil Sands and the Race to Secure North America's Energy Future*. Wiley Canada, 2010.

Takach, Geo. *Scripting Environmental Communication: Oil, Democracy and the Sands of Time and Space*. Routledge, 2016.

——. *Tar Wars: Oil, Environment and Alberta's Identity*. U of Alberta P, 2017.

——. *Will the Real Alberta Please Stand Up?* U of Alberta P, 2010.

Turner, Chris. *The Geography of Hope: A Tour of the World We Need*. Random House, 2007.

——. *The Leap: How to Survive and Thrive in the Sustainable Economy*. Random House, 2011.

——. *The War on Science: Muzzled Scientists and Wilful Blindness in Stephen Harper's Canada*. Greystone Books, 2013.

Walker, Deb. "Comment on *Tar Sands* by Andrew Nikiforuk." New York Public Library, 4 Jan. 2011, nypl.bibliocommons.com/item/print_item/18587367052_tar_sands. Accessed 27 Jan. 2013.

Wall, Derek, editor. *Green History: A Reader in Environmental Literature, Philosophy and Politics*. Routledge, 1994.

Warner, Jessica. "Book Review: The War on Science, by Chris Turner." *National Post*, 11 Oct. 2013, news.nationalpost.com/arts/books/book-reviews/book-review-the-war-on-science-by-chris-turner. Accessed 20 Nov. 2016.

Alberta in the Alberta Novels of David Albahari

George Melnyk

David Albahari (b. 1948) is an Alberta novelist, short story writer, essay-ist, and translator, who now lives in Zemun, a suburb of Belgrade, Serbia, where he had lived since the 1950s before coming to Canada. In the fall of 1994 he arrived at the University of Calgary as the international writ-er-in-residence under the auspices of the Markin-Flanagan Distinguished Writers Program.[1] He continued to live in Calgary until 2012, when he returned to Zemun. During the eighteen years that he resided in Alberta, he published three novels set in the province. The first was *Snežni Čovek* (1995), published in English as *Snow Man* (2005). The novel parallels his own life because it describes a man who flees war by becoming a writ-er-in-residence at a foreign university. "Whatever happened in *Snow Man*," he explained in an interview, he himself felt except "… on a smaller, less intense level" (Melnyk, "Lost in Translation" 41).[2] *Snow Man* is an early representation of Albahari's view of Alberta because it is based on first impressions by a writer who was uncertain about his future relationship to this place. Would he stay? Would he go back? Would he write in English? Would he continue to write in Serbo-Croatian?

The second novel is titled *Mamac* (1996), which was co-published in 2001 in English by Northwestern University Press and Bayeux Arts of Cal-gary under the title *Bait*. The work is more reflective on the status of a writ-er in a foreign country than *Snow Man*, expressing what should be con-sidered a mature engagement with North American reality. It is a classic representation of how Albahari understood Alberta and Canada because it contains an extensive discussion of the contrast between European and North American mores and sensibilities. The third work, *Svetski Putnik* (2001), was published in English translation by Yale University Press in 2014 under the title *Globetrotter*. One ought to consider *Snow Man* an early representation of Albahari's literary displacement, *Bait* a classic example because it reflects his adjustment to life in a new cultural, linguistic, and physical environment, and *Globetrotter* his late or post-classical period of understanding Alberta. Taken together the three novels were produced during the first six or seven years of his life in Calgary. After that he did not write any other novels set in the province. It is as if he had come to an end point in positioning himself in its psychic landscape, though he continued to live in Calgary for another decade.

During the eighteen years he lived and worked in Calgary, he published more than twenty books (novels, short story collections, and essays) averaging more than one book per year. This is a prodigious output, reflecting the tranquility that Alberta afforded him. My focus on his three Alberta-related novels does not constitute a proper literary discussion of his impressive body of work while in Canada, nor his international stature as a writer. It is simply a study of how a writer's displacement from one geo-cultural context to another generated literary work that was influenced by that displacement. The immigrant/exile writer sees the world of Alberta differently than does a writer formed from birth by the province and nurtured by its historical milieu. Alberta is the home of numerous immigrant groups and writers from those groups must reconcile all sorts of socio-cultural and linguistic factors in order to "explain" the meaning of the new land to themselves and their readers. Albahari comes from the Jewish minority in the former Yugoslavia. Its tragic history is part of the Holocaust that engulfed and decimated European Jewry in the Second World War. His mother was a survivor. Later he experienced the early years of the civil war that destroyed Yugoslavia, the country of his birth with which he strongly identified. In a sense, he had become psychologically stateless when he arrived in Alberta.[3] That is the sensibility that haunts each of these novels.

While his novels and short story collections had been translated into numerous languages prior to his coming to Alberta, English translations began to appear only in the late 1990s and were originally published by small presses (Bayeux Arts, Calgary, and Northwestern University Press,

Chicago). This limited their audience, but later on the English translations of his novels *Götz and Meyer* (2004) and *Leeches* (2011) came out with major publishing houses, giving him a wider access to the English-speaking world, especially in North America. Stylistically, Albahari is very much a writer's writer. His narratives communicate through avant-garde structures. His novels are usually written in a single paragraph extending over a hundred pages or more. This unconventional style is disconcerting to readers of more traditional fare, but for those who are willing to enter its stream-of-narrative consciousness, Albahari's work provides a powerful and engaging experience. At first the reader may feel trapped in a singularly voiced consciousness or wrapped in an all-encompassing world that critics have termed "metafictional." Because there are no "natural" breaks in the text, the reader has to create virtual chapters and paragraphs as they see fit. The reader becomes a phantom co-creator by stopping, starting, and reflecting at any point in the text without any structural guidance from the author. He is not the first European writer to use this format. The Austrian writer Thomas Bernhard influenced Albahari in this technique. While fond of first-person narrative, he tends to identify key characters not by name, but by relationship (such as Mother, Wife, and so on). Because of these features, Albahari's writing was not easily accessible to an Alberta or Canadian audience. His style became another hurdle for local readers.

Albahari played a successful game of incognito while in Alberta, partially by writing in Serbian and then waiting for English translations to appear, and partially by remaining active in Serbia, which he visited each fall for the Belgrade Book Fair to launch his latest title or titles. His Serbian audience grew to expect an Albahari book every year. But the sporadic appearance of his works in English translation resulted in a much lower level of recognition in North America and Britain. The end result is that the scholarly response to his work is primarily in Serbian by Serbian scholars. There are also reviews in English-language periodicals and newspapers and critical studies by Northern American and British scholars of Serbian origin, who are able to read his work in Serbian. His work has also appeared in anthologies of fiction by exiled writers, a term he himself is reluctant to use.

The context of his writing about Alberta is a specific and short period in the literary history of the province. This period (1994-2001) was one of increasing recognition of diversity in Alberta writing, post-colonial interest in works by writers from minorities, and lively debate around the concept of being an Alberta writer. Albahari did not participate actively in this emerging consciousness. Instead he was an invisible witness to it and an observer of his own voice as it struggled with an alien environment. This positioning had a certain trajectory that followed a quickly rising arc launched in 1995 with *Snow Man* that reached its apogee a year later with *Bait*, and then became a gradual glide, touching ground with *Globetrotter* five years later. The implications of this asymmetrical trajectory are what this essay explores.

Snow Man

The novel begins with this sentence—"The driver was waiting for me at the airport, just as I'd been told he'd be" (Albahari, *Snow Man* 1). The driver was me. I was using a University of Calgary vehicle when meeting him at Calgary International Airport in October 1994. In this sentence the key word is "airport" because of its signification of travel, distance, passage, departure, and arrival. Airports are places of tension when they are, or represent, unfamiliar places. Airports are places of entry, a kind of border that is crossed to enter another realm. By using the term, Albahari recalls for the reader the reactions that come from either leaving for, or arriving in, a foreign place. The narrator is not being met by a friend or family, but an anonymous figure—a driver. He writes:

> The whole airport was no more than a cluster of sentences, I was on my feet thanks to words, something I would never have believed if someone else had told me. I was kept in one piece by letters, words held me; I breathed thanks to punctuation. (3)

On one level this is a poetic way by which Albahari announces that the narrator is a writer, an unidentified writer. On another level the equation of the airport with language suggests both the new language (English) that the airport represents and also that it is language and his ability as a writer that brought him to the airport in one piece. Being a writer saved him. In a letter that he wrote to the Alberta writer Myrna Kostash on 10 February 1993, he referred specifically to the issue of language in his writing and how it might affect him should he come to Canada:

And now we come to the old question: how does a writer feel when he has to go to another country, another language? Should he surround himself with his own language, and most probably sink, or should he try to mutter in his new language? There is probably no single answer to that question; there must be many of them. But most of them tell very sad stories. (Albahari / Kostash correspondence, 1993, courtesy of M. Kostash and D. Albahari)

It was Kostash who pushed for his getting the writer-in-residence position, and so he entered the no-man's land between two languages, where "clusters of sentences," as he says, are the only definition he has. He did not look forward to his new life, but he also did not think his old life was viable. As he said in an interview only a few months after arriving in Calgary, "The only homeland for a writer is language" (McGoogan B11). This is the homeland he embraced in Calgary.

An anonymous stranger (the driver) brings him to the new life at the university in an unnamed land. This lack of naming is Albahari's way of lifting us into a purely existential position with very few reference points by which to orient ourselves in the narrative, other than the perspective of the narrator, whose voice holds us with its narrative. The narrator hates his new situation and academe itself, where he is forced to play out a Kafka-esque navigation of his new life as "writer-in-residence." Surely, the term itself is loaded with connotations of alienation from the familiar, of being housed in an institutional setting with concomitant demands, and the idea that one is in a public role with an office like some official might have. What brought him to this point is part of the mystery and whatever we are told about the mysterious writer, except his immediate thoughts and reactions, unfolds with obliqueness. The narrator is apprehensive about the whole enterprise he is about to embark on, grateful for small gestures, initially rejecting the value of the new land, and feeling a need to hide his true feelings because he doesn't know the culture. All this is personalized in the appearance of an adversary, an unnamed professor of political science, who pronounces like a Machiavelli on politics and offers explanations of why the writer's homeland is disintegrating.

What immediately strikes the Alberta reader of the novel is the lack of identification of Alberta in the text. Only those who know Albahari's biography can identify Alberta in the text, where it is presented as an anonymous, imagined place without a name, though the references to foothills and mountains do help locate it. Since I was the driver who picked him up at the airport to take him to his rented home and the University of Calgary, I can vouch for the novel's Alberta locale, and having visited him often in this home, I can vouch for its description in the novel. He writes: "The living room faced eastward, the bathroom looked to the north, and the kitchen looked to the west" (Albahari, *Snow Man* 19). So it was. What is also present from early on is the way the narrator views his new home as the Other. Since the book was written for a Serbian audience, who would have a stance similar to Albahari's toward Alberta, the narrator's strategy of making the locals the alien ones makes sense to his readership. But for those of us who see the world from the viewpoint of our Alberta experience and who know Albahari's relationship to, and history with, Alberta, the narrator is the stranger, the Other.

The novel then moves into a mediation/dialogue on the narrator's former country with the professor of political science pontificating in curious metaphors, while the narrator bites his tongue in despair. The first person narrative is so dominant that the other voices in the text seem distant, almost irrelevant echoes. The advantage of our being so fully absorbed into the narrator's perspective is our identification with that narration. The disadvantage is the limitation of a singular point of view. For example, the novel's description of the university sounds more like a guide to an alien planet's civilization. The new world is so shockingly different and discombobulating that the narrator tells us: "I thought it would be best for me to shut myself in the refrigerator and come out when all this was over" (45). Especially galling to the narrator is the casualness with which the students and professors discussed the disintegration of his country. For Albahari's Serbian readers this smug Canadian casualness and ignorance must have been irksome and disappointing. The novel captures the poignant divide between one who has experiences of war and one who sees it from afar. Clearly his audience could identify with the narrator since they knew where he had gone to live. It was public knowledge.

A mantra throughout the novel is the recurring sentence: "I will grow old here." In fact, Albahari did grow old here. He was forty-six when he arrived and sixty-four when he left, an age at which he could begin thinking about collecting a pension. While this fictional prophecy was no doubt a literary device expressing the sadness of the narrator's situation rather than a prediction of his autobiography, it is circumstance that was realized in his own life. This fear of growing old in an alien place is a common enough theme in the life of emigrants and the exiled. One feels that one belongs to the place that one left and one does not wish to die in a foreign land. In Albahari's case, he was to return to Serbia, a country that he could never fully identify with as he had with Yugoslavia. He returned to a physical universe he knew (the apartment in Zemun), but the post-Yugoslav reality was one that troubled him. He never was a Serbian nationalist.

At one point in the novel the narrator is given *A Historical Atlas of Central and Eastern Europe* by the unnamed professor of political science, with the admonition that political identities and boundaries in the region are forever changing. "During one century alone," he says, "every town became several, no language stood firm, people went to bed at night without knowing what place they would wake up in the morning" (57). The whole narrative to this point positions the reality of the body and its suffering against the abstraction of ideas. "I have never hidden the repellant quality history holds for me," the narrator confesses (65). Not only does the narrator hate academe, but he also hates history. Turning to the atlas, he asks: "What do I do with you?" He is asking what do I do with my particular history which is not a book but a living experience. The answer is on the beads of sweat that appear regularly on the narrator's brow as he tells his story. He describes history as a "dislocation" and an "evasion" (68). It is history that has driven him to this new place where he doesn't want to be.

The image of the atlas as a book is quickly transformed into an atlas as a map, another abstract face of history. It was a German language map of the Roman Empire, which is an actual map that hung in his home in Calgary for all the years he lived in it. It had been left by the previous owner. The narrator mentions other maps that he has discovered in the home and they serve as a backdrop to his emotions about his life there and here. Maps have their own language, the shorthand of cartography, which is a language the narrator finds impenetrable. And then it begins to snow, a symbol of Canada. Snow means something to the body and in the novel snow signifies that magical moments are to unfold. The following description of the narrator's first encounter with snow in this new place is worth recounting:

> Then I went back to the snowball, which was lying on a gentle snowy incline. Like a tiny frozen meteor, it lay at the bottom of a shallow crater; as it rolled, once it completed its trajectory, it picked up another layer of snowflakes; the track it left behind, piecemeal, uneven, reminded me of the path of a snail over crumbly soil." (89)

The comparison between the path of a snowball and the path of a snail captures the narrator's bridging his former world with that of his new one. I cannot imagine a Canadian writer making that sort of comparison, but a Serbian audience would understand it. He brings the snowball home and says, "I arrive like a snowball, I disappear like a snowball, and all that is left is a puddle" (91). The new land may be as firm as a snowball at this moment, but it is destined to dissolve like his former country is dissolving. Only books and maps do not dissolve. So the narrator attempts to change the maps, to draw borders that separate "the Illyrians from the Slavs, the East from the West, the Arabs from the Jews" (93), but all he feels are the rivers that people are not allowed to cross and the mountain passes that are shut, all the barriers to the movement of bodies put up by these lines on a map. He concludes mournfully:

> "The only story that is alive is one that has not been given over to language ... just as the only history alive is the history that has not been given over to maps ... Words are merely ... phantom riders in the sky ... just as borders are only unreal scribbles ..." (105)

The juxtapositions of life, of language, and history are matrices that hold the narrator in a trap. Maps are a matter of phantoms and scribbles of lines on paper that have no body, no life but they can kill us.

The novel concludes with the narrator's world falling apart, of his questioning who he is in this place. He is saved by seeing a rabbit in the snow. It is the narrator's *Alice in Wonderland* moment as he pursues the rabbit. "I didn't know what I was exiting from and what I was entering into," he tells us, "but something kept opening behind me, just as something else kept opening before me" (117). The world is now magical rather than prosaic as the tempo of the final pages increases. He chases the rabbit to the summit of a hill—Albahari's home was situated just below Nose Hill in Calgary—and turns to see the city, which disappears before him. The narrator enters an existential void. He is free.

It is a dramatic and fitting end to a novel about a nameless world, where what is real are snow and a rabbit, physical representations of the body that the narrator can identify with, rather than the abstractions of professors, history, and maps. There is a powerful mystical and visual quality to Albahari's writing and imagery. His paradoxical speculations and quizzical attributions have a poetic logic. They levitate the reader, float him above reality as a way of expressing Albahari's own existence in the homeland of language. While the narrator cannot bond with the university or his new home through ideas, he does bond with a snowball, a physical metaphor that means something to him. Perhaps it is its temporality and fragility that appeal to him. Perhaps it is simply a literary device symbolizing Canada for his Serbian readers. But my preference for understanding the power of the snowball image is its whiteness and its lightness. It can fly through the air like an angel. Albahari is one of the few writers who can turn a snowball into a mystical symbol. Its ability to change form is something that resonates for him, mirroring his own life.

The *Atlas* is the only object with a proper name in the novel and having a name it torments the narrator with its historical definiteness. It is not even an atlas of the place he is in, but the place he came from. There is no map to this new alien land, Alberta. The immigrant/exile only understands the new world through its functional identities—dean, professor, woman, neighbour, house, basement, room, and street. For him their proper names do not matter, as he himself slowly becomes nameless to himself and turns into a snow man. Snow does not appear on political maps. Nor does Albahari. In an interview in 1998 he called himself "an invisible writer" (Longinovic 33).

Bait

The form of *Bait* follows that of *Snow Man*. It has a first-person narrator and an antagonist named Donald, who is the foil to the narrator, much like the professor of political science was in *Snow Man*. But now he has a name. Even the narrator's mother has no name, and she plays a vital role in the narrative. The novel recounts the life of his mother (and his father to a lesser degree). He identifies his father as someone who "found himself behind a barbed wire fence in a German camp for captured officers," which is what did happen to Albahari's father (Albahari, *Bait* 4). The autobiographical element continues when the narrator tells us: "It was two years already I hadn't heard my own language, I wasn't able to hear it often being this far away in the West of Canada, in a city in which everyone is an immigrant ..." (5). On the previous page he had identified his nationality by referring to the *Dictionary of the Serbo-Croatian Language*. The immigrant now has a specificity that was lacking in *Snow Man* and the novel itself becomes slightly more illuminated by the reference to Calgary, not by name, but by circumstance as a city "... raised on the surrounding hillocks that had once been part of the prairie at the foot of the Canadian Rocky Mountains, and the high-rises were on a flat stretch of land bounded by a narrow river [the Bow] and its still narrower tributary [the Elbow]" (10). The rivers are narrow because the rivers of Belgrade, the Danube and the Sava, are wide indeed. The narrator's mother has provided him with tapes of her life story, which he has brought to Western Canada. Her story symbolizes Europe and his being in Calgary becomes a place of displacement from his past. The reference to language is fundamental because the narrator expresses anxiety about losing his language and without it he believes he vanishes. Albahari's commitment to writing in Serbian during his eighteen years in Calgary is a confirmation of the narrator's concern. He admitted in an interview that "I can't create in English" (Melnyk, "Lost in Translation" 40). The growing specificity of the protagonist in the novel seems to parallel his affirmation of writing in Serbian rather than in English. Grudgingly he has adopted being in a new place, but not a new language. "I don't even want to consider writing prose in English," he told an interviewer after being in Calgary for four years, "especially because I have been developing my own style in the native language" (Longinovic 32).

While *Snow Man* is a novel of confrontation with the Other, *Bait* is a novel of loss, memory, and explanation. It is mellower in tone and less stringent in its judgements. Places and identities are named so that it is much easier to orient oneself in the work because naming creates a kind of map. What was vaguely suggested in *Snow Man* becomes specific in *Bait*. The battle between the two worlds remains, but now it is more a dialogue or debate rather than an angry, emotional exchange. For example, on page 41 of *Bait*, Albahari mentions Belgrade and Banja Luka, places that carry historical connotations for his Serbian readership, while on the previous page the words "Bosnia," "Yugoslav," and "Muslim-Croat formations" appear. The Yugoslav civil war of 1991-99 is here. He is finally able to write about it from the distance of Canada.

The narrator goes into a bookstore to search for a book about the Canadian soul and meets a writer named Donald, with whom he starts a debate. The narrator is particularly concerned about the relationship between identity and language: "I felt the other language taking over me, adapting me to its requirements, myself becoming another person" (28). The reference to English continues the concerns first expressed in *Snow Man*. The tapes from his mother explain the person he is, including his birthplace (Peć in Kosovo) and his military service. While saddened by the history of war in Yugoslavia and how it impacted his family and himself, he finds Canada a curious culture. The narrator talks about "Canadian kindness" as being made up of "polite phrases and so many thank-yous" (32). But this commentary on niceness leads the narrator to an unnerving conclusion: "Nothing so much frightens as kindness, nothing so much leads one to suspicion as a smile" (37). The cultural divide that this sentence expresses is a gulf that has the narrator feel total isolation ("I haven't met a single neighbour" [37]). This rather bleak social existence is then applied to the whole city where the narrator claims, "Life is invisible" (37). So in his second fictional description of his Alberta experience, two years into it, the alienation seems to have deepened. The city of Calgary is further described in a continuing tone of disinterest:

> ... a city on the edge of the prairie and the rim of the North, where the sun, especially in winter, moved uncertainly and low across the horizon, in the same way as I moved through the city center and the scattered suburbs. (47)

The narrator presents himself as having an uncertain and low profile, suggesting his passage through the city as being surreptitious, either out of fear or out of dis-attachment. This furtive presence seems to have been brought on by the weight of his mother's narrative that he listens to on a tape-recorder. What seems real to the narrator is the family history in Yugoslavia rather than the place he currently inhabits. The family story is the fundamental element, while where the narrator resides is unimportant and simply a place where he can reflect on that story and its tragedies. This may be the way that Alhabari actually viewed his own situation—his Serbian situation being the important one, and Alberta being simply a place where he could reflect on it. In a Canadian interview several years after *Bait* was published, he is quoted as saying:

> My present situation is a blessing and a curse at the same time. It is a blessing because of the experiences offered by the new culture … the curse is in losing touch with one's native language while surrounded by English speakers … (Longinovic 32)

Later on in the interview he presents a more positive view of what has happened to him. He says that his "physical absence" from Serbian literature has liberated him from certain roles he had within that literature. "The burden of being a writer in the East European way has also been lifted off my back" (32). But, of course, his Serbian audience is more interested in how he deals with his voluntary exile in Canada, imagining themselves in his shoes, and he graciously plays to that interest.

When the narrator explains his mother's story to Donald, he encounters a certain blankness that frustrates him. He concludes mournfully: "I will always be a European, as he will always be a North American, and about this nothing can be changed; we will always remain as different as night and day" (Albahari, *Bait* 62). This black and white metaphor suggests that in the continuum of existence and the daily passage of time the transitions offered by morning and evening are inconsequential. It is the two opposites that matter. Then the narrator shifts the parameters toward the elusive so that the reader is left wondering. He describes Donald as "a shady creature from the North" and himself as "a shady creature from the land of no return" (62). The characters in the novel are simply shades rather than reality, just shadows of real people. This shift gives his fictional world a certain indefiniteness. What Albahari wants the reader to experience is that in-between world where he himself is standing or trying to stand. He wants the reader to live in the space created by his writing, to be at home in a "cluster of sentences." One critic describes the point of view of the novel as looming "over the void" (Aleksić 54).

That Albahari felt comfortable enough in 1996 to write about the civil war that was raging in Yugoslavia was an indication of how his residence in Calgary had given him both peace and purpose. The relevance and power of the novel were such that it won the Nin Prize in Serbia for best book of the year, the most prestigious award that his work had received to date. It tells his personal story, though disguised and piecemeal. The tone of the novel is highly confessional and this approach, also true of *Snow Man*, brings the narrator close to the reader. V.G. Petković, writing in *Belgrade Language and Literature Studies*, describes the persona of the narrator as "articulate, but helpless and listless" (95). There are then two features of the narrator—first, his articulateness and second, his vulnerability—that encourage the reader to reach out to him. Because of the narrator's uncertainty and ambivalence, the interplay of history and identity becomes quite fluid and indeterminate. Expressing a viewpoint and then discounting it are typical for the narrator, whose life is losing its centre, just as his former country is disintegrating. Albahari's depiction of Alberta (he never uses the name) is wrapped up in terms such as "Canada" and "North America" which have currency among his Serbian readers, but not "Alberta." This is an important feature of his Alberta novels. They may be situated in the province, but they do not participate in its existence other than as a backdrop or as a symbol of a wider identity such as North America. That is why a Serbian critic like Petrović makes no mention of Alberta in her article. From her perspective the province is not a relevant player other than as the nameless "émigré environment … duly reflected in his fiction" (94). While the narrator in the novel recounts his mother and father's history and his own in Yugoslavia through various selected episodes, the narrator's history in North America deals with his futile attempt to make that previous history understandable to the figure of Donald. This obvious refusal to engage with the history and character of his new home, other than to see it as the opposite of Europe, reflects Albahari's unalterable commitment to his European identity. In the Longinovic interview, Albahari confirmed that it was the "theme of exile" that dominates the novels written in Calgary (33). He describes the novels as being about "isolation and existence in a linguistic and cultural in-between" (33).

The lonely voice of the exile is the voice of *Bait*. Lost in remembering, tied to events that traumatized, formed by the vagaries and horrors of history, the exile finds his new home empty, dull, and blind to his pain. For his European readership this portrayal is meaningful and relevant because of their own experiences. For his Alberta or Canadian readership, or even a wider English-language one, there is sympathy for the narrator's plight, but also a certain disappointment about his refusal to engage with the history and identity of the city on the edge of the prairie. The narrator excuses this failure by claiming he cannot adapt "... to North American standards" (Albahari, *Bait* 79). If he tried to adapt, he would lose whatever authenticity he has. That the narrator's story exists on a tape that he winds and rewinds, stops and starts, characterizes the past as an oral history as opposed to an official history, and the narrator's relationship to that history is one of memorializing family events and family attitudes. It is war, the narrator tells us, that has driven him to Canada and it is war that he cannot forget. It has formed him against his will and rather than glorify the refuge he has received, he tries to ignore it by reliving the past "of my onetime country" (94). The narrator describes these memories as "... the ballast that pulled one violently toward the bottom" (101). The heaviest of this ballast is the narrator's story of his mother's first husband who was a victim of the German occupation during the Second World War. He was Jewish. The baggage that this history has imparted to Albahari and which he does not want to jettison results in his cultural immobility.

The weight of European twentieth-century history lies heavy on this novel and on the reader. Its overpowering presence pushes aside the desire of his new home for a real presence in his work. It makes Alberta and North America feel lightweight and irrelevant to the pain of European history. However, Albahari's literary style is so engaging, his narrative so genuine, and his philosophical meanderings so endearing that the absence of the name Alberta in this Alberta novel does not matter. Albahari maintains his style by encouraging us to be lost in the anonymous narrator's voice as it mulls over possibilities, dithers about this and that, and goes back and forth in a mood of indecision. The humanity of the narrator is never in doubt, even if his reality sometimes is. Because of the novel's precision and its confessional style, it offers a concreteness that *Snow Man* lacked. The explanation of life in Alberta (the discussions with Donald) and life in Belgrade (the pronouncements of his mother) that is at the centre of the novel is both effective and moving. After five years of silence about Alberta, Albahari produced a third work, resulting in an unplanned Alberta trilogy. *Globetrotter* represents his final coming to terms with his years in Alberta.

Globetrotter

The novel follows the same format as the previous two. Instead of a professor of political science or the writer Donald acting as foils to an anonymous narrator, we have Daniel Atijas, an anguished writer from Belgrade, who is staying at the Banff Centre. Daniel is described in the novel as a Jew and an outsider (Albahari, *Globetrotter* 45). He also happens to have the same initials as Albahari. The unnamed narrator, who is a painter from Saskatchewan, meets Daniel and they become temporary buddies supposedly because they both come from flat terrains—the narrator from the western Canadian prairie and Daniel from the flatlands of Vojvodina, a geographic feature shared by parts of Serbia and Hungary. Adopting a Canadian persona for his narrator is a reversal for Albahari, whose first two Alberta novels had narrators from Europe. While Daniel and the narrator have their different points of view, they have an innate compatibility as they delve into the mysterious nature of their respective countries. They discuss and compare politics, multiculturalism, the nature of history, much like the discussions in the previous two novels, but the Canadianization of the narrator and the sympathetic treatment of Daniel give the novel a less antagonistic tone overall. The reader can easily identify with both characters.

Since Albahari was at the Banff Centre in the summer of 1994 when he was approached to become the Markin-Flanagan Distinguished Writer-in-Residence at the University of Calgary, *Globetrotter* should be considered a homage to Banff, to that moment in his life, and to the mountains that he hiked while living in Calgary. The work is full of Banff place-names (Wolf and Bear Streets) and other easily identified locales in the town and on the campus of the Banff Centre (Lloyd Hall). It is ironic that Albahari's most self-evidently Alberta novel should not have found an Alberta or a

Canadian publisher, and had to wait for more than a decade to find an English translation and an American university publisher. However, its publishing history may very well be a reflection of his "invisible" status in Canadian letters.

On the surface, any Albertan reading it would feel instantly at home in its descriptions, its movements through the town, and its appreciation of the mountain landscape, but the discussion of European and North American politics and history which is continued from the previous two novels seems tedious to Canadian readers. This may not be the case for Yugoslav readers, for whom the civil war had come to an end in 1999 with the NATO bombing of Belgrade and Kosovar autonomy. The main focus of the story is Daniel and the narrator's discovery of Ivan Matulić, a globe-trotting Croatian who signed the guest book at a Banff institution back in 1924. His grandson, who has emigrated to Canada and now lives in Calgary, comes out to Banff to meet with the two men. The three men begin a conversation about immigration, what happened to Yugoslavia, and what, if anything, nationalism means to Canada. This tripartite dialogue is a departure from the dualism of the first two novels. It adds to the complexity of the novel and Albahari's adroit representation of their points of view in a seamless text. The idea that a non-ethnic Canadian, a European visitor to Banff, and an ethnic Canadian engage in a conversation about national identities indicates that Albahari had reached a certain degree of comfort with identity after having lived six years in Alberta. The novel was published in Serbian in 2001.

This troika of characters hang out together for a few days, during which the Canadian narrator, much to his chagrin, sees a growing affinity between Daniel and the grandson. Albahari has created three personae (the foreigner, the immigrant, and the native) as representatives of the Euro-Canadian part of Canadian identity and he plays them off against each other, while acknowledging their mutual foreignness to Canada since they are all non-Aboriginal. The clash of European pre-occupations and Canadian issues, already covered in the previous two novels, is repeated when Daniel mentions the philosophers Nietzsche and Kierkegaard, the writers Borges and Rilke, and the artists Bosch and Dürer in reference to art and museums, after which the Canadian narrator counters with comments on Quebec separatism and western Canadian alienation (64). It is the same story of colliding worlds we have heard before. What is different is the mix. Because this is a late period work, relative to the other two, it has become debased by external elements not present in the first two novels. Having a Canadian narrator is a debasement of the classic Albahari-in-exile stance because the explanation of Canadian history and attitudes, while being outwardly correct, lacks a visceral quality when read by an Alberta or Canadian reader. The narrator does not ring quite true as a western Canadian to a western Canadian like myself, though he probably rings true to a Serbian audience, whose knowledge of Canada is either non-existence or very limited. The narrator's historical meanderings and political commentaries on Canada lack the depth of passion that he gives Daniel and the grandson. I find the narrator to be someone who is wearing a western Canadian disguise. Albahari is trying to offer a genuine portrayal of a figure from a place where he had been resident, but which he has not fully absorbed. Claiming a Saskatchewan identity for the narrator could be his way of acknowledging that there may be something not quite right about the narrator's credentials, since Albahari had no experience of Saskatchewan. It is a way of acknowledging a certain inevitable distance from the subject.

There is a plot to the novel. Eventually the grandson tells the narrator and Daniel about his search for the history of his grandfather, the globetrotter, by going to Croatia in the 1990s and later in Canada, when he digs through a box of his grandfather's effects in which he finds a diary. Unfortunately, the information that he gains puts his grandfather in a bad light. This revelation leads, at first, to a long discussion of historical guilt and how little history Canada has. Then it leads to a more tragic conclusion. But before this happens, there is a scene at which Daniel gives a reading along with other writers at the Banff Centre. The narrator describes the story in this way:

> There was no story to it, no events, no central or marginal characters, it even seemed to have no beginning or end. It was all about passages, language itself—endlessly beautiful and endlessly powerful—and if it had sounded this good in translation I had to wonder what it sounded like in the original. (97)

The passage is Albahari's tried and true voice about his own writing. In the second half of the novel there is more of this kind of writing, along with general pronouncements on history, creativity, art, and even communism. These discussions and commentaries provide a lengthy interlude before the novel moves toward its climax. Daniel announces that he must climb Tunnel Mountain before he returns to Europe. He is joined by the narrator and the grandson. The three manage the ascent easily enough, since it is not a difficult route.[4] However, the descent is something else. A storm appears out of nowhere and in the wind and rain, the grandson falls to his death. It is left to the narrator to make sense of what happened as he searches through the things left behind by the grandson, much like the grandson had earlier done with his grandfather's effects. What he finds makes him want to leave the mountains for his prairie home.

It is not surprising that Albahari did not attempt another Alberta-based novel while living in Calgary because *Globetrotter* is so place-specific and western-Canadian oriented that it would be difficult to surpass it, unless he were to drop the whole European segment of his novels. Being full of place names and named characters is the complete antithesis of his first work, *Snow Man*, which had only one name. This specificity suggests a late phase work because Albahari prefers to inhabit general categories, where he can roam backwards and forward without really venturing outside his narrator's mind and emotions. This orientation toward abstraction may have contributed to his work not developing a significant English-speaking Canadian or American audience while he lived in Calgary. But as *Globetrotter* clearly shows, he had absorbed the history, the ambience, and specific locales that are part of Alberta. Yet his language and thought-structures remained Serbian and these continued to be evident in the English translations. It is not just the references to so much of recent Yugoslav history in these novels that make that case; it is the way the novels journey through his personal experience of Alberta—initially, a fierce rejection in *Snow Man*, then a mellower emphasis on differences between Europe and America in *Bait*, and, finally, an attempt to articulate a Canadian identity in his main character, the unnamed narrator, in *Globetrotter*. The journey had to end at some point, and in the case of *Globetrotter* the two remaining characters either go home or are about to. Return to one's roots, willingly or unwillingly, is an abiding theme in all three novels. For Albahari, Alberta never became the home that was Serbia, though *Globetrotter* was his attempt to display what he had learned about this alien place and what he understood to be its preoccupations and formative elements. In the end the concreteness of the novel has to be measured against the innate sense of absence, of silences, of omissions, of spaces in-between that Albahari prefers to inhabit and to re-create. In the case of all three characters there are histories that undermine identities and attitudes that are magnetized, pulling each figure backwards to something that is haunting, yet inexpressible.

Foreignness, Exile, and Alberta Writing

Alberta writing by Euro-Canadians began with the publication of travel journals, so there has always been a component of "passing through" in Alberta literature. But David Albahari spent a long time living and writing in Alberta, without surrendering the foreignness in his writing by writing in Serbian. Because of his orientation toward his European, Serbian-language audience, his significance for Alberta letters is not easy to assess. A 2005 issue of *Serbian Studies: The Journal of the North American Serbian Studies Society* (vol. 19: no. 1) was devoted to articles on the work of Albahari by Serbian-born scholars teaching in North American universities. In these articles the theme of exile is prominent, and it may well be that this theme can explain Albahari's reluctant relationship to Alberta.

Radmila J. Gorup, in "The Author in Exile: Writing to Forget," states that those, like Albahari, "... who voluntarily live in an alien country ... do not suffer as much as those forced into exile, [but] they share the solitude and estrangement of exile" (4). Albahari's stance toward Alberta, an alien country, begets a feeling of solitude and estrangement. That is why his protagonists, according to Gorup, "are in a state of extraterritoriality, being neither *here* nor *there*, but rather in-between things that cannot come together" (6). This in-between state makes one feel alone and resentful of those who are not exiles and "belong to their surroundings" (6-7). Albahari's characters struggle with a people and a landscape that are unfamiliar and strange, and with their own sense of no longer belonging. Zoran Milutinović, writing in the same issue of *Serbian Studies*, confirms Gorup's view by describing the narrator in *Bait* as being caught in "... a no-man's-land between the past, present and future ..." (20). Not being able to identify with Alberta may well reflect the writer's personal response to his situation of voluntary exile.

What the Serbian North American scholars unanimously support is the division of Albahari's work into two phases—his pre-Canada phase and his Canadian phase. Damjana Mraović calls the works discussed here his "Canadian cycle" (40). It is clear to scholars of Serbian literature that Albahari's being in Canada did have an impact on his work because of the subject matter in these works. These scholars comment on how history and identity issues seem to dominate the Canadian cycle (Ribnikar 53). The narrators in the first two Alberta novels appear as traumatized human beings struggling, often without success, to determine who they are now that they have left their formative home. The narration of the past becomes an obsession because they cannot identify with the present. Their bodies occupy this new space, but their minds and memories resist. Petković sees the preoccupation with history and identity by Albahari's protagonists as a direct result of his own "dislocation" and "the need to re-define or explain his identity" (97). To understand Albahari's novels as a product of dislocation and an internal struggle with identity goes a long way in helping grasp what the writer is expressing in his Alberta novels. Because his native country and its audience for his work remained open to him while he lived and wrote in Calgary, his dual status (he carried a Yugoslavian passport when he first arrived in Calgary, and both Serbian and Canadian passports later) encouraged the dislocation, the neither here nor there of his writing. He occupied his own country while he was in Alberta. His body was here, but his mind was there. The result is a view of Alberta that is based on reluctance, uncertainty, and loneliness. The quest for a safe haven for his literary spirit was both met and not met by Alberta. That the place provided a refuge in which he led a prolific literary existence is true, but it is also true that the place did not offer him the audience that writers need. This means that an alien country that remains alien to the expatriate writer can be a wonderful stimulus to literary creativity. That this creativity finds the alien country a negative space is not surprising. What is surprising is how that negativity was able to generate a literary reputation that continues to grow.

Serbian scholars writing in English focus on what they read as the Serb-in-exile theme of Albahari's Alberta novels. North American reviewers and critics take a slightly different approach. They view his work and his presence from the welcoming country's viewpoint. David Berlin, reviewing a book titled *Room for All of Us* by Adrienne Clarkson, which has a chapter about Albahari, states: "Canada offers a tradition of benign neglect that allows a Calgary-based Serbian writer named David Albahari to carve out the space he needs …" (R28). The idea here is that Alberta is a refuge, a sanctuary, where émigrés, expatriates, immigrants, and exiles can find peace. It is a place of welcome and security. Eric Volmers, of the *Calgary Herald*, quoted Albahari as saying in 2011: "I feel like a double personality because I am here in one sense and in another sense I'm not here because I am not writing in English" (C1). This duality is consistent with the legacy of other Alberta writers who did not write in English like the Icelandic poet Stephan Stephansson, the Ukrainian novelist Ilya Kiriak, or the French novelist Georges Bugnet. As immigrant writers they became a part of Alberta literature because of their writing about this place in their work. Albahari has done the same but only to a limited degree. Stephansson, Kiriak, and Bugnet were immigrants who died in Alberta. They embraced their identity as immigrants and wrote about that experience. Albahari never saw himself as an immigrant and preferred to write about the angst of voluntary exile. Considering this view, his return to Serbia in 2012 was not totally unexpected.[5]

When the *Hudson Review* published a review essay of a number of Albahari's novels, the reviewer wrote that *Bait* was a hybrid novel, "unified by the narrator's consciousness" (Lewis 374). My own experience of his Alberta novels suggests that they actually display a highly limited sense of hybridity, because the narrator's antagonists, who represent the Canadian reality, are portrayed in a negative light as lacking in understanding or whose understanding is superficial. Albahari admitted as such when he said in a 2005 interview that he used "stereotypes and prejudices" in creating the conversations between his narrators and Donald (*Bait*) and Daniel (*Snow Man*) (Mraović-O'Hare 184). His purpose was to expose the misunderstanding between cultures. In the same interview, he talked about his protagonists in the Alberta novels as experiencing "cultural shock" as they struggle with loss and adjustment (178). This shock only heightened their struggle with the issue of identity. Because Albahari was born, raised, and became a writer in a multinational state called Yugoslavia, which is now no more, his struggle with identity issues and the meaning of being a Serbian writer was more profound. If Yugoslavia had not disappeared in a civil war, I suspect that he would have remained in Yugoslavia and be known today as a Yugoslavia writer. There would not have been any Alberta novels and Albahari would have explored other realities in his work, as he has done in numerous other novels and short stories. His attempt to describe the clash of two worlds gave both worlds familiar and unfamiliar characteristics. In the end, the only space that he occupied in his Alberta novels was a personal internal space of belonging and not belonging simultaneously. This was most apparent in his engagement or rather non-engagement with the English language. Albahari continued to translate English literature into Serbian, for he was also a fluent speaker of English, and yet, he steadfastly refused to write fiction in English. This refusal became a hallmark of his Alberta novels. It also became a sign of choice of the writer using place for his own ends, and then determining which place mattered at a certain point in his life. Because Albahari chose to live for a time in an English-speaking world while writing in Serbian, he was dependent on translation to reach the world he lived in. This may be the key concept in understanding his Alberta novels. In Yugoslavia he was the founder and editor-in-chief of *Pismo*, a magazine of world literature. He also did numerous translations, especially of English-language fiction. So one can think of his Alberta novels as his "translation" of Alberta to his European home audiences. He was speaking to them with a sensibility they understood about a place they did not know. They could grasp what he was trying to say because he and they came from the same roots. This was not the case with Canadian readers who read him in translation. We had the sense that we were reading a foreign writer. This idea of translation is something that I very much associate with the nature of Alberta writing, where writers, whether anglophones or not, had to tell others what this place was all about. In an essay dealing with Albahari's translation of his own words, I wrote:

> I believe it is best to see David, the writer, as the consummate translator attuned to disparate audiences. He translates his hidden inner self into acceptable external categories (*First Person Plural* 110).

The power of language to both express and repress is captured in this quote from an interview with Albahari conducted by Mraović-O'Hare in 2005, and published in 2008:

From a technical point of view I could write in the English language, but I don't see the point of such a move, and, practically speaking, I would just limit myself." (180)

The importance of native language to Albahari is such that using a language, like English in which he is fluent, would still be limiting to his expression. In fact, in an interview in *Books in Canada*, Albahari makes the point that the Czech Canadian writer, Josef Skovrecky, did not need to write in English as he eventually did. It wasn't "necessary," he says (Longinovic 32). But Skovrecky's choice to write in English gave him a literary profile in Canada that Albahari never achieved. Albahari's emphasis on publishing in Serbian, in Serbia, became self-fulfilling and made him a foreign writer in Alberta.

This emphasis on describing and situating his Alberta novels using Serbian makes the relationship of these novels to Alberta literature problematic. During the time he spent here, he wrote numerous works. The specifically Alberta-located novels represent a minority of the total work he did here. The novels express conflict and uncertainty and their contribution to Alberta letters also seems conflicted and uncertain. Alberta as an alien land that produces emotional and mental conflict for the narrator is the basic structure in the novels, and yet Alberta remains peripheral because it was mostly a nameless Other that could have been any strange place. Albahari wanted his readers, whether in Serbian or in translation, to feel tied to language itself and its power. What is certain is that his Alberta novels contributed to his journey as a literary hero in Serbia, but they did not contribute to his profile in Canada. It would seem that the borders between national literatures are still in place and a writer, like Albahari, who wants to live in the no-man's land between them, in a map of his own imagination, has to pay a certain price.

Albahari's residency in language rather than place is a sign of the diasporic literary imagination. His diaspora is not just his years in Canada, but, more importantly, his diaspora is Serbia itself. How can that be? Because his national literary identity was Yugoslavian, a multicultural and multinational society in which he felt at home. When Yugoslavia disappeared as a nation-state, Albahari became stateless in his heart. For him, Serbian national identity was something he had to struggle to accept. Being Jewish and aware of the horrific history of Balkan nationalism in the twentieth century, how could he not be wary and distrustful of the new/old identities. It is important to note that his diasporic imagination is not a simple Serbian-Canadian duality; it is a complex of disconnections and connections that he had to navigate in a civil war and postwar environment. Later, watching history unfold from the safety of Canada did not make the process any simpler or easier. In fact, it made his retreat into himself and away from nationality an uncertain, even indeterminate, exercise in self-understanding and identity. His Alberta novels were profound expressions of that journey into absence, an inner space where only he could reside.

Notes

1 The program is currently titled The University of Calgary Distinguished Writers Program.

2 One must be careful in accepting Albahari's self-interpretation. The claim of less intensity is something that is difficult to assess by a third party because of the interiority of the author's mindset.

3 It would not be till the new millennium that the name of Yugoslavia would disappear and be replaced by the nationalities (now countries) that had made up its multinational identity—Bosnia, Croatia, Slovenia, Montenegro, Macedonia, and even Kosovo.

4 While David was writing *Globetrotter*, he invited me to go with him to Banff and Tunnel Mountain so that he could accurately describe the situation he had envisaged for the fall. We did go and he confirmed the climb *in situ* as this was part of the nature of the novel with its emphasis on geographic accuracy.

5 Even after his return to Belgrade, he has made periodic visits to Calgary, most recently in 2016. He still has a house in the city and family to visit. Whether this experience will ever find its way into fiction is unknown.

Works Cited

Albahari, David. *Bait*. Translated by Peter Agnone, Northwestern UP, 2001.

———. *Globetrotter*. Translated by Ellen Elias-Bursać, Yale UP, 2014.

———. *Götz and Meyer*. Translated by Ellen Elias-Bursać, Harvill, 2004.

———. *Leeches*. Translated by Ellen Elias-Bursać, Houghton Mifflin Harcourt, 2011.

———. *Snow Man*. Translated by Ellen Elias-Bursać, Douglas & McIntyre, 2005.

Albahari /Kostash correspondence, 10 Feb. 1993.

Aleksić, Tatjana. "Extricating the Self from History: David Albahari's *Bait*." *The Journal of the Midwest Modern Languages Association*, vol. 39, no. 2, Fall 2006, pp. 54-70.

Berlin, David. "The Canadian Dream." *Globe and Mail*, 19 Nov. 2011, R28.

Clarkson, Adrienne. *Room for All of Us: Surprising Stories of Loss and Transformation*. Allen Lane, 2011.

Gorup, Radmila J. "The Author in Exile: Writing to Forget." *Serbian Studies*, vol. 19, no. 1, 2005, pp. 3-13.

Lewis, Tess. "Mystifying Enlightenment: The Fiction of David Albahari." *Hudson Review*, vol. 64, no. 2, Summer 2011, pp. 372-79.

Longinovic, Tomislav. "The Post-Yugoslav Diaspora: Tomislav Longinovic Speaks with David Albahari." *Books in Canada*, Nov.-Dec. 1998, pp. 32-34.

McGoogan, Ken. "A Writer in Exile." *Calgary Herald*, 14 Jan. 1995, p. B11.

Melnyk, George. *First Person Plural*. Frontenac House, 2015.

———. "Lost in Translation: An International Luminary Writes in Obscurity in a Calgary Suburb." *Alberta Views*, vol. 13, no. 7, Sept. 2010, pp. 38-43.

Milutinović, Z. "The Demoniacism of History and Promise of Aesthetic Redemption in David Albahari's *Bait*." *Serbian Studies*, vol. 19, no. 1, 2005, pp. 15-25.

Mraović, Damjana. "The Politics of Representations: *Mamac* by David Albahari," *Serbian Studies*, vol. 19, no. 1, 2005, pp. 35-53.

Mraović-O'Hare, Damjana. "Interview with David Albahari," *Canadian Slavonic Papers*, vol. 50, nos. 1-2, 2008, pp. 177-92.

Petković, V.G. "History, Identity and Masculinity in David Albahari's *Bait*." *Belgrade Language and Literature Studies*, vol. 4, 2012, pp. 93-103.

Ribnikar, Vladislava. "History as Trauma in the Work of David Albahari." *Serbian Studies*, vol. 19, no. 1, 2005, pp. 53-81.

Volmers, Eric. "Calgary's Literary Man of Mystery." *Calgary Herald*, 12 June 2011, p. C1.

Science and the City: The Poetics of Alice Major's Edmonton

Neil Querengesser

"A city comes to life only after writers have invented it."
—Robert Fulford

"To find a city, accept
the guidance of whatever calculating god
has taken you in care"
—Alice Major, *The Occupied World*

Alice Major, Edmonton's first poet laureate (2005-07), is one of Canada's finest poets. Since her arrival in Edmonton in 1981 she has been dedicated to an intimate exploration of her city and its people, crafting the details of her acquired knowledge into a body of powerful and original poetry. Indeed, she has made her poetic career in Edmonton where over the past twenty years she has published twelve books of poetry and a stimulating study on the relationship between poetry and science. Having made Edmonton her home through both her life and her words, Major has the advantage of seeing this city from fresh and imaginative perspectives, many of which, while revealing a deep and abiding passion for the intricacies and complexities of human nature, are from the viewpoint of the natural and social sciences, often in unconventional or indirect ways. Despite a common misperception that poetry and science are at odds with each other, Major demonstrates the contrary, contending that both science and poetry "are central to understanding how human beings fit into the world" (*Intersecting* xv). She echoes Nobel prize-winning chemist Roald Hoffman who invites recognition of "the deep humanity of the creative act in science" (Hoffman 57), when she says: "The human world is awash with emotion. Poets merely give that feeling a little structure" (*Intersecting* 236). In her Edmonton poems, Alice Major gives more than a little scientific structure to this emotion, drawing deeply upon her knowledge of both the social and the natural sciences—including psychology, sociology, anthropology, archaeology, physics, mathematics, geography, and geology—to support some remarkable poetic images.

The perspectives of these images vary. In *Scenes from the Sugar Bowl Café* (1998), Major adopts a sociological perspective in the titular restaurant formerly located on Edmonton's 124 Street, watching and commenting on the world as it passes by, comes in, and leaves. In several deft and sometimes satirical verses she vividly captures the essence of selected people and scenes from 1990s' Edmonton. The poems from this collection are reprinted in *Tales for an Urban Sky* (1999), wherein Major seeks to create a unique mythology of Edmonton (here an unnamed "northern Alberta city that is like and unlike any other place" [7]). *The Office Tower Tales* (2008), set in Edmonton's Commerce Place, recalls the themes and structures of framing tales like *A Thousand and One Nights* and *The Canterbury Tales* through the sociological and anthropological perspectives of its narratives. *The Occupied World* (2006) contains sequences devoted to a contemplation of Edmonton from the perspectives of archaeology, anthropology, mathematics, physics, and geology. Most recently, in *Intersecting Sets: A Poet Looks at Science* (2011), she weaves together a number of informative and essential references to herself and to her city in a deeply philosophical study connecting the arts and sciences to the universalities of human life.

A significant exploration in *Intersecting Sets* concerns the science of empathy, a study that reflects her earlier comments at the end of the 2010 Edmonton Heritage Symposium. In this speech Major contends that emotion is "our mental filing system," tagging various, often idiosyncratic, narratives as parts of a web "that extends over time." We can share these emotions with others and create a sense of shared space through the process of empathy. As she puts it,

A city's heritage is created not just through a memory-like tagging-with-significance but also through empathy. Heritage is a web of *shared* stories/memories. By making those stories conscious, by *noticing* them we can enter into the lives and minds of others who have shared this place, then and now. (Major, "Concluding Remarks")

In *Intersecting Sets*, Major draws on the work of neuroscientists Decety and Lamm to develop this idea, arguing that from a scientific perspective "empathy is not the wishful domain of poets but a real phenomenon in our brains," normally involving three steps: first, when we witness a display of emotion in others, the same areas of our brain actually "light up" as they would were we to experience the same stimulus directly (6). Then adjacent brain cells responsible for our sense of objectivity begin to signal a rational separation between the observer and the observed, and finally the areas of the brain involving "judgment and social context" contribute to, and shape, the ongoing empathic response (6-7). Thus as the poet shapes her response to her city and its people, she is first stimulated by an essential emotional connection, then partially separates her observing self from this response, and finally, through the completed poem, achieves a complex aesthetic and objective structure of the original empathic response.

How does such empathy help her to form the idea of Edmonton? *Scenes from the Sugar Bowl Café* (reprinted, as mentioned, in *Tales for an Urban Sky*) offers several instances where her deliberate notice of specific people becomes an entry point into their lives that, however briefly, opens the possibility of shared stories. For example, in "Persephone on 124 Street" she structures a familiar Edmonton early spring setting with the materials of both classical myth and contemporary allusions. Edmontonians are bound together by many stories, especially those of its ever-changing weather, and in particular its annual spring thaw. Their emerging from the darkness of six months of winter recalls the mythical annual emergence of Persephone from her six-month imprisonment in the underworld. In this poem, as water from the melting snow "goes running down the street" (Major, *Tales* 79), an interesting parade of men likewise figuratively "limbo into summer" to Harry Belafonte calypso tunes broadcast from the café's CD player, all the while being watched from the darkened café by a contemporary Persephone, a "punk" girl in a "Six Inch Nails" T-shirt,[1] who in turn is being observed by the narrator. As the girl with "sunlight in her hair, a ragged nest / of straw spun suddenly to gold" (80) watches these men, one of them, helping to carry a coffin-like sofa, "turns to gaze / at the girl's hair shining through the glass," at which she "smiles and waves, and suddenly / gets up to go … [leaving] the café / door open and lipstick on her cup" (80). While much of the description appears objective, the narrator reflects her empathy by sensing the men's feelings of freedom as they walk by with jackets either open or completely off, and as a policeman's walkie-talkie incongruously swings on his hip like a grass skirt twitched by a hula dancer. As Persephone leaves the underworld café, the narrator's empathetic connection to the scene becomes more pronounced:

> It feels like summer's dancing up
> from ritual darkness. All the nails
> and manacles have popped loose
> and we're the lucky ones who got away. (80)

These and other denizens of the Sugar Bowl Café are unique individuals but also typical of the narrator's fellow citizens. She portrays them with an insight that, while sometimes droll or otherwise ironic, is nevertheless based on an initial empathy and a desire to create a heritage of shared stories that enliven both the city and their many other textual references.

Such shared stories also proliferate in *The Office Tower Tales*, which brings the concept of various medieval framing tales to modern-day Edmonton. Tales narrated by three office workers—Pandora, an accounting secretary; Aphrodite, a receptionist; and Sheherazad, a public relations agent—unfold in the food court of Edmonton's Commerce Place. Like the Sugar Bowl Café, this food court becomes a locus for observation of a variety of Edmontonians, although the stories shared from these observations are not limited to Edmonton but range throughout time and space, with many literary and mythological connections. Empathy is created as these central female narrators, again unique individuals but also obviously types, form ever stronger personal bonds as they recount their tales over the course of half a year, while the outside river valley landscape slowly transforms through the seasons. Similar to *The Canterbury Tales*, each of these tales, such as "The Police Candidate's Story," "The Waitress's Tale," and "The Tale of the CEO's Daughter," is introduced with a prologue by one of the three framing characters, and several conclude with an epilogue. However, unlike Chaucer in *The Canterbury Tales*, the author writes herself into the narration only obliquely, disguised in one of the prologues as a street woman.

In the "Prologue to the Tale of the Gingerbread Girl," the three narrators focus their attention on a small poverty-stricken woman begging quarters from passers-by in the food court. The woman, named Alice, is likely drawn from the same street woman portrayed in "Alice, Downtown" (Major, *The Occupied World* 96-97) and strongly suggests a manifestation of the author's Jungian shadow. She evokes almost immediate and intense reactions from the narrators. The degree of empathy evident in their responses varies quite considerably, so much so that it is possible to read this section as the author writing herself into her own narrative as a shadowy challenging figure, unignorable by her own created characters. Like a scene from a Pirandello play, the relationship between characters and author is playfully yet seriously inverted. Aphrodite "shivers" at the sight of her

> as though the mystery of biography
> has sent a chill
> into the summer sky. *That woman freaks*
> *me out,* she says. *She's always there.* (Major, *Office* 138)

Even when Sheherazad tries to calm her fears by explaining that Alice once did her a good turn by giving her change for the bus, contending "*She's not a maniac, / Just ill, a bit*" (139), her friends are not appeased. Indeed, this challenging figure may also elicit complex empathetic reactions from the readers such as those experienced through encounters with actual marginalized people. Their ensuing discussions of social responsibility and the ethics of biological reproduction (as well as thematic suggestions of artistic production) complicate this encounter between the central narrators and their unrecognized author. Like her fictional counterpart and other characters in Lewis Carroll's famous identity tale, this Alice also eludes our attempts to fix her objectively. She remains just out of range of her characters, and of our control, appearing like "Hecate" (138, 140), the triple-formed goddess whose appearance here belies her powerful creative powers, compelling Sheherazad, just through her "stare from her triune space / at the corner" (142), to begin her next tale. The triune nature of Hecate thus parallels the triune aspects of Alice as author, narrator, and character, intimately involved in the complex process of both acquiescence and resistance to the empathetic response she evokes, from both characters and readers.

Major has argued that the feeling of "yearning" that motivates a poet to write a poem is closely connected to the feeling of empathy. As she acknowledges, her thesis about the relationship between empathy and poetry/storytelling is similar to Wordsworth's famous definition of poetry as "emotion recollected in tranquility" (qtd. in *Intersecting* 15), but with this essential difference that "the gap between emotion and recollection is not the wide span of years but the narrow cleft in a human being between 'me' and 'her'" (15). In *The Office Tower Tales*, the triune Alice invites readers to consider the implications of such a cleft; the author's comments on neuroscience and psychology in *Intersecting Sets* offer the possibility of supplementary insights into the poetry beyond the literary and mythological, even while they complement such aspects.

Scientific perspectives, particularly the archaeological, anthropological, and geological, also structure some of the poetic sequences in *The Occupied World*, providing perhaps initially disorienting but ultimately thought-provoking views of Edmonton. The sequence of poems entitled "Contemplating the City" (originally published, with slight variations, in *The Malahat Review* as the award-winning "Contemplatio") was inspired in part by Joseph Rykwert's *The Idea of a Town* (1976). Rykwert argues that the planning of modern cities and towns is governed, to their detriment, by an emphasis on the physical elements: "The way in which space is occupied is much studied, but exclusively in physical terms of occupation and amenity. The psychological space, the cultural, the juridical, the religious, are not treated as aspects of the ecological space with whose economy the urbanist is concerned," leading, Rykwert continues, to "a pattern of interaction between the community and its outward shell which will be disastrous for both" (24). In her sequence, Major explores what would happen if one were to graft ancient patterns and rituals for establishing a city upon what already exists in Edmonton. The result is an interesting palimpsest of the city's real and imagined pasts and its present poetic evocation.

The word "contemplating" in this context has rich and complex implications. Rykwert notes that it referred to "the ceremony of *contemplatio*"

(45), the root word of which, *templum*, from the Greek *temenos*, has various meanings. According to Varro, the word is derived from *tueri*, to observe, with "reference to nature, in the sky; to divination, on the ground, and to resemblance underground" (45). All three observations inform this sequence. But *templum* also denotes a sacred enclosure, "a piece of land defined by boundaries and devoted to a particular purpose" (46). Throughout this sequence Major demarcates her city as she re-enacts these ancient rituals.

Despite theories of how best to establish a city, as Rykwert remarks, "the injunctions of the theorists do not seem to have been followed" (43) in the ancient cities any more than in the modern ones. The rituals, although interesting, seem more theoretical and ideal than practical. For Rykwert, "[w]hat the city founder thought he was doing and its mythical 'rightness,' or what his followers saw him do is more interesting in this context than his historical success or failure. It is the *idea* of the town which concerns me here" (44). Similarly with Major's sequence, there is little evidence, if any, to suggest that Edmonton's founding was overseen by oracles or augers familiar with the ancient rituals, or that her own poetic rituals have made any observable difference. However, what matters is the *idea* of what these rituals stood for and their impact on the psyche of the poet as she establishes intimate connections between herself and her city. Through these poems she is establishing a new pattern, a new way of "contemplating" the city.

The sequence contains eleven poems, ten titles of which begin with imperative verbs, instructions for establishing the ideal city. The poet serves fittingly as a modern day augur in poems republished soon after she became Edmonton's poet laureate in 2005. Each poem normally begins with italicized paraphrases of classical instructions for establishing a city. The first, "Locate the Site," begins with a bird's-eye view of the North Saskatchewan River that flows through Edmonton, "the only city in a thousand miles of river" (Major, *Occupied* 12), a view that zooms to a panoramic perspective of the North and South Saskatchewan Rivers, which conflow into the Saskatchewan River east of Prince Albert, as "long legs / of a compass splayed across the prairies" (12), at once both geometrical instrument and female archetype. As the poem progresses, the speaker attempts to empathize with her newly adopted city, trying through a "chance encounter" to find the "X" that "marks the spot" (12) as a means of orientation. She describes the final approach of her plane in geometrical and physical terms that locate this spot spatially and temporally:

> Runways mark a skewed cross
> on prairie. Wheels rush at tarmac.
> We arc in seats—thrust
> forwards and backwards at the same time. (13)

Mathematical and physics terminology—"cross," "arc," and "thrust"—and in other lines—"Arithmetic of river" and "ratio of circle to the line" (13)—are deftly interwoven with the speaker's personal imagery and emotions. In the final stanza in particular, the speaker appears to have blended with the northern leg of the Saskatchewan River compass, as her passage from the baggage claim to taxi stand moves like the current, guided by *"whatever calculating god / has taken [her] in care"*:

> I collect my circulating luggage
> from the baggage belt's meander,
> cut through the swirl of strangers
> and their bright foreign chatter,
> head for the taxi stand. (13)

The speaker creates her own version of her new city, identifying herself at first with the point of her landing, the X of the landing strip, and then the city's bisecting river. This is her beginning.

The next poem, "Assess the appearance of portentous animals," portrays Major's portentous animal, the ubiquitous black-billed magpie (*pica hudsonia*). She describes Edmonton as "a city of magpies, a parliament / presided over by the bold-robed birds" (14) to which she comes as "a foreigner—/ a white magpie," wanting to know "that he will be accepted by his kind" (14). This part of the ritual has its ancient counterparts, as in the founding of Rome by Romulus and Remus who "each went on a hilltop to watch for the auspicious birds" (Rykwert 44), in this case vultures, and having sighted them, "determined their exact significance" (45). But, like the white magpie, the foreign poet/augur is sometimes hard to spot. She will, however, make her presence felt by subtly blending into the background, conjuring the city in unusual ways.

"Envision the outline" builds upon the "x-marks-the-spot" motif. The poet as augur creates what the ancients referred to as the *conrectico* (Rykwert 46), establishing the city's "*cardo* and *decumanus*" (47), its intersecting north-south and east-west axes. Already having connected herself with the river, she now positions herself close to the city's centre and, like Varro's augur (Rykwert 46), faces south where not far below the river runs, "the city's hinge, its east-west line" (Major, *Occupied* 16). She completes the north-south axis with an empathetic skyward view:

> Crossing it [the river] from south to north
> geese make their high way overhead,
> a silent, migrant beat
> from the heart. (16)

In "Set up a boundary stone," with reference to the *temenos* or *term*, an ancient boundary marker, she adds a third, vertical axis to the intersecting axes of the geese and river as she moves down to the Rossdale power plant, now a designated historic site close to the original Fort Edmonton as well as to a recently discovered aboriginal burial ground on the north riverbank east of the 105 Street Bridge. The poem chronicles an archeological dig on the site as the cyclists, rollerbladers, and skateboarders "swoop" past (17). Unearthed after a variety of two-centuries-old trade good fragments is a "quartzite knife" dropped by the river bank "eight thousand years ago," the marker of "*our human boundary of time*" (18). The speaker has now, through her empathetic attachment to the river, the geese, and the knife, completed her identification with the city in all three spatial dimensions as well as one terminus of the temporal dimension.

A more recent segment of the temporal dimension, the appropriation of Indigenous land by European settlers and its often unacknowledged but nevertheless underlying guilt, is forcefully expressed in "What is buried under the walls." Here, remembering ancient fratricides and murders connected with the establishment of cities through figures such as Cain and Remus, the speaker is awakened by a woman's three a.m. scream on a quiet Edmonton residential street: "'You're on Indian land, man. / You're all on fucking Indian land, man. / This is fucking Indian land'" (19). The poet, who has by now strong ties to the city, reflects on the "uneasy and hedging" (19) feelings that complicate her empathetic connections to its various peoples.

"Fix the city's regions, from west to east" further connects writer and city through the metaphor of the "*lituus, the seer's wand*" (20) for the North Saskatchewan River. Rykwert says that, according to Servius, the augur was forbidden in his surveys to gesture with the empty hand, being required to use the *lituus* throughout the ritual (47). In this poem the river thus becomes surveyor's instrument, augur's wand, and poet's pen. Moreover, during spring the river is filled with ice floes, described as deeply translucent, each with a "white frill, / a ruffed margin" (Major, *Occupied* 20). The metaphor of the ice suggests fancy, perhaps formal clothing, glass plates, and indirectly, writing paper. The river and floes signify the writer's flowing imagination that captures or freezes aspects of the city scenery. It serves as a bisecting axis of the city and also as a connection to the prairie beyond, where finally, as it "makes always for the east, / [it] ushers us to the feet of the sun" (20). But if the river is metaphor of augury and poetic creation, it can also play the opposite role, as its "[i]ce plates scrape, shushing, shushing" (20), silencing and perhaps erasing what had gone before. It was also the augur's responsibility to consider the "*patterns in the sky*" (21) in an attempt to fulfil the imperative of the next poem, "Align the city with its stars" (21), where the stars have counterparts in the city's bridges, whose foundations serve as still nodes "on a vibrating string" (22), the still points on the ever-changing river, whose current and curves parallel the curtains of aurora borealis through which can be seen the fixed stars. Thus the North Saskatchewan River, its ice, and its bridges acquire foundational significance for the poet's overall vision of the city, a foundation that will also predominate in a later sequence.

In "Give the City Its Three Names," Major adapts Rykwert's quotation of John Lydus's isolated assertion that "'A town had three names: one secret, one priestly, and one public'" (qtd. in Rykwert 59). She calls Edmonton's familiar public name a "polite gesture / to mother country, mother company" (Major, *Occupied* 23), based on the possibility of the city's being named after a north London suburb. For its "priestly" name she selects that which was once proposed by Fort Edmonton's factor John Rowand, "*Fort Sanspareil*" (24), meaning *peerless*, "from the tongue of the missionary priests / who strung their rosary across the prairies" (24), harking back not necessarily to Roman foundations but indirectly to the influence of the Roman Catholic Church in the development of the Canadian West. And just as Lydus and perhaps Pliny suspect that Rome itself had a secret name (Rykwert 59), so Major invokes the city's significant yet often unacknowledged ties to its Indigenous history, in the lines "*We hear but do not recognize / our secret name*" when "Into the aching dusk / Coyote cries again" (24).

Mundus grows out of Rykwert's description of the creation of a ritual hole, or *mundus*, whose origins and purpose are uncertain but which he generally equates with "the mouth of the underworld" (59). Major fashions such ambiguities into modern images of sacrificial pits and propitiative fires, marshalled into the augur's service atop the riverbank as she watches it in the reflected sunset cut "like a slow torch" (*Occupied* 25). To the west, beyond the high-rise apartments, "Clouds on fire / [are] like the entry to a blast furnace"; in the centre "The city's hearth burns red / as the blood of trapped animals"; and to the east "Refinery Row / creeps to the lip of the river," the "gas wells flaring" beyond (25). The flaming vision encompasses significant details of the city's heritage, connecting it surprisingly and powerfully to ancient rituals. Both Edmonton's modern oil industry and its historical fur trade are built upon trapped vegetation and trapped animals respectively. And like the ancient augers and modern oil drillers the poet probes dangerously at specified times throughout the year into these secrets of surface and underworld.

While not explicit in Rykwert, the idea of a public parade involving "*rites of regeneration*" (Major, *Occupied* 27) appears in the sequence's penultimate poem, "Arrange Processions," where Edmonton's traditional parade to mark the beginning of its summer exposition, Klondike Days (later renamed Capital Ex and now K-Days), is seen in both modern and ancient light. A key image in this multicultural poem is that of a parade dragon chasing its tail, "a giddy ourobouros [sic]" that also serves as an apt symbol for the parade route, which "takes us back / where we started" (28). In this parade which "commemorates / a time less history than myth" (27), the ancient priests become "Clean young men" marching beside an gospel church float and "robed monks" on the Buddhist temple float who "wave peaceably / beside a lotus flower of cardboard painted pink" (28), sharing the procession equally with, among others, the Captain Hook pirate ship float and the city fire engines, ambulances, and street sweepers that comprise the parade's tail. While some of these connections to the ancient

Roman rites may seem tenuous at best in a literal sense, the poem reminds us that many of our communal activities are governed by anthropological patterns of behaviour stretching back to early times.

In the final poem, "Set the Gates Open," Major compares the retired oil derrick at Edmonton's southern boundary to Janus, *"two-faced overseer of beginnings, / or the sphinx of Thebes—human head / on a beast's crouched haunches"* (29). However, this *"monster at the gate"* seems to embody more than the sphinx and Janus; Augustine has suggested in his refutation of Roman gods that the second face of the two-faced Janus, the god of beginnings, should logically be that of Terminus, the Roman god of endings and boundaries (351-52) to whom, as Rykwert notes (62), were often offered blood sacrifices. The monstrous aspect of the derrick's penetration of the ancient Devonian sea is enhanced by the reference to a catastrophic event southwest of Edmonton on 8 March 1948 when the surface casings of oil well Atlantic No. 3 ruptured and "all hell blew in" (Major, *Occupied* 29). It was the worst oil disaster in Alberta's history, as millions of gallons of oil spread through surrounding farmland and beyond, the main rupture igniting in September 1948 with a "column of fire visible at night for nearly a hundred miles" (MacGregor 274), causing extreme environmental damage before being extinguished later that fall. This was an inauspicious beginning to Alberta's oil industry with apocalyptic signs of its ending, embodying the Janus-Terminus duality. Moreover, the well's name, Atlantic, also recalls the classical god Atlas, another boundary god of sorts, as well as the ocean, most obviously the Atlantic, but also perhaps the Cretaceous Sea, which once flowed from the Arctic across almost all of present-day Alberta to the Gulf of Mexico. Finally, the reference to the sphinx of Thebes, the terrifying boundary creature consuming those unable to answer its riddles, is also associated with this derrick. The sequence ends with a powerful series of questions as the monster,

> *a mirror of ourselves*[,]
> *... riddles us:*
> *Who comes to enter through these gates?*
> *What brings you? What do you bear?*
> *What will you bury here?*
> *What will you keep alive?* (Major, *Occupied* 30)

These profound questions are perhaps even more disturbing for the modern reader than the traditional riddle posed by the ancient sphinx to hapless travellers. The final lines of the sequence challenge the city's residents as well as the poet/augur, its subtly unobtrusive "I" who is at last both questioned and questioning.

These archaeologically based poems are complemented by a geologically structured sequence entitled "Root Zones," demonstrating just how deep Edmonton's relatively young "roots" extend. Edmonton's history is often framed in terms of its three-hundred-year development by European fur traders and settlers and several millennia's inhabitation by Indigenous peoples; but the geology of the Edmonton region, consisting of two kilometers of compressed sedimentary rocks above the "basement" of the Precambrian Canadian Shield, predates all human presence by two billion years (Godfrey 3-5). Like "Contemplating the City," this series is primarily centred on the North Saskatchewan River valley, but with an emphasis on the valley's geological connections to the present-day human element.

In the first poem, "Foundation," the speaker personifies downtown Edmonton rising from the river valley as a sentient organism. Cars driving up the hillside through the valley fog are compared to "nerve impulses" (Major, *Occupied* 104) moving up from the unconscious toward the high-rise buildings that

> stare over prairie
> as if their glass thoughts floated
> unconnected to the ground,
> unfounded. (104)

Yet as subsequent poems demonstrate, the connections of these buildings and their inhabitants "to the ground" are profound. The river valley, often overlooked in the daily life of the city, is rendered as a critical if unconscious part of this living organism. The form of the next poem, "River Our Bedrock," suggests a sonnet, but the seven couplets which comprise it also reflect the "steep terraces slung like slipped rungs" (105) that comprise the banks of the river valley. The title's oxymoronic imagery reflects Edmonton's geological reality. The North Saskatchewan River valley began to form through erosion twelve thousand years ago, slowly for the first thousand years and then rapidly over the next three thousand until it stabilized at its approximate modern level about eight thousand years ago (Godfrey 31), when the river reached the hundred-million-year old cretaceous bedrock over which it flows and which erodes much more slowly than the upper strata. Major likens the river to a "workman" and a "Quarryman" (*Occupied* 105) carving out this immense valley over time, until it is conflated with the "Bedrock" that it has finally reached.

This valley, eroded over several millennia, reveals layers of geological history that Major transforms into urban poetic foundations. "Empress Formation" appropriately references two imposing structures: the architectural formation of the Fairmont Hotel Macdonald which rests atop the downtown north side of the river valley; and the pre-glacial geological formation of a sedimentary layer above the cretaceous bedrock extending from central Alberta into southern Saskatchewan, taking its eponymous name, originally proposed by geologists Whitaker and Christiansen (354), from the village of Empress, Saskatchewan. The Empress Formation underlying Edmonton is exposed in many places along the river banks, notably beneath the Hotel Macdonald. Although the hotel is named after Canada's first prime minister, here Major invests it with the regal feminine characteristics of Macdonald's contemporary, the reigning Queen Victoria, one of whose titles was Empress of India:

> The old hotel surveys the valley—
> Her Eminence, in limestone challis
> and ornate moulding. (*Occupied* 106)

The hotel is described analogously to the geological formation on which it rests. For example,

> Below her sculleries and basements,
> below her buttoned boots' complacent,
> genteel footing,
> is bedrock formed of sands and baggage
> washed from elsewhere. (106)

The "sands and baggage washed from elsewhere" is an apt poetic description of the geological Empress Formation, which actually underlies several layers of glacial sediment and extends downward to the cretaceous bedrock. Like Shelley's "Ozymandias," the poem reminds us of the tenuousness of empires and that we are "Simply the latest wanderers / on paths that others carved for us" (106).

This reminder of our human and geological antecedents segues elegantly to poems that guide the reader along historical paths. In "Ice Road," Pleistocene inhabitants during the deglaciation of the Edmonton area some twelve thousand years ago call down the millennia to modern readers, alluding prophetically to future place names near Edmonton:

> And we have left the tips of our stone spears
> buried in cages of bone.
> You will discover them—
> you wanderers to come—
> as you seek your rumoured Edens,
> your flowing wells,
> your Rich Valleys,
> your Glory Hills. (107)

"Coal Beds" and "Flour Gold" take the reader to the more recent past, where coal mining and gold dredging along the riverbanks of the North Saskatchewan were viable activities, particularly in the mid- to late-1800s, recalling current place names such as "Gold Bar" and "Clover Bar," named after gold-panner Tom Clover. "We Have Feet of Clay" recalls the clayey mud that "our grandparents" used to experience more directly, still underlying Edmonton's lawns and streets. This clay's source was "the clotted residue / of glaciers rubbing silicate to powder / to pave the basement of a vast and ice-rimmed lake" (110), now called Glacial Lake Edmonton, created when natural drainage from the retreating glacier was blocked to the northeast and then filled with sediment from the surrounding meltwater rivers (Godfrey 28). Its residual clay has been used to form the bricks that now "lift the city sky" and "model / a new world," even as we remain mired in our chthonic origins with "feet of clay" (Major, Occupied 110). "Mazama Ash" describes a white layer in the river valley sediment produced about six thousand and eight hundred years ago from the eruption of Mount Mazama in Oregon, most visible just upstream from the Light Rail Transit bridge on the south bank of the river (Godfrey 115, 118). Major refers to this as "Diaspora of dust / from a ruptured mountain / that scattered this funeral pall / millennia ago" (*Occupied* 111). Overall, the series draws powerful connections between Edmonton's extensive geological history and its much briefer human history. The lives that cling superficially to these ancient geological foundations are emphasized in the sequence's concluding poem, "Root Zones," portraying the struggle between the exposed roots of trees at the edge of constantly eroding riverbanks and the trunks of trees that curve back against "the bank's / persistent slippage" (112).

In many and various ways, then, Alice Major creates new and unconventional perceptions of Edmonton through a variety of scientific perspectives, enlightening her readers through the pleasures of poetic form to a possibly more humane awareness of the city's contextual reality as well as its hitherto unconsidered possibilities for the future. Science has been an important influence on Major's work from the beginning (Querengesser 53-54), and it continues to play an important role in all of her poetry today. But it is ultimately the voice of the poet that predominates, perhaps most powerfully in these lines from the Afterword to *The Office Tower Tales*:

> Touch me and touch this place, this great plain,
> these city lots fenced around with carragana
> where we construct our lines from the wordless
> like windbreaks. Where we make the edge
> bite like the knife that shapes the quill.
> We lay down our evolving alphabets
> against this white, anxious to preserve our being
> here. Our letters take their shapes
> from magpie flight, from aspen's wintry silhouettes,
> *from the stone quarry of cities, the width of steppes.* (251-52)

While this literary alchemy may in some respects remain independent of "the huge edifice of innovation and knowledge [of] the scientist's vocation" (Major, *Intersecting* 233), it nevertheless demonstrates, like so much of her poetry, the powerful ties between the arts and sciences, and just "how enormously complex it is to move, to recognize a pattern, to tell a story, to love" (233). Alice Major's scientific empathy—indeed love—for Edmonton is apparent throughout her work.

Notes

1   Major is not unaware of the famous industrial rockers, Nine Inch Nails, but in a conversation the author suggested her preference for the acronymic connotations of the fictional Six Inch Nails in this context.

Works Cited

Augustine. *The City of God*. Books I-VII. Translated by Demetrius, B. Zema, S.J., and Gerald G. Walsh, S.J., *The Fathers of the Church: A New Translation*, vol. 8, Catholic U of America P, 1950.

Decety, Jean, and Claus Lamm. "Human Empathy Through the Lens of Social Neuroscience." *The Scientific World Journal*, vol. 6, 2006, pp. 1146-63, doi:10.1100. Accessed 17 Sept. 2012.

Fulford, Robert. "The Wonderful Enigma of Raymond Souster." *Globe and Mail*, 24 June 1998, www.robertfulford.com/souster.html. Accessed 16 Nov. 2012.

Godfrey John D., editor. *Edmonton Beneath Our Feet*. Edmonton Geological Society, 1993.

Hoffmann, Roald. *The Same and Not the Same*. Columbia UP, 1995.

MacGregor, J.G. *Edmonton: A History*. Hurtig, 1967.

Major, Alice. "Concluding Remarks: Heritage, Innovation and Livability: Address to 'Heritage, Innovation & the Livable City.' Edmonton Heritage Council Community Symposium." 2 Oct. 2010, www.alicemajor.com/poetry-writing/heritage-innovation-the-livable-city/. Accessed 14 Sept. 2012.

———. "Contemplatio." *The Malahat Review*, vol. 135, Summer 2001, pp. 5-25.

———. *Intersecting Sets: A Poet Looks at Science*. U of Alberta P, 2011.

———. *The Occupied World*. U of Alberta P, 2006.

———. *The Office Tower Tales*. U of Alberta P, 2008.

———. *Scenes from the Sugar Bowl Café*. BS Poetry Society, 1998.

———. *Tales for an Urban Sky*. Broken Jaw, 1999.

Querengesser, Neil. 2005. "Domestic Science in the Poetry of Alice Major." *Canadian Poetry: Studies, Documents, Reviews*, 56, Spring-Summer 2005, pp. 53-64.

Rykwert, Joseph. *The Idea of a Town: The Anthropology of Urban Form in Rome, Italy and the Ancient World.* Faber & Faber, 1976.

Whitaker, S. H., and E. A. Christiansen. "The Empress Group in Southern Saskatchewan." *Canadian Journal of Earth Sciences*, vol. 9, no. 4, 1972, pp. 353-60, doi: 10.1139/e2012-041. Accessed 22 Nov. 2012.

Double Vision in Betty Lambert's
Jennie's Story

Cynthia Zimmerman

Betty Lambert's *Jennie's Story* is set in a southern Alberta farmhouse in 1938-39. The demands of the Second World War would soon change everything, but at this point the prairies are in the grip of the draughts, plagues, soil erosion, and despair known as the Great Depression of the 1930s. Politically, it is the time of the Social Credit and Premier William Aberhart (1935-43)—a premier known for his outspoken religiosity and fiery speeches. Originally a Baptist minister and school principal in Calgary, "Bible Bill" preaches the doctrine as a way to end the Depression. Also in existence is a particularly insidious law which Betty Lambert spent much time researching. Getting it right would be critical to the underpinnings of her play, *Jennie's Story*. The legal information about that law is included as "Author's Notes" to the play publication:

> For the legal background for this play, see "The Sexual Ster-
> ilization Act" (Alberta, 1928), especially Section 5, which
> concerns "multiplication of the evil by the transmission of the
> disability to progeny." In 1937, just before the time of the play,
> an amendment [to the Sexual Sterilization Act] was passed,
> making it possible to sterilize a person without his or her con-
> sent, provided consent was given by an appropriate relative or,
> if the appropriate relative did not exist or was not resident in
> Alberta, by the Minister of Health. This law was repealed in
> 1971. (Lambert, "Jennie's Story" 304)[1]

The Statute on Sterilization (1928), which is based on the eugenics argument, states that a person can be sterilized to prevent "the transmission of evil." "Evil" includes everything from promiscuity, to alcoholism, to feeble-mindedness. Lambert's protagonist will refer to the statute which is used against her explicitly in Act I, Scene v. Speaking to her husband, she says:

> See, I was 16, and so they had ta get. … Ma had to sign the paper. … See, Harry, when I wrote the letter to that doctor, the one who done it, he said he didn't know what to think. That's why he wrote back so fast, come up to see him in Calgary. He's in private practice now. He was just startin'out then, ony job he could get. Anyways, he said, he said, he said … he didn't have no idea I could write a word of English. (*Tries to laugh, numb with shock.*) See there's this law, Harry. Against "the transmission of evil." And they said I wasn't too—No, they said I was feeble-minded. 'n' the other … I was evil. (342)

The central story of the play is based on one that Betty Lambert was told by her mother when she was growing up on the prairies. A true story, it concerned a young prairie girl who had worked as a domestic for the local priest who sexually abused her. During this time, at some point she was taken to Calgary for an appendectomy. Years later she married, happily, but she could not conceive. After investigating, she discovered that she had, in fact, been sterilized years before. It was not an appendix that they removed. She returned home and swallowed sufficient amounts of the household cleanser, lye, to commit a wrenching suicide. Lambert was haunted by the awful incident. In an interview she confided:

> That is a story that I had been told since I was a girl, and I knew the husband, so that when I came to write … I mean, it's always bothered me, it's something I knew I'd have to deal with one day … it seemed to me that men could cut you out for being sexual. I mean literally eviscerate you. (Worthington 60)

In another interview she also said about her work that:

You write almost therapeutically. There are things you want so badly to understand—it's not at all a matter of me knowing what's wrong with me and wanting to set it out on the page … it's a matter of me NOT knowing and wanting to find out. (Wyman 6)

Jennie's Story is an example of just that: of NOT knowing and wanting to find out. Imagining it, writing it out, creating her own scenario as a route to understanding, Lambert retains the basics of the original for her play.

The first production of *Jennie's Story* was staged for the Canadian Theatre Today Conference held in Saskatoon in 1981. It was produced by Vancouver's New Play Centre, directed by Jace van der Veen. The same production was later mounted in the fall of 1981 at the Waterfront Theatre in Vancouver. *Jennie's Story* was a finalist for the 1982 Governor General's Literary Award. Subsequent productions, all directed by Bill Glassco, were at the National Arts Centre (February 1983), the St Lawrence Centre in Toronto (April 1983), and the Canmore Opera House, produced by Alberta Theatre Projects (January 1984).

Lambert's play includes a cast of five: the priest Father Edward Fabrizeau, Jennie and her mother Edna Delevault, Jennie's husband Harry McGrane,[2] and one more: fifteen-year-old Molly Dorval, who is brought to the farmhouse to help feed the farmhands during harvest threshing. As Harry says, unaware of its portent: "Here's Miss Molly Dorval come to save the homestead!"(323). "And the Dorval girl, Ma. My, she's a pretty one" (322), Jennie says. Stage directions indicate that Molly makes "(a quick conspiratorial glance at HARRY; a smothered laugh)" when they enter. "JENNIE, at the door, notes this, and is slightly disturbed" (323). Molly arrives immediately before Jennie is to leave for her visit to the doctor in Calgary, the same doctor who did her surgery several years before. During the four days Jennie is gone, Molly proves she is incredibly competent:

MOLLY: Everythin's done! My goodness, Miz McGrane's goingta drop dead, everythin' done and 18 threshers fed mornin' noon 'n' night. I never worked so hard my whole entire life, an' nothin' dirty to start with! (332)

When the harvesting is over, she stays. Molly is a lovely and lively uneducated farm girl. She is a Thea to Jennie's Hedda Gabler: strong, resourceful, life-affirming, cheerful, and adaptable. But unlike Thea, she is also fertile. In fact, Jennie's mother guesses Molly is already about four months pregnant when she first comes to the farm.

> MOLLY: How could you tell, Mrs. Delevault?
> EDNA: I kin tell.
> MOLLY: (*Drinks tea.*) Well. I guess I'll hafta kill myself.
> EDNA: (*Pause.*) Fine idea. Don't be a stupid girl, suicide's a sin, and you know it, yer a good Catholic. If you're a bad girl, yer still a good Catholic. (*Pause.*) Let's think it out. You leave it to me. God works in mysterious ways. There's a way outa anything, if you don't let go. (*Pause.*) How old're you, Molly? (329)

Edna is quick to think that perhaps Jennie and Harry could adopt Molly's child, an idea Harry will not be adverse to. That Edna is thinking *this* way, even before Jennie returns home with confirmation of her hysterectomy, indicates Edna knows the truth and explains why Jennie's planned trip to Calgary has frightened her so: as Jennie will say with horror upon her return, "You knew all along" (336).

Molly is clearly a double for Jennie. Also a local farm girl hired to help out, she has the same desires as Jennie for a husband, family, and home. She is light-hearted, unreflective, and in tune with the natural world. She too is considered prescient, as Edna notes just before Jennie's return:

> EDNA: You heard truck come over bridge?
> MOLLY: Just now. (*Moves kettle to hot part of range.*)
> EDNA: Bridge's a good piece away.
> MOLLY: Oh I got good ears. My da says I can hear grass grow.
> EDNA: (*Speaks as if JENNIE were dead.*) My Jennie used to hear things.
> I better get away this waxing brick then. (*Gets up stiffly.*) Yes, my Jennie was like that. My Jennie could allus hear things. ... (331)

However, Molly's character differences from Jennie are more to the point than her similarities. She is not as readily obedient, as "biddable" (320) as Jennie, nor is she as timid. Stage directions indicate Edna is aware that "MOLLY is not going to be a meek slave" and Edna "grudgingly likes her for it" (323). Molly gets very excited about the technology Harry has introduced to the homestead, repeatedly turning the lights on and off with glee, unlike Edna and Jennie who stick with the kerosene lamp. When she tells Harry about her sly adventures at the hot spring at her uncle's place and how "My Uncle Charlie, he's got it all wired off so's us kids won't get at it. But we do anyways," Harry says: "But you aren't scared off" (330). Molly is a feisty, spirited one compared to Jennie. She is also less reverent and brazenly tells them all that her cousin, Father Fabrizeau, is "cursed" (324). Most importantly, although Molly is the same age as Jennie was when Jennie was working for the priest, Molly's sexual mishap will not have tragic consequences. In fact, Molly will ultimately replace Jennie in the homestead and in the marriage bed.

Harry honours Jennie's wish to be cremated, to go up into the skies and not into the cold, dark earth. He completes his prison term for the "desecration of the dead" (361) and, several months after Jennie's awful suicide, Harry returns to the farm. It is the closing scene of the play. Molly waits on him; her babe, Ben, is in a nearby basket. The marriage bans have already been announced. What are we to make of this closure to the play with its apparently happy ending? That is to say, after witnessing a transformed and vehement Jennie extract confessions from her betrayers, after watching her heroically overcome the pressures to withhold a revelation which involves religious authority, and knowing the desperate measure soon to follow this climactic confrontation, this nice domestic scene comes as a shock. I certainly found it most unsettling, as did others.

In their published conversation, director Bonnie Worthington tells Lambert it is a "tacked-on happy ending" (65) and totally unnecessary. Critic Rosalind Kerr argues the ending is necessary but that instead of a "healing catharsis," this ending "demonstrates to us how insignificant and nontragic the lives of women are" (99). Furthermore, the substitution of Molly is a way "to represent the state of bitter competition that [Lambert] believes exists between women" (110). Lambert expresses this clearly when she tells Worthington, "look at what I was saying—you bloody women, you'd better not kill yourselves, because there's going to be someone there moving into your place!" (65). Nonetheless, I would argue that Lambert's response to Worthington is a defensive reaction to a specific charge: the charge that that scene should be removed, that it is unnecessary and tacked-on. What Lambert means—and she says so—is that "suicide is not an answer" (64).

> In *Jennie's Story*, for example, she is not a completely evolved character. She is not at all a role model for women, because what she does is she accepts. She doesn't see any way of breaking out of her world, and she turns her anger inwards. (62)

People are NOT replaceable but life goes on. In direct reaction to Worthington, Lambert says, "No, it wasn't supposed to be that, it was supposed to be—look, she killed herself and it was not the answer. It is not an answer" (65). The ending of the play is problematic. How does one understand the gap between the effect Lambert wants and the way, in fact, so many have responded? Could it be because, as the writer, she was "recollecting in tranquility"? She had the distance, the overview, but the reader/audience is given no time at all between the experience of the terrible tragedy and the happy ending. Lambert brings us into painful intimacy with the main character, only to draw back at the climactic moment, like a camera suddenly pulling back from a close-up.

Young Jennie had been the priest's perfect victim: naïve, obedient without questioning, supposedly "not that bright," and sworn to silence. Her mother's consent, her betrayal, as well as Jennie's silence, aid the sterilization procedure. Later, Jennie's time with her husband is happy. She is a sensual and sexually satisfied woman. Ignorance is bliss. But once she knows the "truth" everything falls apart: ejected from the natural cycle, unable to reproduce, Jennie feels herself damaged, "dirty" (Lambert, "Jennie's Story" 345), "no good for anything" (346), both unnatural and undesirable. Representing innocence and vulnerability, being the one who went to work for the priest so her mother would not have to, the one who needs a child to confer value and identity as a female, Jennie embodies complex feminist ideas. And yet does her sacrifice redeem anything? No, not for Lambert. Jennie's heroic "moment of truth" is "largely overshadowed," as Rosalind Kerr says (111). When Max Wyman asks Lambert about the final scene, she explains it to him as well. She says she could not let the play end with the woman's suicide, though many people would like her to. "I can't," she says," I don't like that classic tragic form. That's no answer to human suffering" (6).

In the "Introduction" to the first publication of *Jennie's Story*, Pamela Hawthorn refers to what she considers characteristic of Lambert's talent: "an intense, emotional connection to the material that poured out" (8). In *Jennie's Story*, the personal connection is not simply that the plot is based on the upsetting anecdote told to Lambert as a child; it is also that the play theatricalizes her personal philosophy with its deep roots in her religious upbringing. This view is fundamental to Lambert's intended meaning. Although Lambert admits to Worthington that "[she is] not sure that final scene does what [she] want[s] it to" (66), understanding her spiritual premise illuminates what otherwise might appear a too-sudden switch from searing individual tragedy to a signal that for the others there is the possibility of ongoing happiness. In the same way that Molly is the life-affirming "double" to Jennie, Harry is the life-affirming "double" to Father Edward Fabrizeau. *Jennie's Story* has more than one priest onstage. Harry is the one who embodies the spiritual way of seeing of that other priest, Gerard Manly Hopkins, the priest whose poetry is recited and referred to repeatedly in the play. It is Harry's philosophical perspective that Lambert finds compelling.

My appreciation of Lambert's "double vision" came about as a result of archival work on the Betty Lambert Papers held by Simon Fraser University.[3] In her personal diaries and journal entries, I read what a fighter Lambert was—how she refused to give in to the polio that hit her as a child; how she fought the poverty she was born into. I saw her letter to Joy Coghill written shortly after she was diagnosed with cancer. She explained that she would never, even though she knew her illness was fatal, never, ever commit suicide and I realized how many of Harry's lines spoke to her purpose:

JENNIE: It happened, so it happened, forget it.
HARRY: (*Pause.*) No, you don't forget something like that. But you can't brood on it. You can't just lie up here and brood on it.

JENNIE: I want to die.
HARRY: (*Angrily.*) Don't talk like that! (*Pause.*) Things happen to people. Bad things. You can't give in. You got to keep your hope. (80)

Then I learned that the poem which frames this play, "God's Grandeur," which Harry teaches to Jennie and then to Molly, was Lambert's favourite poem and the one she requested be read at her Memorial Service. Beginning with man's plight as "Crushed," blighted, "seared," the poem ultimately celebrates nature's plenitude. I want to argue that the spirit of its comfort is actually woven throughout the fabric of the play and offers, subtly—perhaps too subtly—a more hopeful way of accommodating the tragedy. To access this alternative framework is to shift focus away from Jennie's heroic, though futile "sacrifice," away from any sense of her as a "kind of everywoman" (Kerr 103). It is to look instead to her husband, the one who has learned the painful rituals of atonement, the reconciliation of God and man, which can sustain him. It is Harry who will prove to be the play's most evolved character.

Therefore, while the play is called *Jennie's Story*, it is not something pertinent to Jennie's life which opens the play or closes it. It opens at harvest time with Jennie's intuitive knowing that Billy, the hired hand, has died a natural death. Billy's death is set in obvious contrast to the suicide. Jennie's death occurs offstage while the others, preoccupied with the blessing ceremony, have momentarily forgotten about her. The play concludes in the spring, with a recent birth and a wedding planned for the next day. The play pays close attention to the changing seasons and to the natural cycle of things. The setting is the remarkably prosperous farm of Harry McGrane. Somehow his farm has been spared the blight. Even Father Fabrizeau remarks on Harry's good luck:

FATHER: (*Pause.*) The whole district hailed out last summer except for you.
The whole country in a black depression and you get a new truck and electricity. ... (312)

Harry has been so successful, so lucky, that he is putting in electricity—he has put technology to good use. Associated with light, with bringing in the light, he represents positive change. "That's right," he says to the priest, "ever since you married us, Jennie's brought me nothin' but luck" (312).

Unlike Father Edward Fabrizeau, the other man in Jennie's life, Harry, is not dark, brooding, morose. He is a believer and observant, conscious of the importance of ritual, but he is his own man and his own kind of priest, a Gerard Manly Hopkins kind of priest who believes in joy and loves the physical world. As he puts it,

> God help me, I love the world, Jennie. I love the world. I love it all, the way the thunderhead comes up dark and purple and the still before it breaks, everything holding its breath, I love it though it'll flatten my field. (344)

For Lambert, Harry McGrane, with a name that links him to the land, represents the physicality of the Dionysian side of our natures. He has learned how to hang on to hope and how to celebrate life.

But his is not a naïve optimism. Harry has known violence in his past. His father had been a brutal man, a "bully" he says, who beat his brother so bad that "Jamie was never right in the head" (350). Moreover, Harry has spent time in prison for killing a man (341, 362). Lambert does not explore his crime, but it is an interesting addition to Harry's story and to his character. He is no coward (although Jennie will accuse him of being one), and he burns his own hand to keep him from taking revenge. His past means that he can say to Jennie, "You're not the only one things happen to" (344). He can also honour her wish to be cremated, knowing he can take the consequences—another prison term. He will let Fabrizeau bear the burden of belief that Jennie is "in danger of her immortal soul" (353). Harry will act according to his own conscience, pay the price, mourn his losses, and accept the unalterable facts of nature.

Moreover, Harry is an unusually generous and free-thinking man: he will love and marry Jennie although he knows about the rumours; he is prepared to adopt the child of an unwed mother so they can have a family; he frequently makes reference to what is natural—whether it be Billy's manner of dying or Jennie's true nature or the ways of the world. In fact, he says that what the priest did *as a man* he can understand: "it's ony nature. The Church says it's bad, but it's ony nature. But what happened after, what he did to you"—that Harry *cannot* understand, "It's even against the Church" (345). Harry is not moralistic, and although he is described as having "an edge of steel in his voice" (310), he is definitely a Lambertan, if not a Lawrentian hero. He will be moved to the breaking point, and he will not break. He is strong, successful, proud, self-educated, tender, playful, and compassionate; he has known deep suffering and he is moved by literature and poetry. As Molly is the adaptive, life-affirming double to Jennie, Harry is the life-affirming resilient double to dour Father Edward Fabrizeau. Eddie is the farmer's son who cannot remember to shut the gate, who cannot control his desire or his despair, and he falls apart in a most unseemly fashion. "What can I do," he cries. And Harry says, "You can live and do yer job an' make the best of it. Molly will have her baby and we'll take it. … You're a bad priest but you're our priest. So, bless this place and go. … Damn you, Eddie, be a priest!" (360).

At this point it is useful to turn to the first version of *Jennie's Story*, the unpublished, unproduced, undated play for CBC Radio called "Fire People."[4] The major characters, the plot outline, and all of the main script details are the same. However, there are revisions, significant alterations, and additions. First of all, Molly has increased visibility in *Jennie's Story*. Jennie "watches this girl taking over her kitchen" (338); Jennie notices Harry's attraction to her. In the original, Harry does NOT come to Molly's bedside the first night Jennie is away. He does not listen to her tell the seductive little anecdote about swimming naked in an underground hot spring while Edna sleeps soundly beside her. In "Fire People," Molly tells the anecdote directly to Jennie and simply reports that she had also told Mister McGrane. The revision alerts us to the potential for intimacy between Molly and Harry.[5]

However, to support my reading, the most important changes are to the confrontation and the closure. In the radio play, Jennie comes downstairs to see her mother and the priest. It is a radio play and nothing is said of her appearance, although she has something in her hands. In *Jennie's Story*, Lambert carefully describes Jennie's appearance:

> JENNIE appears behind MOLLY. She is wearing a new flannelette nightgown, buttoned to the neck, long sleeves. Her feet

are bare, her hair is cropped off, and in her hands she holds a long fiery-red braid of hair. (353)

She takes the scarf from her mother (a Christmas gift) and "puts the scarf around her neck so it hangs like a vestment" (353). About her cropped hair she says, "Don't mind, Mother, it's ony what they do to nuns" (354). The change in her appearance marks the dramatic change in identification: gone is Harry's sensuous young wife, his "pagan lady" (308). Here now, is the nun, the desexualized one outside the cycle of generation. In this role, she says:

> ... I feel free 'n' I can think, and what I think is, it was an untrue blessing, and Harry can annul me. ... Harry can annul me and marry Molly Dorval. (*Turns and goes to MOLLY.*) Molly Dorval, may your union be holy. (*Turns MOLLY to EDNA.*) Molly Dorval, I give you to my mother who will have no more children and you kin be hers, reborn, in the fire 'n' the spirit. Amen. (356)

In the play Jennie herself blesses this union, but having Jennie explicitly endorse this union is not in "Fire People." This is another example of Lambert underlining her central thesis: necessary continuity, the affirmation of life over death.

Similarly, the closing scene of *Jennie's Story* has a poignant, intensely rendered sympathy with Harry. He enters "bone tired" and "sits at his old place at the table" (362). He is in a suit. He does not touch the food placed before him. The laughter and the baby on his lap, which were in "Fire People," have been removed. In fact, only **after** (emphasis mine) Molly recites the lines she has memorized from "God's Grandeur" does he raise his head (363). At this moment of communication, he looks up.

Although Harry says, "Damn it, Jennie, you're alive and life's a miracle! The rest we can swallow" (346), and although he begs her to come back, she cannot. Jennie has swallowed the lye/lie. It is Harry who is to be the play's moral anchor. The real focus of the play is not the revenge or the substitution, but the courage to live, which is central to Lambert's work and to her life: "They won't beat Harry down," says Edna (361). It is through Harry's eyes that we realize a vision of humanity that is harsh, unflinching, and yet cautiously optimistic. Harry's favourite poem, "God's Grandeur," was also Lambert's, with its famous lines of solace:

> The world is charged with the grandeur of God.
>   It will flame out, like shining from shook foil;
>   It gathers to a greatness, like the ooze of oil
> Crushed. Why do men then now not reck his rod?
> Generations have trod, have trod, have trod;
>   And all is seared with trade; bleared, smeared with toil;
>   And wears man's smudge and shares man's smell: the soil
> Is bare now, nor can foot feel, being shod.
>
> And for all this, nature is never spent;
>   There lives the dearest freshness deep down things;
> And though the last lights off the black West went
>   Oh, morning, at the brown brink eastward, springs—
> Because the Holy Ghost over the bent
>   World broods with warm breast and with ah! bright wings.

This poem, lines from which are recited early in the play by Harry and at the end by Molly, provides the frame to *Jennie's Story*; "God's Grandeur" puts Jennie's individual suffering in perspective. The religious abstraction, intended as comfort, can be read as sentimental. But is it not true that, when facing death, people often cling to the common abstractions of love, family, religion? It is the ending that Lambert prefers.

NOTES

1   In 1996, after a court case which lasted six years, Leilani Muir became the first victim of sterilization to win a judgment against the Alberta government. She was awarded damages totaling $740,000. Around her eleventh birthday, she had been admitted to the Provincial Training School for Mental Defectives in Alberta and given a simple IQ test. This was sufficient for her to be deemed "unfit" to bear children. In 1959, when she was fourteen, she was sterilized in accordance with Alberta's eugenics policy. She was one of approximately two thousand and eight hundred victims. For more information, see www.cbc.ca/thecurrent/episode/2011/11/14/leilani-muir-successfully-sues-alberta-govt-for-wrongful-sterilization and the NFB documentary film by Whiting in 1996.

2   Lambert gives Harry the surname McGrane. According to Lambert's sister Dorothy, McGrane was the surname of their maternal grandmother who had been a serving girl

in Ireland. A young man named Thomas Craven fell in love with her and married her. The problem was that this young man was in training to be a priest. He was promptly excommunicated by the Church and disinherited by his wealthy parents. The young couple immigrated to the Canadian prairies, changed their name to Cooper, and began a difficult and impoverished life together. Betty's mother was their first born and, like her parents, she raised her three daughters with a religious sense of life. This story of her grandparents, part of Lambert's history, also contributed to her anger against the authoritarianism of the Roman Catholic Church.

3   Her scripts, journals, and letters are housed with the Betty Lambert Papers at Simon Fraser University. For more information on the author, see Beavington.

4   The manuscript for "Fire People" can be found with the Betty Lambert Papers at Simon Fraser University. One significant alteration is the title, which I do not develop in the body of this paper, but which clearly points to the alternate vision Lambert is embracing. Lambert in fact weaves many explicit verbal references to this alternate way of seeing throughout the play. The title highlights the references to the "firefolk" (Lambert, "Jennie's Story" 343, 361), to Jennie as Harry's "pagan lady," and to his love of her exuberant sexuality reinforced by her long "fiery–red braid." As he says, "it allus gets away on you. It's not in yer nature to braid your hair so tight" (351). When she crops it, she is literally cutting off the pagan, earthy side of her nature. The most explicit identification occurs when she describes the way she wants her life to end: "Ony when I go, Harry, don't put me in the ground. I want to go like the fire-folk, burnin', burnin', burnin,' like those old Fire People made the rings up on the butte. Take me down ta the river and cut me some kindlin,' and let me go up inta the sky like fire-folk" (343). Lambert mentions the "butte" and "the rings" in the "Author's Notes": "The 'Indian rings' referred to in the play are found in southern Alberta, and also in Saskatchewan, along the river, on buttes. As Harry says in the play, they are often found one day's canoe trip apart. Archaeologists guess the age of the circles to be perhaps 100,000 years, and, because of the placement of larger boulders, that they were used as an almanac of some kind" (304).

5   In *Jennie's Story*, just before the Father and Edna arrive, before the final confrontation, Jennie seems to be warming to Harry's "we can still make a life" (351). Then he hears the car approaching and she is shocked to discover that she has not heard it. She quickly goes upstairs "in darkness" (351). In "Fire People" he tells her they can still make a life; he shoots at the coyote and hears the car. He does not say that he likes it "when [she lets her] hair go loose like that" (351), of how he first fell in love with her. The "Fire People" does not include this short-lived softening with its sense that, perhaps, they might still be able to move forward together. It is noteworthy that when Molly greets Harry upon his return from prison, Molly's hair is loose.

Works Cited

Beavington, Lee. Betty Lambert website: www.bettylambert.ca.

Hawthorn, Pamela. "Introduction." *Jennie's Story and Under the Skin*, by Betty Lambert. Playwrights Canada Press, 1987, pp. 7-9.

Kerr, Rosalind. "'Swallowing the Lie' in Betty Lambert's *Jennie's Story*." *Modern Drama*, vol. 47, no 1, Spring 2004, pp. 98-113.

Lambert, Betty. "Fire People." Betty Lambert Papers: Special Collections, WAC Bennett Library, Simon Fraser University, Burnaby BC. Manuscript.

———. "Jennie's Story." *The Betty Lambert Reader*, edited by Cynthia Zimmerman, Playwrights Canada Press, 2007, pp. 303-63.

Whiting, Glynis, director. *The Sterilization of Leilani Muir*. National Film Board, 1996.

Worthington, Bonnie. "Battling Aristotle: A Conversation between Playwright Betty Lambert and Director Bonnie Worthington." *Room of One's Own*, vol. 8, no. 2,1983, pp. 54-66.

Wyman, Max. *The Magazine*, 25 Oct. 1981, p. 6.

Seeing Seeing, and Telling Telling: Framing and Transparency in Robert Kroetsch's *The Hornbooks of Rita K.* and James Turrell's "Twilight Arch"

Harry Vandervlist

American artist James Turrell occupies a prominent place in Robert Kroetsch's 2001 volume, *The Hornbooks of Rita K*. Turrell has been described as a "minimalist" and "conceptualist" artist whose best known works involve the creation of precisely lit, deliberately structured spaces which viewers enter in order to experience light. Often the light appears to form a solid shape, yet this effect diminishes as one approaches more closely. As Turrell has explained it: "these pieces are highly sensitive to your position, and on approach tend to dissolve to reveal their existence. This is like looking behind the stage to find the mirrors, only to discover there are none" (Didi-Huberman 117). In recent years Turrell has been creating such structured viewing spaces within Roden Crater, a volcano north of Flagstaff, Arizona.

Kroetsch signals Turrell's role in *The Hornbook* through one of the book's three epigraphs, which offers Axel Muller's description of Turrell's 1991 piece "Twilight Arch":

> No object can be seen, no shadow. The picture's optical frame-work, made by light, has no foreground, middle or background. Everything is light—even the room. Here a process of perception begins that is hardly describable or nameable. The

gaze is now at rest. The constant and fruitless attempts to fix one's eye on something have been given up at last. (n.p.)

Further references to "Twilight Arch" appear throughout Kroetsch's book, most notably at its centre, where Rita disappears while viewing the artwork at the Frankfurt Museum of Modern Art. The significance and the humour attached to the notion of an absent central image could hardly be more clear:

> There in Frankfurt, on the occasion of Rita's disappearance (and I was standing beside her in the darkened room where one believes one is looking at a framed painting only to discover, as one's eyes adjust to the dark, that one is staring into a faintly lit recession set blankly into a blank wall), I turned to remark that I found James Turrell's "Twilight Arch" compelling nevertheless, for all the absence of an image. I turned and she was not there. (53)

What is implied by this central presence of a singular work of visual art, in a book filled with poems, manuscripts, and correspondence? The critical context in which this question must be explored is, in the large sense, the context of discussions about the relation between textual and visual art. The question of Canadian literature and photography, for example, has been addressed by Linda Hutcheon (*The Canadian Postmodern: A Study of Contemporary English-Canadian Fiction*) and Lorraine York (*The Other Side of Dailiness: Photography in the Works of Alice Munro, Timothy Findley, Michael Ondaatje, and Margaret Laurence*). Within Alberta, authors and artists as diverse as Jane Ash Poitras ("2C Mother = E" and other works), Ernie Kroeger (*Crossing the Great Divide*), and Fred Wah (*Sentenced to Light*) have all forged distinctive combinations of text and image. This critical context is vertiginously enlarged as we move away from Canadian literature specifically, to include works by Rosalind Krauss, Roland Barthes, Jean Baudrillard, and others.

Kroetsch maps out his own distinctive path through this territory. He was of course steeped in the world of international postmodern culture, theory, and art practice from at least 1972 on, when with William V. Spanos he co-founded *boundary 2, a journal of postmodern literature.*

(See Robert David Stacey, *Re: Reading the Postmodern: Canadian Literature and Criticism After Modernism*, for a fuller discussion of this area.) The intersection of photography, video, and other visual arts with text was a mainstay of much work at the time—think of the now-iconic work of Barbara Kruger and Jenny Holzer, or Laurie Anderson, for example. Kroetsch's distinct form of the postmodern conjunction of text and image, however, shows less interest in mass-media imagery and "memes" than in what Donald Lawrence and William F. Garrett-Petts call "picture space," and in particular, vernacular modes of visual imagery. As they point out in *PhotoGraphic Encounters: The Edges and Edginess of Reading Prose Pictures and Visual Fictions*, Kroetsch includes snapshots of himself in his first collection of critical essays, *The Lovely Treachery of Words: Essays Selected and New* (1989). The casual documentary mode of these snapshots shows Kroetsch's interest in what Lawrence and Garrett-Petts call "the vernacular mode of self-representation":

> Like oral story-telling, photography hints at an ostensibly art-less, certainly vernacular, mode of expression … For Kroetsch, the photograph, especially the snapshot, is part of what he calls the "great-given," the flow of vernacular culture, the "particulars of place" that the writer may draw upon: "newspaper files, place names, shoe boxes full of photographs, tall tales, diaries, journals, tipi rings, weather reports, business ledges, voting records … archaeological deposits (*Lovely Treachery* 7). These are the tokens of lived experience; personally invested, these forms of vernacular expression stand apart from the words and images of mass, popular and high art cultures. (219)

Not only has Kroetsch mined such stores of visual vernacular material in his work, but for him the printed page has also often worked as a visual field, as in, for example, *The Ledger* and *Seed Catalogue* with their conjunction of spatially-organized documents with poetic text, but also in poems such as "Mile Zero." In so much of Kroetsch's work, then, visual imagery, spacing, and page layout all "speak" in their interactions with, and their difference from, text itself. I certainly agree with Lawrence and Garrett-Petts's view that when Kroetsch employs visual elements, he does not aim to offer a complement or "counterbalance" to text, resulting in something he critiques in *Labyrinths of Voice* as "equilibrium or stasis" (Neuman and Wilson 126). Instead he aims to "animate, rather than freeze, representation" (Lawrence and Garret-Petts 220) through ambivalent acts of juxtaposition and mutual (re)framing.

Briefly, then, this is the context for Kroetsch's choice of Turrell's work as a crucial reference in *The Hornbooks*—a choice which demands focused interpretive scrutiny, as Turrell is a singular artist. His works rely on sight, but they are not visual art objects in the usual sense. As such they could never be "reproduced" as "illustrations" in Kroetsch's text. Early in Turrell's career, Willoughby Sharp said "Turrell's breakthrough was that he had broken out of the need for material objects to create a highly intense aesthetic experience" (qtd in Adcock 53). Perhaps similarly, *The Hornbooks of Rita K.* is not a poetry collection, a narrative, or a work of poetics in the usual sense, though I believe it partakes of all of them. Indeed Kroetsch's epigraph seems to signal that Turrell's unusual visual artworks and his own unusual book share several interests and strategies: both engage the concepts of framing and transparency in various senses; both direct their audience's attention, not toward represented objects, but toward an awareness of fundamental artistic processes; and finally, both reach toward a common grounding in elements that are ubiquitous and shared, yet somehow not seen or "transcended" in ordinary experience.

While noting these interesting intersections, I think it is important to remain aware of the different types of analysis each form of work seems able to support. For example, an initial point of convergence between Turrell and Kroetsch would seem to be their use of "framing" and "transparency"—but these concepts need to be applied in the slightly different senses appropriate to the verbal and visual arts. In the hornbooks, framing and transparency appear quite literally in the image of the historical artifact, the hornbook itself:

> Framed and wearing a handle, covered in transparent horn, it sets out to fool no one. It says its say. Rita Kleinhart seems not to have got a handle on this realization. What she claimed for her poems was exactly that which they did not provide: the clarity of the exact and solitary visible page. The framed truth, present and unadorned. Not a page for the turning, no,

but rather the poem as relentless as a mirror held in the hand.
(Kroetsch, *Hornbook* 30, 23)

The hornbook as an artifact relies on physical framing—the short texts presented in this limiting, focusing format were used as primers or to teach alphabets—and literal transparency. However, Raymond, as editor, archivist, and also Rita's would-be or actual lover, immediately makes the leap to the figurative notion of transparent clarity of signification. Rita's poems never offered such easy clarity, he says. The idea of "getting a handle on" Rita's poems, of their easy manageability, is also raised only to be mocked.

A new frame, a conceptual one this time, is created through this process of opposing the hornbook's evident straightforwardness to the "real" experience of reading Rita's poems, which Raymond suggests has more to do with obliqueness and opacity than directness and clarity. Now the reader has a nice set of oppositions within which to situate Rita's poetry: clarity versus opacity; directness versus indirection; the isolated page versus the complicating narrative context; the "truth, present and unadorned," versus the fleeting traces of Rita, absent and commented upon at length by Raymond. As an editor—the classic character used in "framing narratives"— Raymond is bound to operate on this kind of interpretive level. He offers a context for Rita's works, he arranges her remains for viewing. But he does not stop there. As a lover, Raymond is preoccupied with Rita herself: with her actual presence. For him the poems are traces of something else, clues even, like the postcards he receives. He desires to read through them to Rita herself, to what he wants to read as their story. Yet they remain, insistently, themselves: mounds of paper, perhaps even burial mounds recording a vanished presence.

The structure of Kroetsch's book, with its two key figures Raymond and Rita, along with the work performed by this kind of conceptual framing, is what makes the book into a "trace structure" (to use Dawne McCance's term for it). McCance describes the way the book's two central figures operate as "two hands at once" which create "a hesitation between them" ("Still Life"). But what is this "hesitation," this space between: is it a gap which readers fill? Is it blankness, absence, "nothing?" Does this space make Rita's "disappearance … a mode of entrance," a space "for play and entrance?" (McCance, "Art of Building" 168). Is it a "transparency" through which significance can be glimpsed? Is it, as McCance describes it, the space in which we realize that "the poem is not constituted by the idea of the poem or the idea of the poet, but by the sociality of writing, the poem as materialized supplement ceaselessly reinventing itself as it moves through the world" ("Still Life"). Just as historical hornbooks realized themselves, not through aesthetic contemplation but through social use in bringing children into the realm of language, does *The Hornbooks of Rita K.* realize itself by bringing readers into the realm of writing?

These questions can perhaps be illuminated by a glance at the parallels and contrasts offered by Turrell's visual works. If Kroetsch's book evokes a set of conceptual oppositions in order to frame the absent Rita, to make a question of her, of her work, and of our reading and *writing* of it—then how might this correspond in any way to the procedures behind a work such as Turrell's "Twilight Arch"?

Turrell makes use of literal frames, just as the historic hornbook did, in order to direct attention. "Twilight Arch" is framed within architectural space. As viewers enter a room, their sight is oriented toward what Raymond called "a faintly lit recession set blankly into a blank wall" (Kroetsch, *Hornbook* 53). Yet the viewer's experience has little in common with the conventional experience of viewing a physical art object. In response to the question "what is Turrell's art about?" Daniel Birnbaum writes:

> About light and perception, one is tempted to answer. Perhaps it would be more correct to say: his art is light and perception. Turrell's works do not represent anything. They are themselves: light and darkness, space and perception. His installations manipulate the conditions of our perception rather than present object of aesthetic contemplation. This is art liberated from all objects. It is not about what is before but rather what is behind our eyes—about the preconditions of seeing and the limits of perceptions. (227)

Turrell himself has said, "I am really interested in the qualities of one space sensing another. It is like looking at someone looking. … As you plumb a space with vision it is possible to see yourself see. This seeing, this plumbing, imbues space with consciousness" (Adcock 227). The profundity of such perceptions may be suggested by Jacques Lacan's contention that "consciousness, in its illusion of *seeing itself seeing itself*, finds its basis in the inside-out structure of the gaze" (82).

Here we can begin to see one potential correspondence between Kroetsch's and Turrell's strategies. Both work, not so much with represented objects, but through manipulating the most fundamental transactions of their artistic activities: in Kroetsch's case, reading, and in Turrell's, viewing. In literature, it may be difficult to imagine "art liberated from all objects," but less difficult to see how a written work might engage "preconditions and the limits of perceptions." (Kroetsch's comments on literature as a game in *Labyrinths of Voice* [Neuman and Wilson 56-57] for example, engage the idea of reading's "preconditions.")

The notion of the frame may serve as one such fundamental precondition, shared by both readers of works in language and viewers of visual artworks. Turrell's installations, at least before the Roden Crater project, were usually situated in familiar types of space: the Mendota Hotel in California, for example, or art galleries. His initial task in creating works was always a kind of "emptying out," something Kroetsch has called "fundamental to any making of art" (*Lovely Treachery* 34). Familiar objects would be removed, all surface decoration eliminated, so that the light installation could fill the space with "absence, and make the work out of it, its opening" (Didi-Huberman 47). This "absence," framed by the familiar viewing space, becomes the space where viewers "see themselves seeing."

Part of what makes this effect possible is the play of the frame. By projecting light in such a way that his fields of colour appear to have solid edges (sometimes solid enough that viewers have attempted to lean against them), Turrell appears to offer a "depth" that is "framed." Daniela Zyman describes one such work as follows:

> Through the powerful blue glint at its very outer edge, the brilliant monochrome color field appears to lose itself in an unfathomable darkness, into a "there" which does not reveal itself. The viewer's vision can take no hold and turns back to the yellow frame in order to re-immerse himself into the depth of the space to define it. (19)

It is between the edge or frame, and the "depth" that the viewer's seeing oscillates, revealing the need for an object, a "there" to focus on, and the need for an edge or a limit. As Craig Adcock has it, "Turrell's homogenous visual fields ... stimulate the eyes but do not provide enough data for "things" or "objects" with names to be perceived by the receiver" (227). In this way, he says, they "present the viewer with something very like "wordless thought" (227).

Turning to *The Hornbooks of Rita K.*, can we discern a similar role for the frame in making visible some fundamental artistic conditions? I would argue that the parallel with Turrell's work emerges in the way the *Hornbooks* contends with the concepts of the writer and the self, and their presence or absence. Rita, the writer, ought to be the "object" at the centre of the framed space set up by a volume bearing her name. Yet Rita is an absent presence: she cannot be finally located, either in her poems or in her house. As Dawne McCance suggests, *The Hornbooks'* version of autobiography, of Rita's autobiography, follows the logic of supplementarity: rather than delivering "a deposit of self-referential content to be hermeneutically unsealed," autobiography, for Rita, "inscribes the writing process itself, the play of the frame, the insistent crossing of inside and out" ("Art of Building" 162).

James Turrell also links his work to this threshold phenomenon, this play "between": he says "I'm interested in the point where imaginative seeing and outside seeing meet, where it becomes difficult to differentiate between seeing from the inside and seeing from the outside" (Didi-Huberman 130). Or, as Zyman puts it, "Turrell reinforces the enigmatic nature of space and its dimensionality by materializing the space in between—the transitory" (18). This formulation recalls McCance's description of "the poem as materialized supplement" ("Still Life"). It is through framing this transitional space, whether it is the space of viewing, reading, or writing, that Turrell and Kroetsch materialize the very artistic activity in which their audiences are engaged.

I've been attempting to suggest how both Turrell and Kroetsch make use of framing in order to manifest some basic processes of their respective art forms. I also suggested at the outset that both artists reach toward a grounding in elements that are ubiquitous and shared, yet which are somehow "transcended" or not seen in ordinary experience. It is here that the differences between their respective forms begin to be clear.

What Turrell's viewers "see themselves seeing" is light, that ubiquitous and fundamental element of all sight, which is itself rarely perceived in its own right. As Craig Adcock puts it, "the centrality of light for existence notwithstanding, seeing light, just light, is unusual." Humans generally "comprehend the information contained in the light that is reflected from objects in the world." Yet in Turrell's works, viewers confront precisely "light as such" and "mere illumination" (221).

Readers of *The Hornbooks* are perhaps invited to experience a different, yet analogous awareness of something whose "centrality for existence" makes it generally invisible. In *The Hornbooks*, the image of the "back door" seems to summarize a complex of notions related to this theme. Rita's project in "collective biography" located itself "literally and momentarily" among whatever is ignored, denied, rejected—that is, invisible—yet also shared. Her references to "back doors," partly through their link to *collective* biography, seem to me to imply sociality. "Back doors," she claims, "are the very locus of discharge and communality" (Kroetsch, *Hornbook* 11). Rita asks "what is more precious to our collective biography than those very things we elect to conceal or discard?" (11). Here at this level commonly denominated "low," she sought, according to Raymond, escape from several things: from "transcendence," "good neighbours," and "possibly from language itself" (9). At the same time Rita is described as seeking, if not escape from language, at least "another possibility in language." Perhaps this other possibility lies in her own writing, which "she reckons ... is freighted with no end of traces that were neither literal nor metaphoric" (14).

But what "language" can escape the territory between those two poles, the letter and all the types of figuration represented by the metaphor? I believe the choice of the hornbook as a central image evokes the idea, if not the actual availability, of a type of exchange that lies *avant la lettre*. The hornbook, as a type of primer, marks that social and linguistic threshold that we cross when we first learn our letters. The hornbooks' association with sheer unmediated directness, mere transparent *monstrance*, suggests a clarity that requires no words. In this way the hornbooks evoke exchanges so primary that they precede or obviate language. Such exchanges may be bodily, like those Raymond says he shared with Rita. They may be gestural. Or they may involve a simple *constatation* of the world: seeing without looking. Perhaps it is this that led Kroetsch to conclude with an image of "not the sought after needle," but the blindingly obvious "haystack in the field by the lane" (91).

If "the poem itself is at best a trace of what is fundamental and now forgotten" (87), how then, "The Hollow Hornbook" asks, to "give it a surface that lets the eye hear?" The question seems compatible with Turrell's project of making visible the fundamental and forgotten properties of light and perception. Perhaps just as Turrell frames absence in order to foreground seeing itself, so *The Hornbooks* frames a gap, a transitional space, in order to make visible some fundamental, forgotten back-door elements of the game of writing. What "mere illumination" is to Turrell, so the body, desire, the absent other, the self as a mere trace may be to *The Hornbooks of Rita K.*

Kroetsch's framed absences in *The Hornbooks* may recall what he refers to in his essay "Reciting the Emptiness," as "the gap" which "tells us more than the bridge" (*Lovely Treachery* 35). Rita seems to me to be evoking a gap, something central or fundamental, yet invisible, something "unspeakable," unreadable. In "Reciting the Emptiness," Kroetsch suggests that the gap "may have a lot to do, not with the stories we share, but with our attempts at sharing stories" (40).

This exploration of framed absence in the *Hornbooks* may suggest some convergences between visual works, such as Turrell's art and Kroetsch's writing—but it also aims to reveal a key difference. Although Turrell's viewers may "see themselves see," and may be brought to a changed awareness of their own perception, this remains an individual affair. Turrell has said that "I feel my work is made for one being, one individual" (Douglas). What is more, Turrell conceives of his work as leading out of language altogether: "My work has no object, no image and no focus. With no object, no image and no focus, what are you looking at? You are looking at you looking. What is important to me is to create an experience of wordless thought" (Turrell). Viewers who cross his carefully crafted thresholds between "inside" and "outside" seeing may do so as solitary perceivers encountering light and space. Private visual perception remains conceivable in a way that private language does not. As a work of language, however, *The Hornbooks of Rita K.* retains irreducibly social elements. The work compels readers to recognize that the thresholds crossed here are those between self and other, reader and writer. They are the everyday, back door thresholds across which the fundamentally social exchanges of language—our not-necessarily successful "*attempts* (my emphasis) at sharing stories"—all take place. The frame of the back door may not contain a static, finished product—a "story," much less "the" story of, say, "Rita K."— so much as it offers a space for further, ongoing telling. Kroetsch's reader can hardly avoid becoming an activated reader, a teller in turn, of stories prompted by the scraps of lived life. In this way perhaps Turell and Kroetsch do converge, despite their differences, in their shared emphasis on leading viewers and readers to something framed and offered, which makes visible or activates within viewers and readers the very processes that generate the work.

Works Cited

Adcock, Craig. *James Turrell: The Art of Light and Space*. U of California P, 1990.

Birnbaum, Daniel. "Eyes and Notes on the Sun." Noever, pp. 219-37.

Didi-Huberman, Georges. "Dark Spaces," Noever, pp. 126-31.

———. "The Fable of the Place," Noever, pp. 45-57.

———. "Space Division Constructions," Noever, pp. 102-21.

Douglas, Sarah. "In Their Words: James Turrell and Andy Goldsworthy," www.blouinartinfo.com/news/story/263666/in-their-words-james-turrell-and-andy-goldsworthy. Accessed 3 May 2007.

Hutcheon, Linda. *The Canadian Postmodern: A Study of Contemporary English-Canadian Fiction*. Oxford UP, 1989.

Kroeger, Ernie. *Crossing the Great Divide*. Banff Centre Press, 2001.

Kroetsch, Robert. *The Hornbooks of Rita K*. U of Alberta P, 2001.

———. *The Ledger*. Applegarth Follies, 1975.

———. *Seed Catalogue*. Turnstone Press, 1977.

Lacan, Jacques. "Of the Gaze as *Objet Petit a*." Translated by Alan Sheridan. *Four Fundamental Concepts of Psychoanalysis*. Vintage, 1998.

Lawrence, Donald, and William F. Garrett-Petts. *PhotoGraphic Encounters: The Edges and Edginess of Reading Prose Pictures and Visual Fictions*. U of Alberta P, 2000.

McCallum, Pamela. *Cultural Memories and Imagined Futures: The Art of Jane Ash Poitras*. U of Calgary P, 2011.

McCance, Dawne. "On the Art of Building in Ten Hornbooks." *New Quarterly: New Directions in Canadian Writing*, vol. 18, no. 1, Spring 1998, pp. 161-73.

———. "Still Life: Dis-figuring the Self-portrait in Robert Kroetsch's *A Likely Story*." 130.179.92.25/canlitx/Framed_Version/Conference/McCance. html. Accessed 3 May 2007.

Noever, Peter, editor. *James Turrell: The Other Horizon*. Ostfildern-Ruit, Germany: Hatje Cantz, 2001.

Neuman, Shirley, and Robert Wilson, editors. *Labyrinths of Voice: Conversations With Robert Kroetsch*. NeWest Press, 1996.

Stacey, Robert David. *Re: Reading the Postmodern: Canadian Literature and Criticism After Modernism*. U of Ottawa P, 2010.

Turell, James. "James Turell." http://jamesturrell.com/about/introduction/. Accessed November 28, 2016.

Wah, Fred. *Sentenced to Light*. Talonbooks, 2008.

York, Lorraine. *The Other Side of Dailiness: Photography in the Works of Alice Munro, Timothy Findley, Michael Ondaatje, and Margaret Laurence*. ECW Press, 1987.

Zyman, Daniela. "The Other Horizon: On the Exhibition at the MAK," Noever, pp. 18-45.

The Mythological and the Real: Sheila Watson's Life and Writing

Joseph Pivato

A Father's Kingdom, a collection of short stories, was the last book that Sheila Watson published (posthumously in 2004). The "father" in the title alludes to Oedipus in the story, "Brother Oedipus," and to the original mythic Oedipus, the King of Thebes. Other figures from the original myth, Daedalus and Antigone, are also referenced in Watson's book, suggesting the closed nature of this kingdom and the power of the king. To a religious reader the title may suggest the Kingdom of God. The title also alludes to Watson's early life growing up in an asylum run by her father, Dr. Doherty. On the first page of the story "Antigone," we read,

> My father ruled men who thought they were gods or the instruments of gods or, at the very least, god-afflicted and god-pursued. He ruled Atlas who held up the sky, and Hermes who went on endless messages, and Helen who'd been hatched from an egg, and Pan the gardener. ... (36)

This double meaning of the title and of Watson's childhood experience is an appropriate place to begin an examination of her life and work because it links her real life with the mythological in her writing. The location and nature of Watson's early life in British Columbia had a profound effect on her writing.

She was born Sheila Martin Doherty, the second of four siblings of Mary Ida Martin and Dr. Charles E. Doherty, in 1909 in New Westminster,

BC. Her father was the medical superintendent of the Provincial Mental Hospital in New Westminster. The family lived in an apartment on the grounds of this psychiatric institution and Sheila received her early education there. Her father died prematurely in 1920 and the family moved to a house in New Westminster. Sheila then went to the convent school of the Sisters of St. Anne to continue her education. Her father had left money for her university education which allowed her to complete two years of university at the Convent of the Sacred Heart in Vancouver. Sheila earned her B.A. honours in English at the University of British Columbia in 1931, and a teaching certificate in 1932. She began writing at about this time and completed an M.A. in English 1933.

In 1934, in the middle of the Great Depression, Sheila's first teaching job was at St. Louis College in New Westminster. Jobs were hard to find and she considered herself lucky to have a second teaching position in the remote BC interior. From 1935-37, she taught in a one-room school at Dog Creek in the Cariboo region, riding her horse back and forth to school. It was here that Sheila Doherty composed her first novel, *Deep Hollow Creek*, which was only published half a century later, in 1992. This valley also provided the setting for her first short story, "Rough Answer," published in 1938 and the location for her iconic novel, *The Double Hook*, which she completed in Calgary in 1952. (All references to *The Double Hook* are from the 1969 edition.)

When the Dog Creek school closed, she moved to Langley Prairie to teach high school until 1940. Then she moved to Vancouver Island to teach in the town of Duncan where she met the poet Wilfred Watson. They were married in 1941 and she became Sheila Watson. From 1942 to 1945, Sheila taught at Mission City while Wilfred finished his B.A. at the University of British Columbia and then served on a navy minesweeper.

By 1945, the Watsons were in Toronto where Wilfred was a full-time graduate student at the University of Toronto. Sheila took graduate courses part-time and taught at Moulton College. It was at this time that the idea for *The Double Hook* began to emerge in her writing. She explained many years later,

> I can remember when I first thought about it, it was right in the middle of Bloor Street—it was in answer to a challenge that you could not write about particular places in Canada:

that what you would end up with was a regional novel of some kind. It was at the time, I suppose, when people were thinking that if you wrote a novel it had to be, in some mysterious way, international. ... And so I thought, I don't see why: how are you international if you're not international? if you're very provincial, very local, and very much part of your milieu. I wanted to do something too about the West, which wasn't a Western. ... ("What I'm Going to Do" 182)

By 1949 the Watsons were back in Vancouver with Sheila teaching as a sessional lecturer at the University of British Columbia and Wilfred teaching with a term appointment. He later moved to Calgary to teach at what was then a satellite campus of the University of Alberta. Sheila joined Wilfred in 1952 and completed the draft manuscript for *The Double Hook*. She had difficulty finding a publisher for such an unusual novel. With a letter of support from Professor Fred Salter of the University of Alberta, Jack Mc-Clelland was convinced to publish it in 1959. The reaction to it was at first mixed, but it won the Beta Sigma Phi Canadian Book Award in 1960 and began to establish Sheila Watson's reputation as an original writer. *The Double Hook* later influenced experimental Alberta writers Robert Kroetsch and Aritha van Herk.

In Calgary, Sheila continued to work on her short stories, completing *And the Four Animals*, which was published in 1980 with Coach House Press and in 1984 as part of the *Five Stories* collection. "Brother Oedipus" appeared in *Queen's Quarterly* in 1954. When Wilfred was offered a position in English at the University of Alberta in 1954, they moved to Edmonton. There Sheila helped Wilfred submit his many poems to journals and assisted him to put together a collection. They submitted the manuscript to Faber and Faber in London, where T.S. Eliot was poetry editor. Wilfred's first collection, *Friday's Child*, appeared in 1955 and won the Governor General's award for poetry and the Arts Council of Britain prize.

Paris, France, was the city where the Watsons worked for the year 1955-56. There Sheila went to see an exhibit of paintings by Wyndham Lewis and she developed an interest in his writing and art works. When she returned to Canada, she began research work (1956-61) for her Ph.D. at the University of Toronto with a focus on Lewis. She met Marshall McLuhan who had known Lewis when he was in Canada during the Second

World War. In 1951 McLuhan had published *The Mechanical Bride*, a collection of studies on popular culture that combines visual images and text. McLuhan became her thesis advisor on Lewis since she planned to study both the paintings and the writing of Lewis. In the meantime, Sheila also continued to publish her short stories "The Black Farm: A Modern Allegory," in *Queen's Quarterly* (1956), and "Antigone," in *The Tamarack Review* (1959). When *The Double Hook* was published in 1959, Sheila was still in Toronto. She joined Wilfred in Edmonton in 1961 where she began teaching at the University of Alberta. With the completion of her thesis, she received her Ph.D. in 1965.

The Watsons were back in Toronto in 1968-69 to work with McLuhan in the Centre for Culture and Technology. The result was the book *From Cliché to Archetype* (1970), a collaboration between McLuhan and Wilfred Watson. After the Watsons returned to Edmonton, they co-founded *White Pelican* with Douglas Barbour, John Orrell, Dorothy Livesay, Stephen Scobie, and Norman Yates. This avant-garde literary magazine featured works by many Alberta authors: Rudy Wiebe, E.D. Blodgett, Chris Wiseman, and Henry Kriesel. Sheila mentored aspiring writers in Alberta such as Caterina Edwards, Myrna Kostash, and Miriam Mandel.

In 1975 Sheila Watson retired from teaching at the University of Alberta. *White Pelican* stopped publishing in 1976, but Sheila continued to supervise graduate students and serve on literary juries. Wilfred Watson retired in 1977. Before she moved to Vancouver Island, Sheila Watson wrote a study guide, "How to read *Ulysses*," for a new course, Modern Consciousness, for Athabasca University's new English studies program. The editor was Mary Hamilton, one of the last graduate students to have Sheila Watson as a Ph.D. supervisor.

Another avant-garde literary journal, *Open Letter*, brought out a special issue devoted to Watson's other prose fiction and essays, *Sheila Watson: A Collection*, edited by Frank Davey in 1974-75. The most significant inclusion in this volume was the publication of Watson's four short stories: "Brother Oedipus," "The Black Farm," "Antigone," and "The Rumble Seat." Also included were a number of literary essays on Wyndham Lewis, Michael Ondaatje, Gertrude Stein, and Watson's only statement on the writing of *The Double Hook*, up to that point, "What I'm Going To Do," which has been quoted numerous times since its appearance. In 1984 the Coach House Press published Watson's *Five Stories*, which included the addition of "And the Four Animals." When in 2004 McClelland & Stewart published Watson's *A Father's Kingdom: The Complete Short Fiction*, it opened the collection with "Rough Answer," which Watson had originally published in 1938.

Soon after Sheila Watson retired, her colleagues at the University of Alberta got together a collection of literary essays in celebration of her literary achievement, *Figures on a Ground: Canadian Essays on Modern Literature Collected in Honor of Sheila Watson* (1978). Edited by Diane Bessai and David Jackel, it included essays by many Canadian writers: Michael Ondaatje, Henry Kreisel, E. D. Blodgett, Marshall McLuhan, Rudy Wiebe, Eli Mandel, Douglas Barbour, and Robert Kroetsch. The three-page biography by Diane Bessai was the first published information on Watson's life, a publicity which she always resisted. As she explained in a 1984 interview with Bruce Meyer and Brian O'Riordan, "I've wanted what is on the page to speak for itself. I've never, not even now, wanted to talk about what I have written ..." (167). She succeeded in living the ideal of the T.S. Eliot poetic persona, "the invisible poet." She gave few interviews. Two of the longer ones are: "Interview, Sheila Watson" with Pierre Coupey, Roy Kiyooka, and Daphne Marlatt (*The Capilano Review*, 1976), and "It's What You Say" with Bruce Meyer and Brian O'Riordan, just mentioned (*In Their Words: Interviews with Fourteen Canadian Writers*, 1984). Sheila and Wilfred Watson moved to Nanaimo, BC in 1980. She died in 1998 and Wilfred died seven weeks later.

Critical Responses to *The Double Hook*

Until the publication of Watson's short stories and essays in a special issue of *Open Letter* in 1974, all critical work focused on *The Double Hook*. In 1985 George Bowering edited a collection of essays, *Sheila Watson and The Double Hook*, which included eighteen articles on the novel. In this volume Bowering selected some initial reviews of Watson's novel which indicate the mixed, if confused, response to this experimental novel. The better early essays are: Margot Northey's "Symbolic Grotesque: *The Double Hook*," which reads the novel as part of the Gothic tradition in Canadian wilderness writing; Leslie Monkman's "Coyote as Trickster in *The Double Hook*," which interprets this mythological figure as an evil presence in the community; and Beverly Mitchell's "Association and Allusion in *The Double Hook*," which looks at Biblical patterns and Christian allusions in the narrative. The best essay is Margaret Morris's 1969 "The Elemental Transcended," which identifies the symbolic structure of the novel based on the four elements and "the archetypal pattern of redemption." Also included in Bowering's volume is Barbara Godard's "Between One Cliché and Another: Language in *The Double Hook*," which looks at Watson's exploration of language in art and communication. In reaction to Godard is Dawn Rae Downton with "Message and Messengers in *The Double Hook*," which looks more closely at Watson's style by analysing some of the secondary characters as messengers.

The most comprehensive bio-critical study of Watson was Stephen Scobie's *Sheila Watson and Her Works* (1984). After a brief biography, Scobie reconstructs the tradition and milieu of modernism which form part of Watson's literary education: T.S. Eliot, Ezra Pound, Gertrude Stein, Dorothy Richardson, James Joyce, D.H. Lawrence, William Faulkner, and John Dos Passos. He points out her reading the mythopoeic theories of Northrop Frye and her studies with Marshall McLuhan, absorbing his mosaic approach to literary interpretation. This methodology directs the reader to analyse a text by linking together the many different references, allusions, quotations, and facts into separate strands in order to arrive at meanings for the whole work. Scobie argues that her spare poetic writing style in *The Double Hook* is a direct reaction against the "clumsy intensities of Frederick Philip Grove; the dreary and derivative banalities of Morley Callaghan; the urbane and academic essay-writing of Hugh MacLennan ..." (6). After a brief review of the critical response to *The Double Hook* up to 1984, Scobie gives a detailed critical analysis of the four stories which appeared together in *Open Letter* (1974). He explains, "Wit plays a great part in establishing the setting of these stories, a setting which is simultaneously local and universal, realist and mythological" (14). In short, he positions Watson as an original writer who refocused the western narrative on language and a sense of place.

Scobie's is also the first comprehensive study of Watson's short stories in which he demonstrates his own sensibility as a poet in his careful reading of these short poetic-prose works. He makes the following striking observation about the fifth story:

And the Four Animals, then, represents a first sketch for the landscape of *The Double Hook*, the major difference being that it is farther back in mythological time, it is not yet peopled—except by the dogs, by Coyote, and the observing eye. For this is a landscape which both exists, autonomously, and also is being brought into existence: it is a landscape created, and landscape *perceived*. (22)

This story, which was first published separately in 1980, was actually written in the early 1950s, before *The Double Hook*, and is a kind of experiment in poetic-prose style and location. The spare language and the peculiar disembodied perspective of "the watching eye" suggest the narrative voice in *The Double Hook*. Scobie correctly observes that the clear link between the short story and the novel is a landscape that is bare, minimal, primitive, and "is simultaneously a specific, localized setting (the BC interior in the drought years of the 1930s) and a symbolic, mythological country ..." (*Sheila Watson* 19). Scobie goes on to give a very detailed reading of *And the Four Animals* and identifies many parallels to *The Double Hook*. He considers the problem of regional versus international writing in terms of Watson's writing style and her balancing the influences of Frye's emphasis on archetypes and McLuhan's mosaic approach full of eclectic references. Two of Watson's favourite authors, James Joyce and William Faulkner, demonstrated that small regional settings can be successfully combined with work of universal appeal and meaning. In addition to examining Watson's language style, Scobie also explores the biblical allusions and religious implications in this story with its final apocalyptic vision.

The final twenty pages of Scobie's study are devoted to *The Double Hook*. Building on his cogent observations of the language and setting of *And the four animals* and Watson's own comments on the genesis for her novel, Scobie gives a systematic reading of the characters. In her talk, "What I'm Going to Do," Watson explained her intentions in *The Double Hook*: "And there was something I wanted to say about how people are driven, how if they have no art, how if they have no tradition, how if they have no ritual, they are driven in one of two ways, either towards violence or towards insensibility—if they have no mediating rituals ..." (183). She is referring to the characters in her narrative, both white and First Nations, who have lost Christian rituals and native traditions. Coyote seems to symbolize this loss of faith in all of the communities in the novel.

In his book, Scobie also examines Margaret Morris's exploration (1969) of the elemental symbolism in the narrative: earth, air, fire, and water. Morris argues that these elements have a real basis in nature and also function symbolically in the novel. For example, we can see that the fire which Greta uses to destroy herself and the Potter house is real, but it also functions symbolically as a ritualistic fire of cleansing and renewal. Fire is also used in many religious rituals, which Watson alludes to throughout the novel. Scobie considers religious symbolism by examining Beverley Mitchell's essay "Association and Allusion" that explores the religious references to the Bible, Catholic ritual, and the Coyote myths. Mitchell argues that nearly all the characters in Watson's novel have associations with figures in the Old Testament and that only Felix Prosper's behaviour reflects the values of the New Testament. This is often indicated by the fragments of the Roman Catholic mass which he repeats as if trying to remember a lost faith, a lost hope.

The most controversial character in *The Double Hook*, Coyote, has been seen as saintly or satanic or a troublemaker who also fools himself. Leslie Monkman's study "Coyote as Trickster" explores the function and meaning of Coyote in the context of American Indian mythology. When Kip remarks "That if you hook twice the glory you hook twice the fear. That Coyote plotting to catch the glory for himself is fooled and every day fools others [and] how much mischief Coyote can make" (Watson 61), he is alluding to the figure of Coyote as trickster, creator and destroyer, giver and taker, deceiver and self-deceived. Coyote and Mrs. Potter spread fear throughout the isolated community in the valley. People like Felix and Angel confront fear and overcome it, leading to the beginning of hope for the future. At the beginning of *The Double Hook* many of the characters are in a state of paralysis, the insensibility which Watson refers to above. With the return of James and his determination to take on his responsibilities to himself, to Lenchen and their unborn child, and to the rest of the community, the regeneration of the valley begins.

Watson's Language Style

The first study that looks at Watson's language style is Barbara Godard's "Between One Cliché and Another: Language in *The Double Hook*" (1978). Godard argues that Watson's work

> might be examined in terms of a "post-modern" rebellion against established order. Such iconoclasm may be detected in the radical exploration of the limits of language undertaken in *The Double Hook* ... a dramatization of the beginning of language and cultural order in a primitive people. ... I should like to suggest that the revolutionary qualities of Watson's writing are a consequence of her femaleness ... [and supported by] her use of a quotation from Gertrude Stein ... remarking that "in this epoch the only real literary thinking has been done by a woman." (149)

In *The Double Hook* Sheila Watson is concerned with exploring the different levels of language and meaning. She uses many different types of language: everyday dialogue, clichés, aphorisms, backwoods expressions, Biblical phrases from the Old and New Testaments, Indigenous myths, Catholic rituals, and parody. "Everyone seems to talk naturally in aphorisms, transforming every particular incident into an occasion for universal truth" (Scobie, *Sheila Watson* 30). There are many examples: "I forget, Kip said. A man can't remember things all his life" (Watson, *The Double Hook* 62). "How can a man know what he wants?" (64). "A man needn't hang himself because he's put his neck through a noose in the dark" (70). "The whole world is a big lot for one girl to wreck," (117) and "We don't choose what we will suffer. We can't even see how suffering will come" (119). Of all the characters, William is the one who speaks mostly in aphorisms: "He was like a gay cock on the outside in his plaid shirt and studded belt" (34). "There's things even a man's brother has to pass by" (74). "Suppose the rock should suddenly begin to move" (76) and "The curious thing about fire, he said, is you need it and you fear it at once" (128). These forms are repeated so often that we soon begin to question the intended meaning of the characters' words as opposed to the ironic meaning. These ritual forms of speech harden into the empty cliché of modern language detached from meaning and emotion. As Barbara Godard explains:

> With its questioning of cliché, its divesting language of associ-
> ations—thus creating a new way of seeing—with its awareness
> of silence, with its dramatization of the origins of creativity,
> *The Double Hook* stands beside contemporary works like
> those of [other women writers who explore] linguistic exper-
> iments. (151)

Sensitive to the thinness of modern speech, Watson finds many ways to disrupt the reader's usual understanding of words and their corresponding links to reality by guiding the reader into a realm of poetic possibilities and aesthetic values beyond the sense of dull quotidian reality. In his 1988 essay, "Originary Grammarians," a comparative study of the Quebec writer Laure Conan and Sheila Watson, E.D. Blodgett examines the language experiments in Watson short stories and argues that the pure bare language of the tribe is more evident in these elemental stories than in the novel. The stories possess only the merest of plots which compel the reader to seek deeper meaning in the language, the allusions, and the symbolism.

Watson in the Digital Age

Since the publication of Bowering's and Scobie's volumes on Sheila Watson's work there has been a continual production of studies, especially in the 1990s. Of significance is the first publication of her first novel, *Deep Hollow Creek*, in 1992, which was written in 1937-38, and the appearance of all her short stories in one volume, *A Father's Kingdom*, in 2004. The "Afterword" for *Deep Hollow Creek* is by novelist Jane Urquhart, and that for *A Father's Kingdom* is by modernist scholar Glenn Willmott.

The 1990s saw no less than nine M.A. and Ph.D. theses on Watson. The explosion in digital communication has re-awakened interest in McLuhan's pronouncements on technology and experiments in writing like *The Double Hook*. This relation is explored in Gregory Betts's article, "Media, McLuhan, and the Dawn of the Electric Age in Sheila Watson's *Deep Hollow Creek* and *The Double Hook*" (2009), and the book he edited with Paul Hjartarson and Kristine Smitka, *Counterblasting Canada* (2016). The following recent studies strike me as interesting to readers and scholars of Watson's work because they benefit from developments in literary theory, feminist theory, and language studies. The 1990s saw whole chapters devoted to Watson, in contrast to the 1970s when *The Double Hook* received only brief comments. In his book *Coyote Country: Fictions of the Canadian West* (1994), Arnold Davidson devotes a chapter to *The Double Hook* and examines it in the context of Howard O'Hagan's *Tay John* (1939) and Robert Krotesch's *Badlands* (1975). This volume makes it clear that Watson is recognized as a major contributor to the creation of a literature about Alberta and the Canadian West. In her book *Imagining Culture: New World Narrative and the Writing of Canada* (1995), Margaret Turner also spends a chapter analysing *The Double Hook* and describes Watson's writing as she "moves between literal and metaphoric planes in her dismantling and construction of new world discourse" (79).

Watson's short stories are the subject of Valerie Legge's article, "Sheila Watson's 'Antigone': Anguished Rituals and Public Disturbances" (1992). In her critical article, "Canadian Letters, Dead Referents: Reconsidering the Critical Construction of *The Double Hook*" (1993-94), Donna Palmateer Pennee examines the canonization of Watson's novel and argues that "sacrifice is central to the canonization of this novel, the formation of a literary-critical community, and by extension, the formation of the nation 'on its way to itself'—or, that beneath the canonization site is a dead woman's body ... a mother is murdered (on the very first page of the novel) so that the son's narrative can go forward ..." (235). The first detailed study of *Deep Hollow Creek* is Glenn Willmott's "The Nature of Modernism in *Deep Hollow Creek*" (1995). As the volume I edited in 2015, *Sheila Watson: Essays on Her Works*, indicates, her novels and short stories continue to garner critical attention, a recognition of the tangible contributions she made in Alberta and beyond. As a student and academic in Edmonton, I personally witnessed Watson's work first hand.

Before her death in 1998, Sheila Watson donated her literary documents to the University of St. Michael's College at the University of Toronto. At St. Michael's was Fred Flahiff, whom she made her literary executor and biographer. In 2005 Flahiff published *Always Someone to Kill the Doves: A Life of Sheila Watson*, which provides valuable information on Watson's personal life, marriage, and writing activities. A long-time friend, Flahiff lets Sheila speak for herself by including a seventy-page excerpt from her Paris diary of 1955-56. In his critical analysis of these seventy pages, George Melnyk links Sheila's writing style with her two novels. Using access to the Sheila Watson Archives, Margaret Morriss published "'No short cuts': The Evolution of *The Double Hook*" (2002), a study of the various revisions that Watson worked on between the completion of the manuscript in 1952 and its final publication in 1959.

In her 1974-75 statement "What I'm Going to Do," Sheila Watson questions the idea "that if you write a novel it had to be, in some mysterious way, international." So she wrote a "very provincial, very local, and very much part of your own milieu" novel (182). In Canada Watson was vindicated by the success of her novel. She was vindicated in another way as well: the international reception of *The Double Hook* which has been translated into Swedish as *Dubblekroken* (1963), into French as *Sous l'oeil de coyote* (1976), and into Italian as *Il Doppio amo* (1992). We also have critical essays on the novel in Italian and German (Kuester). The international dissemination of all this information on the writing of Sheila Watson is now made easier by the internet.

Sheila Watson spent most of her life trying to be the invisible writer. Nevertheless, her reputation grew and has continued to flourish. With the publication of *Deep Hollow Creek* and *A Father's Kingdom*, her status in Canadian literature is assured.

Works Cited

Bessai, Diane, and David Jackel, editors. *Figures in a Ground: Canadian Essays on Modern Literature Collected in Honor of Sheila Watson*. Western Producer Prairie Books, 1978.

Betts, Gregory. "Media, McLuhan and the Dawn of the Electric Age in Sheila Watson's *Deep Hollow Creek* and *The Double Hook*." *Essays on Canadian Writing*, 84, Fall 2009, pp. 254-64.

Betts, Gregory, et al., editors. *Counterblasting Canada: Marshall McLuhan, Wyndham Lewis, Wilfred Watson and Sheila Watson*. U of Alberta P, 2016.

Blodgett, E.D. "Originary Grammarians: Laure Conan and Sheila Watson." *Canadian Review of Comparative Literature / Revue Canadienne de Littérature Comparée*, vol. 15, no. 1, Mar. 1988, pp. 52-72.

Bowering, George, editor. *Sheila Watson and the Double Hook.* The Golden Dog Press, 1985.

Davey, Frank, editor. *Sheila Watson: A Collection. Open Letter,* vol. 3, no. 1, Winter 1974-75.

Davidson, Arnold E. "Coyote at Dog Creek." *Coyote Country. Fictions in the Canadian West.* Duke UP, 1994, pp. 58-73.

Downton, Dawn Rae. "Messages and Messengers in *The Double Hook,*" *Studies in Canadian Literature,* vol. 4, no. 2, Summer 1979, pp. 137-46. Rpr., in Bowering, pp. 177-84.

Flahiff, F.T. *Always Someone to Kill the Doves: A Life of Sheila Watson.* NeWest Press, 2005.

Godard, Barbara. "'Between One Cliché and Another': Language in *The Double Hook,*" *Studies in Canadian Literature,* vol. 3, no. 2, Summer 1978, pp. 149-65. Rpr., in Bowering, pp. 159-76.

Kroetsch, Robert. *Badlands.* New Press, 1975.

Kuester, Martin. "(Post-)Modern Bricolage: Classical Mythology in Sheila Watson's Short Stories." *Zeitschrift für Anglistik und Amerikanistik,* vol. 42, no. 3, 1994, pp. 225-34.

Legge, Valerie. "Sheila Watson's 'Antigone': Anguished Rituals and Public Disturbances." *Studies in Canadian Literature,* vol. 17, no. 2, 1992-93, pp. 28-46.

McLuhan, Marshall. *The Mechanical Bride.* Vanguard Press, 1951.

McLuhan, Marshall, and Wilfred Watson. *From Cliché to Archetype.* Viking, 1970.

Melnyk, George. "Touching Sheila Watson: Always Someone to Kill the Doves." Joseph Pivato, ed. *Sheila Watson: Essays on Her Works.* Guernica Editions, 2015, pp.149-162.

Mitchell, Beverly S.S.A. "Association and Allusion in *The Double Hook.*" *Journal of Canadian Fiction,* vol. 2, no. 1, Winter 1973, pp. 63-69. Rpr., in Bowering, pp. 99-113.

Monkman, Leslie. "Coyote as Trickster in *The Double Hook.*" *Canadian Literature,* vol. 52, Spring 1972, pp. 70-76. Rpr., in Bowering, pp. 63-69.

Morriss, Margaret. "The Elements Transcended." *Canadian Literature,* vol. 42, Fall 1969, pp. 56-71.

———. "'No Short Cuts': The Evolution of *The Double Hook.*" *Canadian Literature,* vol. 173, Summer 2002, pp. 54-72.

Northey, Margot. "Symbolic Grotesque: *The Double Hook.*" *The Haunted Wilderness: The Gothic and Grotesque in Canadian Fiction.* U of Toronto P, 1976, pp. 88-94. Rpr., as "Symbolic Grotesque" in Bowering, pp. 55-61.

O'Hagan, Howard. *Tay John.* 1939. McClelland & Stewart, 1960.

Pennee, Donna Palmateer. "Canadian Letters, Dead Referents: Reconsidering the Critical Construction of *The Double Hook.*" *Essays on Canadian Writing*, vols. 51-52, Winter 1993-Spring 1994, pp. 233-57.

Pivato, Joseph, editor. *Sheila Watson: Essays on Her Works.* Guernica Editions, 2015.

Scobie, Stephen. *Sheila Watson and her Works.* ECW Press, 1984.

———. "Watson, Sheila." *The Canadian Encyclopedia.* McClelland & Stewart, 1999.

Turner, Margaret E. "Sheila Watson: On Soft Ground." *Imagining Culture: New World Narrative and the Writing of Canada.* McGill-Queen's UP, 1995, pp. 64-78.

Urquhart, Jane. Afterword. *Deep Hollow Creek*, by Sheila Watson, New Canadian Library edition, McClelland & Stewart, 1999, pp. 113-18.

Watson, Sheila. *And the Four Animals.* The Coach House Press, 1980.

———. "Antigone." *The Tamarack Review*, no. 11, Spring 1959, pp. 5-13.

———. "The Black Farm: A Modern Allegory." *Queen's Quarterly*, vol. 63, Summer 1956, pp. 202-13.

———. "Brother Oedipus." *Queen's Quarterly*, vol. 61, Summer 1954, pp. 220-28.

———. *Deep Hollow Creek.* 1992. McClelland & Stewart, rpr. 1999.

———. *The Double Hook.* 1959. McClelland & Stewart, rpr. 1966, 1969.

———. *A Father's Kingdom: The Complete Short Fiction.* McClelland & Stewart, 2004.

———. *Five Stories.* The Coach House Press, 1984.

———. "Interview." With Pierre Coupey, et al. *The Capilano Review*, vols. 8-9, Spring 1976, pp. 351-60.

———. "It's What You Say." With Bruce Meyer, and Brian O'Riordan. *In Their Words: Interviews with Fourteen Canadian Writers.* Anansi, 1984, pp. 157-67.

———. "What I'm Going to Do." Davey, pp. 181-83.

Watson, Wilfred. *Friday's Child.* Faber and Faber, 1955.

Willmott, Glenn. "The Nature of Modernism in *Deep Hollow Creek.*" *Canadian Literature*, vol. 146, Fall 1995, pp. 30-48.

Gwen Pharis Ringwood and Elsie Park Gowan: Writing the Land 1933-1979

Moira Day

Introduction

"'What a piece of work is man,' cried Hamlet, and for centuries the world echoed his admiration," noted Elsie Park Gowan in the 1930s. "'Frailty, thy name is woman,' exclaimed the same Prince, and for years they have been making us believe it" (Gowan, "Woman" 307). Thus Gowan succinctly outlines not only the ongoing historical challenges confronting women, but the larger pattern of conflicts, ironies, and contradictions surrounding the lives and careers of herself and her contemporary, Gwen Pharis Ringwood. They were women writing plays in a classical humanist tradition that regarded playwriting and theatre alike as dominantly male domains. They were Canadian regional writers forging a native tradition of playwriting in the face of an imperial British and older central and eastern Canadian tradition of letters that viewed not only men, but also Hamlet and all of Shakespeare's princes and kings, as the measure of all things.

Yet, paradoxically, if Laurier declaimed in 1904 that it was Canada that would "fill the twentieth century,"[1] he might equally have asserted the same of women and the opening western provinces. Elsie Park (Young) Gowan, born in Helensburgh, Scotland (1905), and Gwen Pharis Ringwood, born in Anatone, Washington, USA (1910), moved to the new "boom" province of Alberta—Gowan to Edmonton in 1912, Ringwood to McGrath in 1913—when waves of immigration and new forms of feminism and populism were radically transforming its social, political, intellectual, and physical landscape. It was a richness that left both playwrights "writing the land" and its people long after many of the other great possibilities hinted at, in 1904, had failed them.

Gowan: Depression and War 1933-46

With *Homestead* (1933) Gowan became an Albertan pioneer of the new folk play genre favoured by the Irish Renaissance and American Little Theatre movements. As Sam Selden, later one of Ringwood's mentors at Chapel Hill, explained:

> The term "folk," as we use it, has nothing to do with the folk play of medieval times. But rather it is concerned with folk subject matter: with the legends, superstitions, customs, environmental differences, and the vernacular of the common people. [...] The chief concern of the folk dramatist is man's conflict with the forces of nature and his simple pleasure in being alive. (60-61)[2]

Gowan also became one of its first Alberta defenders when a 1935 Dominion Drama Festival adjudicator attacked "God Made the Country," a revised version of *Homestead*, as representative of a new school of local playwriting seemingly intent on reducing Canada to "a land of kitchen stoves from end to end" peopled by "old ladies sitting in rocking chairs" moaning and groaning, while surrounded by "those wide open spaces" just "waiting to claim a victim in time for the curtain to fall" (Morley 12). Gowan's spirited riposte certainly defended the folk play as authentically Canadian:

> It's just Mr. [Malcolm] Morley's bad luck that we misguided playwrights have tried to create a drama distinctively Canadian. We believed that the quality of our lonely land might be found in its far places [...] that its reality might be best known by those close to its prairies and forests and mountains. We

imagined a dramatic theme in the impact of these tremendous forces on the spirit of man. (Gowan, "Another" 8)

However, as Wagner indicated in 1987, the discussion was not just about aesthetics. If Gowan resented Malcolm Morley's implication that Canadian playwriting should mimic, if not Shakespeare, at least the best of British drawing-room comedy, she breathed fire over his suggestion, especially in the midst of the Depression, that the quintessence of Canada was to be found in the glittering circles of privilege he had encountered in "our best hotels and transcontinental trains" (Gowan, "Another" 8) as an indulged guest.

By 1992, Gowan had mellowed enough to agree about the rocking chair and kitchen stove: "you don't stay in the log cabin forever." But she still felt Morley had never understood "those wide open spaces" and what constituted "the main problem in Canada. Land" (Day, *Hungry* 42). In analyzing the 1930s prairie drama of Minnie Bicknell, Elsie Park Gowan, and Gwen Pharis Ringwood, Arnd Bohm argues that in their eagerness to refute Morley's argument about the narrow, provincial nature of the folk tragedy, Canadian critics have sometimes fallen into the opposite trap of "[r]eading these plays in terms of universal symbols and abstracted myths" that can filter out "their specific historical meaning" (257). Without that contextualization, one can miss the significance of the dramas not only as sophisticated, compact analyses of the social, political, and economic assaults on the family unit by the global crisis of the Depression, but as feminist critiques presenting women as frequently more resourceful and resilient than men in their response to breakdowns in the patriarchal system. Similarly, without due regard to "specific historical meaning," one can miss the increasing complexity of Gowan and Ringwood's approach to "Land" long after they had left the "log cabin" behind.

Gowan credits her own near-fatal encounter as a rural teacher with falling trees in a storm, and then preoccupation with Thomas Hardy as the initial inspiration for *Homestead* (Day, *Hungry* 38-39). The ending of the play may indeed suggest the cruel and arbitrary nature of the environment, as Freda, having decided to leave her brutal spouse for their sympathetic neighbour, Hugh Forbes, finds her happiness and escape thwarted by a falling tree that kills her lover rather than her husband. But arguably, the real turning point is the refusal of Freda's husband, Brandt, to consider

Hugh's neighbourly proposal to adopt a more co-operative approach to managing their respective lands. Despite Hugh's pleas, as seconded by the desperate, pregnant Freda, that such a scheme would alleviate their crushing work load, terrifying physical and human isolation, and vulnerability to political and economic exploitation, Brandt holds stubbornly to his individualistic and proprietorial approaches to property, chattel, and wife, and goes out (illegally) hunting. Had Brandt stayed to talk the proposal through, likely none of them would have been out in the lethal windstorm when the tree fell.

Gowan's preoccupation with the conflict between those who see land as a beginning point for building co-operative human, social, and economic community, and those who exploit it to build personal empires maintained by oppression, violence, and self-interest, accelerated in her 1937 *Building of Canada* radio series. The three episodes dealing with the settling of Manitoba cover a sweep of times, countries, and families over three generations, starting in 1812 Scotland and ending in 1870 Manitoba. If Gowan contrasts the initial romantic image of "the log shack in woods" that lured *Homestead*'s Freda into her marriage—"I thought how pretty it would be, like on a calendar" (54)—with the grueling reality of the life she finds there, Gowan draws a similar contrast in "X The Silver Chief " between the romantic, beautiful Scotland for "successful poets" that Sir Walter Scott can still afford to live in, and the far more brutal one now inhabited by the McLeods and the McKays, representatives of those "Highland crofters" (1) who have been pushed off the land by the Enclosures. "XI Seven Oaks" shifts the action to 1814 and the arrival of the Selkirk settlers in the Canadian Northwest, but hardly to an empty land. Having been violently dispossessed of their own land in Scotland by the mercantile forces of the Industrial Revolution, they now find themselves in turn being viewed suspiciously in Manitoba as potential dispossessors by the English Hudson's Bay, French Norwesters, Métis, and Aboriginal communities that already occupy the land. The settlement eventually finds its own place, but only through cooperation and negotiation.

Both episodes paved the way for Gowan's unusual "take" on the 1870 Red River Uprising,[3] "XVIII Red Star in the West." Jean McLeod, a descendent of the original Selkirk settlers, is the maternal voice of moderation and reason. Given her own crofter ancestry, she sympathizes with the Métis cause and approves of Riel's standing up to the Canadian surveyors.

But the same communal memory running back to 1812 also leaves her suspicious of potential Empire-builders, whether she finds them in Thomas Scott, Riel's implacable Orangeman enemy, or in Riel and his growing dictatorial and military aspirations. In their escalating conflict, she sees unfolding yet another cycle of the violence and irrationality that threatens family helping family in a free and co-operative fashion, regardless of race, ethnicity or gender. While Jean mourns the loss of both young men—one left dead by the hand of the other, and the other fled to escape retribution—she nonetheless closes the play with the thoughtful words, "I pray we'll have no more dictators on the Red River ... or anywhere else in the country ... from this time forward" (18).

There are echoes of Riel's 1869 defiance of the federal surveyors on the Red River in the comic 1930s confrontation between the dim but likeable Davys and the local surveyors sent by a scheming lakeside developer in Alberta. But while inspired by an actual incident of a family commandeering "a pile of stones, a club and a fierce dog and a Boer War shotgun" (Day, *Hungry* 149) to defend their lakeside property from all comers, Gowan's first full-length comedy, *The Last Caveman* (1938), was even more transparently than *Red Star*, a parable about the growing international threat of fascism. *Caveman*'s message, that sovereign nations could no longer settle their differences like "cavemen" given their greater capacity for destruction, had become even stronger by 1946, when the play, in a revised form, was launched on a professional five-month western Canadian tour. The idealistic young professor of 1938 promoting his book on the concept of a co-operative world government had been replaced in 1946 by an angry, somewhat cynical war veteran; his sweetheart, Miranda, also having seen two major wars in less than twenty years, and this "brave new world" of postwar prosperity threatened by a shadow of the nuclear bomb, was even more insistent that her publisher father spread the book's urgent message. Otherwise, she suggested, it would be neither trees nor surveyors dropping next on Alberta's little "two-by-four piece[s] of land" (Day, *Hungry* 148):

> I don't call it freedom when we're all afraid. Deep down in ourselves, even when we're doing happy things—sailing the boat, working at our jobs, dancing and laughing—somewhere inside us we know it's only a breathing spell. The horror will come back. Bombs will fall, children scream, boys will die in

flames. [...] I've got a high enough opinion of the human race to believe we could extend our loyalty to a federation of mankind. (*Caveman* 208-09)

Ringwood: The New Alberta 1949-56

In February 1949, Leduc No.1 blew, and Joe, the young crewman in Gowan's *Who Builds a City*, crowed, "On the horizon ... the smoke and the flame—Nothing around here's going to be the same!" (Gowan, *Who* 43). If Gowan's 1954 civic pageant managed to usher in the Oil era on a celebratory note (Nothof, "Making" 176), Ringwood seemed more ambivalent about "the change in the landscape, a change in the sky" (Gowan, *Who* 43). She had made her reputation at Chapel Hill writing lyrically on the influence of drought, hardship, and the Depression on the land and its community in such folk tragedies as *Still Stands the House*, *Pasque Flower*, and *Dark Harvest* (1938-39), and at least superficially, the Alberta Folklore Project plays, written between 1944 and 1946—*The Jack and the Joker*, *The Rainmaker*, and *Stampede*—seemed a continuation of that phase. In truth, she was later to confess to theatre scholar Anton Wagner, land remembered as historical myth became her sanctuary from a war that had devastated her personally. If her husband's enlistment left her a single parent for most of the durance, other losses were more permanent and profound:

> My two eldest brothers were in the Air Force and both were killed in action while Barney [her husband] was overseas. [...] I think my youngest brother Bob never got over his grief entirely, and from that time suffered severe depressions which later resulted in his death. (Letter to Wagner 1979)

Confronted with the magnitude of a human evil and violence seemingly beyond personal comprehension or healing, the Alberta Folklore plays allowed her to retreat into an idyllic semi-mythic world of the past, "symphonic," full of "music, color, bigness" in which the elements of celebration considerably lightened the darker, sadder, or more menacing undercurrents in the material. "[W]ith my personal life so torn by the war [...] it was a relief to write plays about Alberta's past" (Letter to Wagner 1979).

But after 1949 she was forced to consider how unexpected prosperity might paradoxically prove as destructive to land and community as deprivation. In her folk farce, *A Fine Colored Easter Egg* (1950), it is too many resources rather than too few that threaten the Ukrainian-Canadian Nemitchuk family. Ironically, both marriage and farm are saved when the oil wells drilled on the property prove dry. Nonetheless, given the allure of the encroaching cities, Wasyl's dream of bequeathing the land to his newborn grandson may prove as illusory as Olga's dream of it yielding a gusher of new furniture and appliances.

Ringwood's first full-length comedy, *Widger's Way* (1952), turns to Plautus' *Pot of Gold* for its basic story of a miser who sacrifices his own and everyone else's happiness for the love of his gold. However, Ringwood's parsimonious, anti-social farmer gives the Roman archetype an Alberta twist by blaming the lean years of the Depression followed by the trauma of the war and its aftermath for curdling his character:

> And the world changed. The world was a giant, Docket, waiting to crush a man. The thing to do was hide, be small and careful. [...] And yet for all my care, at his own time, the Giant closes his fist on Widger. Since it's so, I'd wish myself a bigger fistful. (326)

Similarly, Ringwood not only translates the Roman pot of money into a prospector's bag of gold nuggets, but also playfully suggests the real hidden "gold" in the Alberta earth lies in its long-dead dinosaurs. Ringgo Dowser, a wandering pedlar who embodies the free natural spirit of the land, offers to find or "divine" water for Widger, but it is oil that springs up instead, this time as a happy *deus ex machina* that salvages a much-chastened Widger's fortunes, and allows the young folks to marry. Still, by suggesting that the fossils on Widger's land ignite the passion of Roselle's geology student suitor as much as Roselle herself, the play remains a cautionary tale about preserving human values and community in the face of a new Giant threatening to fill Alberta with Widgers.

For playwrights toiling in the wilderness of inadequate performance and production opportunities, the Giant had its benign aspect. By the 1950s, both Gowan and Ringwood seemed poised to become the first significant playwrights of the new urban, professional theatre starting to emerge in Alberta's cities. Instead, they virtually vanished: Ringwood into northern BC in 1953, Gowan into teaching to support herself after her husband's death in 1958. Their stage writing over the 1950s and 1960s, while innovative, paradoxically led them back into the wilderness rather than into the new professional theatre structures. Unlike earlier decades when their respective stage and radio writing drew them in different directions, they gravitated towards writing large, epic community dramas where the community itself was the protagonist, the dramaturgy a mix of song, words and dance—and the land an interactive presence in its multiplicity.

"The Jasper Story" (1956-60, 1976-79), "Look Behind You, Neighbor!" (1961), "The Road Runs North" (1967)

Gowan had always loved radio's ability to resituate the human action of the play from the confines of the box set to the vast expanse of a Canadian Northwest created through sound and imagination. "Who Builds a City," featuring a cast of three hundred local actors, dancers, singers, and musicians to tell the story of Edmonton from 1904 to 1954 gave her valuable experience in adapting the same epic technique to live theatre. Writing a script for the Edmonton Gardens arena that required the driving of real vintage cars before a crowd of six thousand ("6000" 24) was good practice for the "total theatre" of "The Jasper Story," with its use of "all the theatre's resources of dialogue, song, music and spectacle" (Gowan, "History" 8). Since "the basis of history is economics, the saga had three chapters—Fur, Gold and Steel": the impact of the fur trade on Jasper's human story motivated The Fur Brigade—1825, Act One, Scene One (Chapter One); the lure of the gold rush drove The Overlanders—1862, Act One, Scene Two (Chapter Two); and the arrival of the railway stoked The Twentieth Century—1908, Act Two (Chapter Three).

Aware of the spectacular theatrical success story of another small, rural town in Canada, director/producer/composer Jack McCreath argued that Jasper had arguably produced something even more "unique" (qtd. in Bill 21). In featuring over one hundred members of the Jasper community "in a spectacular Canadian setting" enacting their own story and singing "songs from an all-original Canadian score," in an "all-Canadian show"—that is, one that is also written, directed, and produced by Canadians—"The Jasper Story" actually offered a show that was "much more authentically Canadian than the Stratford venture" (McCreath); while Gowan resorted to her old radio technique of using a narrator/guide as a framing device and arranging the historical narrative around the fortunes of several representative families—as dominated by their own share of strong, assertive historical women like Katy O'Hara Schubert and Mary Shaffer—the epic use of cast and environment was strikingly different. Particularly in its 1956-60 manifestation, the "musical Historama" placed cars, horses, and a cast of well over one hundred local performers, singers, dancers, and musicians on a huge "two-hundred foot stage at the foot of the Palisades, with one of the most magnificent ranges of mountains in the Rockies as a backdrop" ("History" 9). At least one reviewer, John Dafoe, considered the combination of Gowan's text—which had a knack for catching the human element within the historical incident—and the setting, which allowed the human and historical narrative to be shown within the natural environment where the events had actually occurred, gave the show an unusual poignancy:

> The production succeeds admirably in telling these stories in human terms, in bringing into vivid relief the everyday problems which faced the men and women on the trail west. [...] Strengthening this added element of depth is the site itself. The events which make up this drama actually happened at or close to this spot. (Dafoe)

Being close to the spot sometimes had its drawbacks; several reviewers (Bill 21; Deacon 5) joined Stephen Franklin in complaining of real trains arriving "50 yards away and 50 years ahead of time as an entirely unwelcome and deafening show-stopper" (Franklin). Still, even Franklin agreed with Dafoe that the presence of the rails added a strong note of authenticity to the 1908 sequence, which was actually staged on the original Swift property, "on almost the exact spot on which the lone homesteader defied the railway to build its line through his property. Behind the stage lies the line the railway finally did build after surrendering to the stubborn man's defense of his home" (Dafoe).

It is difficult to believe that "The Jasper Story" did not influence near-by Edson's decision to commission its own 1961 historical musical from Gwen Pharis Ringwood (book) and Victoria's Chet Lambertson (music) to mark its fiftieth anniversary. Although "Look Behind You, Neighbor!" lacked the natural sweep of the mountains to forestage its action and condensed the historical survey from eighty-three to ten years in favour of concentrating on its two central romances, it resembled the Jasper play in binding history and land together in a three-act human narrative, dominated by strong women. Act One, which begins in 1909 with the arrival of the first settlers, Kathleen Freeman and her family, documents the period from 1909 to 1910, when Edson, chosen as the railroad terminus over Wolf Creek, begins to boom. Ringwood also introduces her first Asian-Canadian character, Johnny Boniface, the "Chinese gentleman" (22) who erected Edson's first building, a two-storey hotel in 1910. Act Two follows the arrival of the railroad and the beginning of a rocky romance between Kathleen's sister, Melissa, the new teacher—who acts as a metaphor for the "civilizing" influence of culture, education, temperance, and morality arriving with the women—and Lance Delaney, who is representative of the rollicking male adventure, energy, and anarchy of the frontier. Both forces are needed to build a town, joyously incorporated in 1911. Act Three, which documents the hardship of the war years, ends happily with Delaney, now a wounded veteran, returning to start life—and the cycle of fertility and regeneration—anew with Melissa on their own farm.

Calling on Edson's citizenry to contribute everything from newspaper research, oral history, period costumes, hats and props to a quickly-formed town band ("More" 9; "Period Costumes" 1; "Period Items" 6; "Once" 12), and a cast of seventy-five, ranging in age from seven to seventy, "Neighbor," not surprisingly, sold-out locally ("Warm" 9; "Finale" 1). However, as was the case with "The Jasper Story," the all-Canadian aspect of the show, a quality still missing from the Stratford success story, also contributed to "Neighbor" attracting a surprising amount of national and even international attention. Condensed versions were broadcast over CFRN-TV, Edmonton ("Warm" 9) and CBC Radio as a "genuine piece of Canadiana […] a marvelous example of how a group of people in a small town can rise to great heights" ("CBC" 5). Additionally, in the spring of 1962, "Neighbor" toured to Edmonton for the Duke of Edinburgh Second Commonwealth Study Conference to serve as a "typical representation of how a community in Western Canada developed during the push of the railway West just after the turn of the century" while demonstrating "what local talent, combined with competent music and writing can do toward putting history in a palatable form" ("Pageant Cast" 1; "Pageant Being"16). Gordon C. Garbutt, one of the conference coordinators, wrote that despite weary "days of travel across Canada and a series of tightly packed programmes" that left most of the three hundred delegates on the twenty-day cross-country event dreading the prospect of two hours of amateur drama, "'I wish I could put into words just how moved we were.'" Few items "succeeded as well in establishing cordial understanding among people from 35 countries, of many races, of many tongues" or at conveying "the Conference theme: The human consequences of the changing industrial environment" ("Edson Story" 16).

Arguably, the "human consequences of the changing industrial environment" had become a pressing concern in Ringwood's drama as early as *Egg* (1950), then *Widger* (1952) where a bag of miners' gold fuels greed and murder. She developed the theme at greater depth in her next historical musical "The Road Runs North," written with composer Art Roshomon, to celebrate the Canadian Centennial year (1967) and the establishment of Barkerville and the Gold Rush era (1861-64). Drawing on almost one hundred members of the Williams Lake community working onstage and behind the scenes, "Road" relied on many of the same dynamics of strong local involvement as "Neighbor." However, in Anthony's estimation, Ringwood's experience "with the Edson musical aided her in writing [...] [a] new musical [that] was more mature and had greater sweep and depth" (102-03).

While the same war of the sexes continues into "Road" with two feisty chorus girls landing their men on the frontier, the racial relationships are more complex. Unlike Johnny Boniface ("Neighbor"), the nineteenth-century Chinese prospector Lo Chen ("Road") faces deep-rooted personal and systemic prejudice. Reflecting the larger aboriginal population of Williams Lake, Ringwood, who also directed the play, incorporated a sympathetic romance between Hilt Ryland, a young man from Ontario, and Mayla, a young aboriginal woman whose family saves his life. In addition to indicating that actual dance, song, and drumming by aboriginal performers be incorporated into the play, Ringwood also specifies that Mayla's father (51-57) speak only in his own aboriginal tongue. In the scene where Hilt, now healed, leaves again, Mayla, who, along with her brothers, has been learning English from Hilt, serves as translator, both literally and metaphorically, between worlds. In a similar translation between worlds in "The Jasper Story," Gowan's Overlanders seeking Cariboo gold in 1862 are saved from starvation only by native-speaking Shuswap and the ability of the pregnant Katie Schubert, the only woman in the party, to move beyond the mercantilism and territorialism of her fellow travellers to negotiate successfully for food (29).

However, where Gowan wryly contrasts the absurdity of the little party's grandiose dreams with the reality of quiet female and indigenous resourcefulness and the immensity of the wilderness, Ringwood more clearly aims at juxtaposing the option of a life lived close to the land, with the capitalistic pillaging of it represented by the Gold Rush. While the impulsive, good-natured Barker eschews the cruelty and greed of many who follow him, the life and marriage he builds on his own idiosyncratic "strike" prove as ephemeral as Barkerville itself. As his wife sneers upon her leave-taking, only "a fool" would expect that luck twice, especially by 1864 when only "the big outfits with machinery" are "taking out gold now" (100). It is the outsider, Lo Chen, who first talks to Hilt about the importance of "having place." For him, it is his wife and child in China; Hilt has to find his own: "You get wife, have son. You feel part of earth then. Like tree with roots. You have place" (33). For Hilt, "having place" means buying a ranch to live close to the land (a choice similar to Delaney's in "Neighbor" and John Ware's in *Stampede*) and marriage and children with Mayla; since he has no other family (32-33), hers will also become his, and their descendants the true treasure embedded in the land.

The Lodge (1977), *Mirage* (1979), and "A Treaty for the Plains" (1977)

Forty years after Gowan and Morley's confrontation, the kitchen stove and the creaking rocking chair may have been less in evidence, but Alberta's "wide open spaces" had never been more the site of heated debate, both in life and art. Physically, socially, economically, politically, ethically, spiritually, mythologically, and artistically, "Land" continued to be a locus of physical and human commonality striking community out of a growing diversity of genders, races, ethnicities, classes, times, and spaces. While remaining on the margins of the new professional arts, theatre, literature, and dance scene, the 1970s work of both women was the richest and most multi-dimensional in its treatment of an increasingly complex regional voice, employing song, dance, and music.

Ringwood's 1977 comedy, *The Lodge*, focuses on a family reunion organized by Jasmine Daravalley, the family's beloved matriarch, at Wilderness Lodge to celebrate what she has mysteriously heralded as "her last birthday" (453). It soon becomes apparent that Jasmine means this in the apocalyptic sense of a Day of Judgement, marking the passing away of old lives and selves, and the coming into being of new ones. Again, land and community and "having place" are central to that process of revelation and transformation. Ringwood again returns to Greek myth to ground the surface realism of the action in archetypical structure. She transforms Shelley, her young *alter ego* as an artist, into a Persephone figure descending from the airy realm of youth and artistic freedom to the underworld of marriage, pregnancy, and increasing responsibility. Shelley must judge whether her husband, Allan, has dragged her Hades-like into a dark, unnatural spiritual realm and physical wilderness from which she must escape or eventually smother; or whether the earth, to which both her marriage and co-ownership of the land bind her, is a source of deep hidden riches that will allow her to become a "tree with roots [...] and have place" ("Road" 33).

Jasmine, Ringwood's aging *alter ego*, by contrast, is re-ascending from the world of experience, back to that of light and freedom to pursue her Muse; however, transformed by her own journey through the earth, she emerges not into spring in her younger guise as Persephone, but into the cooler autumnal light of Indian summer as Demeter, the older nurturing maternal figure associated with the fertility of the earth and the fulfillment of the harvest. As an artist, she is closely connected to the spiritual force of the land, eager to sketch the beauty and colour of the autumn woods. She also shares, with the aboriginal Lashaway family, an intuitive sense of the restorative nature of the waters of the Soda Spring on the property, and their power as a site of visions.

However, as in the case of "Neighbor" and "Road," it is a view of land complicated by the forces of industrialization, urbanization, commercialization (including logging and entertainment), and economic self-interest.

When Jasmine's son-in-law Eardley looks at the Soda Spring, all he sees is "Sasquatch Hot Springs" (479), part of a "Canadian Disneyland"—"an empire devoted to recreation, stretching from this lodge right up to that spring" (481). It is one of the reasons that Jasmine has decided to turn her birthday into a day of reckoning, and to dispose of her own property and person on her own terms while she still can. She informs her surprised family that she will be moving, not to assisted living, but to the Antipodes "to teach and study Maori art" (486). She also advises them that the two family properties she has held in trust for many years will also be moving out of their grasp: the High Valley Ranch has already been sold to the government as a heritage site, and the money spent endowing a school in Africa, and the soda spring will be returned to aboriginal ownership, "providing it is left as it is now for a hundred years" (488). In a resolution that mirrors both the ending of "Road" and the beginning of *Mirage*, the true inheritors of the earth are Jasmine's heirs, Shelley and Allan, the now-owners of the lodge, who strive to "live off the land" while building and sustaining it for future generations, and the aboriginal Lashaway family, long-time friends of the Daravalleys, who will similarly serve as the stewards of the Soda Spring.

Mirage (1979) resembles Gowan's *Building of Canada* series and "The Jasper Story" in using music, song, text, and a protean ensemble of actors to tell an epic tale of the building of Saskatchewan between 1910 and 1980, through the interrelated fortunes of three generations of family and neighbours in rural Saskatchewan. While divided over the effectiveness of the play's chronicling almost seventy years of Saskatchewan history in two acts, both the Saskatoon and Edmonton critics, aware of Ringwood's reputation as a regional writer with a strong lyrical, poetic sensibility, tended to praise the aspects of the play and production that conformed most to that image (Ashwell C9; Perkins 37).

However, re-examining the play in 1998, Anne Nothof suggests that their very familiarity with Ringwood's early work may have led some critics to underestimate the complexity and nuances of Ringwood's dramatic treatment of land. As Anthony (107) and Nothof ("Gendered" 131-33) both indicate, Ringwood not only uses the families to connect the narrative internally, but she also draws upon characters and motifs from earlier plays to interconnect the narrative of *Mirage* to her larger body of writing. Shelley and Jasmine from *The Lodge* find an echo in Laura Ryland who makes art, "place," and a living from the rich clay of Saskatchewan as a potter and artist. Jasmine's mercenary, self-interested relatives re-emerge most memorably in the Burns family and Marj Blair.

However, the larger link made in both *Lodge* and "Road" between a self-perpetuating cycle of violence to land and to humans, also emerges poignantly in an unusually personal scene in *Mirage*. In one of the very few times in her own drama when Ringwood references the devastating personal loss of her brothers in the Second World War, Jeanne, amidst autumn and harvest, receives the news that her son, Mark, has been killed at sea. Where the response of Gowan's Miranda in *Caveman* to the terrifying human cost of war is passionate, dialectical, and ultimately political, Ringwood's Jeanne's expresses a deep personal pain bearable only by grounding it in the land. Although part of her "lies in the deep ocean with Mark" (530), only the earth can give an answer to the unanswerable question of when the carnage will end:

DOWSER: I don't know, Jeannie. We plough up our land until it blows away into dust. We hurl bombs on our cities until the children blow away in the dust. I don't know. (530)

Acknowledging that "the four winds are heavy with the children that have been blown away, all the wasted children" (530), Ringwood then evokes an image from *Pasque Flower* as possibly the only life-giving response to so profound a grief. Her stage directions indicate that "*[Jeanne] moves forward and slowly begins to plant the tulip bulbs*" (530), a sign of spring and of rebirth and regeneration to come in another season.

From *Widger's Way*, Ringwood borrows the mystical water diviner, Dowser, as a symbol of the ability of the "dreamer" to draw spirit, life, and vision—mirages—out of land that seems empty, dry, or purely material. His vision of the "mystery" that must not be spoiled or defiled lest the land "become your enemy" (*Lodge* 488) frames the action of the play:

No easy gods, and yet they challenge, crying "hunt us down,
Uncover us from beneath your monuments of wood and stone,
Come, dance and sing with us,
For without us you are homeless,
Hunt us down for without us you are forever homeless." (490)

As he does in *Widger*, *Mirage*'s Dowser evokes the remains of the dinosaurs (499), both as a reminder of other giants who have had their day and
passed into the earth, and as a source of hidden mineral treasures that
again will change the meaning of land for a later generation. But the effect
is rendered disturbing rather than comic by his simultaneous summoning
of the spirit of the buffalo bones and prairie grass (499, 506), talismans of
a self-sustaining way of life destroyed to make way for farming, even as
farming itself may one day be swept away to make place for something else.
Curiously, neither the Edmonton nor Saskatoon reviewers commented
much on *Mirage*'s aboriginal characters, possibly, to judge from Ashwell's
comments, because the white ensemble cast had trouble bringing the same
authenticity to their aboriginal as to their white roles (C9). Yet it is clear
that Ringwood intended to establish the same kind of relationship between the Rylands and the neighbouring aboriginal family as she did in
both *Lodge* and "Road." It is significant, in fact, that both families again are
borrowed from earlier plays, which sends their representatives into *Mirage*
already carrying deeper resonances.

The White Calf family comes from *Stampede* (1946), one of Ringwood's
first explorations of the contrast between a more natural ranching world
that equitably encompasses "outsiders"—like the rodeo bronco, Midnight,
turned "outlaw" by bad treatment; the maverick Shorthorn, haunted by
his violent American past; and early Afro-Canadian rancher, John Ware—
and the more exploitive, materialistic forces arriving with the railway and
the commercialized form of the Calgary Stampede. The White Calf we see
exploited in 1912 as a sideshow at the Calgary Stampede, speaking a few
words of "real Indian" (239) while the carnie urges the audience to "Step
right up, folks, shake hands with a genuine vanished American [...] Last
chance for a souvenir of the old West, folks. Last chance" (253), is almost
certainly kin to the aboriginal family we meet in 1911 Saskatchewan. Besides a name, they also share a rapidly changing prairie that sees common
hunting grounds being broken into individual property by fences, treaties,
and land titles, and inconvenient animals, foliage, and people eliminated
or confined (*Mirage* 495-97). From "The Road Runs North," Ringwood
borrows the Rylands. While the John Ryland who arrives in 1911 Saskatchewan with his Scottish wife, Jeanne, never refers to his own background,
the fact that his grandson is named Hilt suggests he is descended from the

same Hilt and Mayla of 1861, and may be linked even distantly by blood as well as land to his aboriginal neighbours.

These older connections give a deeper resonance to the opening and closing scenes set in 1980, in which another Hilt Ryland and a second Jeanne, this time, Jeanne White Calf named affectionately after his grandmother, wrestle with "having place." For Hilt, the family farm may still be a place he can feel rooted in the earth, but the new engineering jobs are luring him northwards at a time when American agribusiness is pressuring him to sell. Jeanne confesses to a similar feeling about the recovery of her language and the Sun Dance at a time when she is spending less and less time on the reserve and becoming immersed in the "Indian Rights" movement: "We didn't even say we owned the land then …we lived on it. A person could carry what he owned on his back or on a horse. At that Sun Dance I almost wished I didn't live now … But it's too late for that … I've got to find some other way to hold myself together now" (493). The play ends with the bittersweet possibility of a wiser and more equitable joint stewardship of the land being forged between most recent descendants of White Calf and Hilt Ryland.

Intriguingly, Gowan wrote what she considered her final and best work about the importance of a joint stewardship and responsibility towards the land at almost the same time. It was a theme that she had explored in the context of historical Aboriginal and Métis land rights as early as 1937. However, an Aboriginal voice that still remains relatively muted in the *Building of Canada* moves closer to the forefront in "The Jasper Story" where Gowan's strong women who protect land and people through marriage and children tend to be Aboriginal or Métis, or, like Katie Schubert, have a strong affinity to them. Babette, in 1825, suggests that her mixed heritage—"My father is Irish, my mother of the Cree people. I am proud of them both and proud to be what I am" (9)—allows her to negotiate more effectively between the cultural tensions of the fur trade war. Similarly, Suzette Swift, in 1908, herself of mixed blood, perpetuates the final scene by reminding the guide that any "dream of the future" requires acknowledgment of those, like the Haida, who first "made place" on the Pacific coast (50).

This was simply a prelude to "A Treaty for the Plains" written in 1977 to mark the one-hundredth anniversary of the signing of Treaty 6 in Alberta. As with "The Jasper Story," the outdoor setting was resonant with layers of human and historical meaning. Dried Meat Hill in south-east Alberta had served first as a traditional site for pemmican-making by both the Blackfoot and Cree, then, after 1893, as a popular site for picnicking by European immigrants, and with the building of Wabel Hall, a social and dance centre for "hundreds of early settlers" ("Expect" 1). Unfortunately, after the hall's demolition in 1915, the hill itself fell victim to industrialization. With its very existence now threatened by extensive "gravel dredging" for road building, the Battle River Heritage group hoped that the pageant and the site repairs needed to stage it, would help get the hill declared a historic site for both cultures (Hartman 1; "Heritage Group" 14; Bartlett 21).

Gowan was commissioned to write the sixty-minute re-enactment of the signing, at least in part, because she "was a former resident of the area" ("I can" 1). Ironically, while her parents (1931-46) were longtime residents of Bawlf ("Party" 19), Gowan portrayed the town negatively as a provincial, materialistic backwater in *The Hungry Spirit*. In hindsight, Gowan felt the 1935 autobiographical play said more about her youthful callowness than the land and community: "today I would recognize the fact that it had been pioneered only ten years before and that these Scandinavian people with whom I felt nothing in common were really giants in the earth" (Day, *Hungry* 70).

"A Treaty for the Plains" gave her an unprecedented opportunity to travel back in historical time to the treaty agreement that had made even the Scandinavian farms possible. Over July, every effort was made to ensure that as many descendants and representatives of the 1877 signing as possible were present. The aboriginal planners, represented mostly by the four bands at Hobbema, committed themselves to erecting "a complete Indian village" on-site and supplying band members in costume to participate in the pageant and perform a program of dances ("Expect" 1). For Gowan, who had spent weeks doing historical research and interviewing old-timers as part of the project ("Treaty" 1), the day of the pageant itself was an electrifying experience. A crowd of over four thousand witnessed First Nations, Mounted policemen, interpreters, trappers, settlers, and government men represented "in the hour-long pageant … dramatically portrayed on the hill where Indians used to make pemmican many years ago" ("5000" 1). Gowan (as reported in both "5,000" 1; Bartlett 21) herself received the most moving review she had ever had:

Tall and erect, Alberta's Lieutenant Governor Ralph Steinhauer strode over and gently kissed Elsie Park Gowan at the conclusion of the pageant. [...] A full Indian chief himself, the Hon. Mr. Steinhauer was expressing the feeling of hundreds, Indian and white alike, as they pondered the closing words of her pageant: "The chiefs have kept their word. Has the white man kept faith with the Indians? Now in 1977, do they live among you in dignity and equality, with equal rights in the Canada that once was theirs?

"Look into your hearts.

"Think of these things as you watch the treaty signed. ... "

While the answer, sadly, was no, noted aboriginal leader, Joe Dion, the very act of coming together to remember and re-enact the past, with a mutual awareness of what still remained unfulfilled now, represented the best hope for further action together; "if the peoples of the province" were to stand together "in the future, as they stood together on Monday [...] we can build one of the greatest nations of the earth ("5,000" 1; Bartlett 21). Reminiscing from the distance of 1992, Gowan commented, "I think that day at Dried Meat Lake was the top of my life as a playwright" (Day, *Hungry* 261-62).

Conclusion

By the time Ringwood passed away in 1984 and Gowan in 1999, they were aware of the extent to which the twentieth century had not fulfilled all that it had promised them either as women or as playwrights. They had come of age when first-wave feminism, western utopianism, and the native Art Theatre movement had suggested that the weight of patriarchal and colonial oppression implicit both in Hamlet's statement and the established gender, class, and racial order that upheld Shakespeare as the measure of all things theatrical, could be successfully challenged, and it was possible to at last be female, Canadian, western Canadian, and a playwright without contradiction or inequity.

It was a dream left unrealized on a number of accounts. In thoughtful letters to Geraldine Anthony (1978) and Anton Wagner (1974), Ringwood suggested that contrary to the feminist rhetoric of her time, women had still remained far more constricted and confined by their sexual, family, and community roles and fragmented in their writing lives, especially after marriage. Gowan, while also happily married, had similar complaints. The Marian of *The Hungry Spirit*, who triumphantly leaves the restrictive domestic world of her mother in 1935 to pursue a university education and career, was ironically apt to find herself by 1952 in the situation of Frances in *The High Green Gate*: forced back into her mother's world once she had married and had children, unless she could snag one of the very few subsidized daycare spots available to working mothers.

Beyond that, both writers expressed insecurities about the playwriting itself and the efficacy of the conventional forms they often wrote in. In her autobiographical short story, "An Appetite for People," Ringwood suggests that she first became a writer because of an insatiable desire to embrace the entirety of the world in all its multifariousness. But her comment in "The Sense of Place," that "[i]n a way it seems that artistic experience is often a search for somewhere where it doesn't hurt so much" (12), was perhaps a tacit admission that there were forms of horror, darkness, chaos, and pain in both the internal and external world that she could not express in life or writing and survive. Of her radio work, Gowan commented, "I often think it was all written on air. As Keats said, 'My name is one—whose name was writ in water.' My name was writ on the air and 'its substantial pageant faded'" (Day, *Hungry* 30-31). Their pioneering efforts paved the way for a professional Canadian and western Canadian theatre that neither playwright was fated to enter.

Land and their work based on land were the only places where their art and vision never ceased to grow. In *Mirage*, Ryan Ryland says, "Those who come after won't know how a man can carry a map of every acre of his farm inside him" (544). The ultimate measure of both Gwen Pharis Ringwood and Elsie Park Gowan as writers is that they not only wrote the land, they "made place" and, in doing so, made us all immeasurably richer by sharing with those who will "come after," the ever richer "map of every acre" of Alberta and the prairies that they created within themselves for over fifty years.[4]

NOTES

1   Laurier's famous assertion, more popularly paraphrased as "The Twentieth Century belongs to Canada," was apparently delivered as part of a speech to the Canadian Club of Ottawa on 18 January 1904. While frequently quoted in many sources, this is taken from *First Among Equals*.

2   Editorial ellipses have been marked [...] to avoid confusion with ellipses actually used by the authors themselves as part of their text. The latter are marked with simple suspension points.

3   While current usage tends to favour "Resistance" over "Uprising" or "Rebellion" as having less colonial overtones, it is not a term that would have been familiar to historians or playwrights of Gowan's era. One suspects that many of them would likely have seen the more passive word "Resistance" as an odd way to describe a conflict where people on both sides had died fighting for a cause they believed in strongly. It is also clear from the justification that Irish-Canadian playwright, John Coulter, gave for writing three influential plays on Riel in the mid-twentieth century, that at least some playwrights of Gowan's generation regarded the term "rebel" as a badge of honour, rather than otherwise, if the "rebellion" or "uprising" was justified by tyranny or oppression: "I see the Metis leader and the rebellions which he led as precursors of later and present uprisings all over the world, particularly the so-called Third World—armed resistance by small nations against forcible take-over by some powerful neighbor [...] in order to be free [...] free to develop in their own way from their own roots"(i).

4   I would like to thank the archivists of University of the Calgary and University of Alberta Special Collections for helping me locate and acquire copies of Gowan and Ringwood's unpublished scripts, some of them on short notice. My thanks as well to editors like Diane Bessai and Enid Delgatty Rutland who have made many of Gowan's and Ringwood's scripts publicly accessible again. In addition, I would also like to credit the very fine previous scholarship of Geraldine Anthony, Anton Wagner, and Anne Nothof that this article builds on.

WORKS CITED

Anthony, Geraldine. *Gwen Pharis Ringwood*. Twayne, 1981.

Ashwell, Keith. "Ringwood's *Mirage* Alive with Prairie Life. *Edmonton Journal*, 18 July 1980, p. C9.

Bartlett, Cathie. "Dried Meat Pageant Ponders Past, Future." *Edmonton Journal*, 2 Aug. 1977, p. 21.

Bicknell, Minnie Evans. *Relief: A Play in One Act*. Macmillan, 1938.

Bill, Desmond. "*Jasper Story* Re-Enacting Life of Rockies Pioneers." *Edmonton Journal*, 14 July 1960, p. 21.

Bohm, Arnd. "Fertile Minds in a Barren Season: Western Canadian Women Playwrights and the Great Depression." *West-words: Celebrating*

Western Canadian Theatre and Playwriting, edited by Moira Day, CPRC, 2012, pp. 147-262.

"CBC Radio Presents *The Edson Story.*" *Edson Leader*, 21 Dec. 1961, p. 5.

Coulter, John. *The Crime of Louis Riel.* Playwright's Co-op, 1976.

Dafoe, John. "Jasper's Colorful Early History Told in Town's Annual Pageant." *Edmonton Journal*, 1957. Clipping in Elsie Park Gowan Scrapbooks. Microfiche. University of Alberta Archives, Edmonton, Alberta.

Day, Moira. "Elsie Park Gowan's (Re)-Building of Canada (1937-1938): Revisioning the Historical Radio Series Through Feminist Eyes." *Theatre Research in Canada / Recherches Théâtrales au Canada*, vol. 14, no.1, Spring 1993, pp. 1-13.

——, editor. *The Hungry Spirit: Selected Plays and Prose by Elsie Park Gowan.* NeWest Press, 1992.

——. "The Portrait of the Artist in Old Age: Gwen Pharis Ringwood's *The Lodge. Theatre Research in Canada / Recherches Théâtrales au Canada*, vol. 25, nos. 1-2, Spring and Fall, pp. 48-83.

Deakin, Jack. "Jasper Opens Pageant On Its Pioneer Days." *Edmonton Journal*, 12 July 1956, p.5

"Edson Story Perfect for Duke's Conference." *Edson Leader*, 7 June 1962, pp. 1, 16.

"Expect 4,000 at Dried Meat Hill." *Camrose Canadian*, 20 July 1977, pp. 1.

"The Finale Brings the Entire Cast on Stage." *Edson Leader*, 16 Nov. 1961, p. 1.

"5,000 Throng to Dried Meat Hill." *Camrose Canadian*, 3 Aug. 1977, p. 1.

Franklin, Stephen. "Jasper Tells Its Romantic Story." *Weekend Magazine*, vol. 9, no. 25, 1959. Clipping in Elsie Park Gowan Scrapbooks. Microfiche. University of Alberta Archives, Edmonton, Alberta.

Gowan, Elsie Park. "Another Kitchen Stove." *Saturday Night*, vol. 50, no. 44, 7 Sept. 1935, p. 8.

——. *The Building of Canada.* ["X The Silver Chief," "XI Seven Oaks," "XVIII Red Star in the West."] Elsie Park Gowan Papers, pp. 87-123. University of Alberta Archives, Edmonton, Alberta. Typescripts.

——. "The High Green Gate." Day, *The Hungry Spirit*, pp. 226-54.

——. "History into Theatre." *Canadian Author and Bookman*, vol. 51, no.1, Fall 1975, p. 8.

——. "Homestead." Day, *The Hungry Spirit*, pp. 45-63.

———. "The Hungry Spirit." Day, *The Hungry Spirit*, pp. 66-102.

———. "The Jasper Story." Music: Jack McCreath. Elsie Park Gowan Papers, pp. 87-123. University of Alberta Archives, Edmonton, Alberta. Typescript.

———. "The Last Caveman," *The Hungry Spirit*, pp.155-223.

———. "Who Builds A City." Music: Bob McMullin. Elsie Park Gowan Papers, pp. 87-123. University of Alberta Archives, Edmonton, Alberta. Typescript.

———. "Woman in the Twentieth Century." Day, *The Hungry Spirit*, pp. 291-309.

Hartman, Mrs. E. "Heritage Day Planned for Dried Meat Hill." *Camrose Canadian*, 25 May 1977, p. 1.

"Heritage Group to Meet Friday." *Camrose Canadian*, 8 June 1977, p. 14.

"History of Athabasca Valley to be Outlined in Jasper Pageant." *Edmonton Journal*, 19 June 1956, p. 9.

"I Can Just See It…" *Camrose Canadian*, 6 July 1977, p. 1.

McCreath, Jack. "Crowds Brave Weather to Witness Pageant." 1957. Clipping in Elsie Park Gowan Scrapbooks. Microfiche. University of Alberta Archives, Edmonton, Alberta.

"More Human Interest Needed For Pageant." *Edson Leader*, 11 May 1961, p. 9.

Morley, Malcolm. "Canada's Kitchen Drama." *Saturday Night*, vol. 50, no. 40, 10 Aug. 1935, p. 12.

Nothof, Anne F. "Gendered Landscapes Synergism Of Place And Person In Canadian Prairie Drama." *Great Plains Quarterly*, vol. 18, no. 2, Spring 1998, pp. 127-38. http://digitalcommons.unl.edu/greatplainsquarterly/2032

———. "Making Community History: The Radio Plays of Ringwood and Gowan." *Edmonton: the Life of a City*, edited by Bob Hesketh and Frances Swyripa, NeWest Press, 1995, pp. 174-77, 351-52.

"Once Again Edson Has Own Town Band." *Edson Leader*, 12 Oct. 1961, p. 12.

"Pageant Being Whipped Into Shape for City." *Edson Leader*, 17 May 1962, p. 16.

"Pageant Cast Invited to Perform in City." *Edson Leader*, 5 Apr. 1962, p. 1.

"Party Honors Mrs. R. Young." *Edmonton Journal*, 26 Apr., 1954 p. 19.

"Period Costumes For Edson's Story." *Edson Leader*, 19 Oct., 1961, p. 1.

"Period Items Supplied for Pageant Authenticity." *Edson Leader*, 21 Sept. 1961, p. 6.

Perkins, Don. "*Mirage* Opens at Greystone." *Star-Phoenix* [Saskatoon], 25 May 1979, p. 37.

"The Right Honourable Sir Wilfrid Laurier: Biography 1841-1919." *First Among Equals: The Prime Minister in Canadian Life and Politics. https://www. collectionscanada.gc.ca/primeministers/h4-3181-e.html*

Ringwood, Gwen Pharis. "An Appetite for People." *Scenes from a Country Life.*

Short short stories and episodes about a child in the country. 13 scenes. 21 Jan. 1980. Gwen Pharis Ringwood Papers, University of Calgary, Calgary, Alberta. Typescript.

———. "Dark Harvest." Rutland, pp. 437-88.

———. "A Fine Coloured Easter Egg." Rutland, pp. 255-70.

———. "The Jack and the Joker." Rutland, pp. 163-79.

———. Letter to Anton Wagner. 23 June 1974. Gwen Pharis Ringwood Papers. University of Calgary, Calgary, Alberta.

———. Letter to Anton Wagner. 29 Jan. 1979. Gwen Pharis Ringwood Papers. University of Calgary, Calgary, Alberta.

———. Letter to Geraldine Anthony. 5 Feb. 1978. Gwen Pharis Ringwood Papers. University of Calgary, Calgary, Alberta.

———. "The Lodge." Rutland, pp. 437-88.

———. "Look Behind you, Neighbor." Music: Chet Lambertson. Gwen Pharis Ringwood Papers, University of Calgary, Calgary, Alberta. Typescript.

———. "Mirage." [Music: Gary Walsh and Alvin Cairns, 1979; Rick Fox, 1980] Rutland, pp. 489-548.

———. "Pasque Flower." Rutland, pp. 45-58.

———. "The Rainmaker." Rutland, pp. 181-204.

———. "The Road Runs North." Music: Art Rosomon. Gwen Pharis Ringwood Papers, University of Calgary, Calgary, Alberta. Typescript.

———. "The Sense of Place." Notes for Co-op Talks, national Tours, Speaking at Colleges and University. 26 Jan. 1977. Gwen Pharis Ringwood Papers. University of Calgary, Calgary, Alberta. Typescript.

———. "Stampede." Rutland, pp. 205-53.

———. "Still Stands the House." Rutland, pp. 26-43.

———. "Widger's Way." Rutland, pp. 287-337.

Rutland, Enid Delgatty, editor. *The Collected Plays of Gwen Pharis Ringwood.* Borealis, 1982.

Selden, Samuel. *Frederick Henry Koch: Pioneer Playmaker.* U of North Carolina P, 1954.

"6,000 Watch City's History Unfold in Colorful Pageant." *Edmonton Journal,* vol. 9, Oct. 1954, p. 24.

"Treaty Signing Ready for Monday." *Camrose Canadian,* 27 July 1977, p. 1.

Wagner, Anton. "Elsie Park Gowan: Distinctively Canadian." *Theatre Research in Canada / Recherches Théâtrales au Canada,* vol. 8, no. 1, Spring 1987, pp. 1-12.

"Warm Afterglow From Pageant." *Edson Leader,* 9 Nov. 1961, p. 9.

Writing Alberta's History

R. Douglas Francis

For over a century, historians of Alberta have chronicled the province's history. This labour has resulted in a rich harvest of books and articles. To date, however, no one has examined the historiography: the differing approaches, interpretations, and themes that Alberta historians have applied to the province's past. This chapter will examine this historiography through an analysis of survey histories of the province. Survey histories provide an overview of their subject and usually incorporate the most recent trends in research and interpretation. To date, there have been six survey histories of Alberta, a relatively small number but in line with survey histories of other provinces with the exception of Quebec where history and identity have consistently played a prominent role.

Archibald Oswald MacRae, the principal of Western Canada College, a private boys' school (and the forerunner of Western Canada high school), wrote the first history, simply entitled *History of the Province of Alberta*, in 1912. His history appeared seven years after the founding of the province and five years after the incorporation of the History Society of Alberta. The Society aimed to "encourage the study of the history of Alberta and Canada, to rescue from oblivion the memories of the original inhabitants, fur traders, explorers, and settlers of the north and west of Canada, to obtain and preserve narratives in print, manuscripts or otherwise of their travels, adventures, labor and observations" (Historical Society of Alberta). MacRae's history fulfilled the aspirations of the Society. His history records extensively the "memories of the original inhabitants" while focusing at length on their contribution to the province's history. He also incorporates the history of the fur traders, explorers, and settlers. As well, his history contains documentation of Native myths and stories, lengthy excerpts from fur traders' and missionaries' accounts, along with extensive quotations from government reports, material that might otherwise have been lost.

John Blue, the Provincial Librarian, wrote the second history, *Alberta: Past and Present: Historical and Biographical*, in 1924. The decade of the 1920s was the heyday of Canadian nationalism, an offshoot of the pride engendered by Canada's contribution to the First World War. Blue reflected this national pride by focusing on the ways that Alberta was an integral part of Canada's history. He set out his aim in his "Foreword": "to trace the development of the political institutions of the newest province of the Dominion and compare it with the development of similar institutions in the older provinces of Canada" (Blue v).

Then a fifty-year hiatus prevailed before the next history appeared. This period was devoted to national history, culminating in the Canadian centennial in 1967. Only after the celebrations had died down did regional, provincial, and local histories come into vogue, along with the histories of specific groups that had not been included or given sufficient attention in national histories, such as Natives, women, and workers. What triggered the shift was an appeal by two prominent Canadian historians. Ramsay Cook urges Canadian historians in an article entitled "Canadian Historical Writing," written at the time of Canada's centennial, to explore ways in which Canadian historians can get beyond their obsession with national history. He recommends focusing on provincial and local history, and on groups that had been overlooked in national history. In a seminal article entitled "Limited Identities in Canada" (1969), J.M.S. Careless made a similar appeal. The term "Limited Identities" has stood for a major shift in Canadian history that took place beginning in the 1960s. James G. MacGregor's *History of Alberta*, published in 1972, was Alberta's contribution to "limited identities." MacGregor, an engineer by training but a historian by passion, wanted to write a popular history of the province that would promote the province as a success story. "Progress" became his mantra, reaching its peak, he believed, in the period in which he was writing.

Howard and Tamara Palmer produced the first authoritative history of Alberta. Entitled *Alberta: A New History* (1990), to distinguish it from MacGregor's, it incorporated the abundance of new historical research of the 1970s and 1980s. It also provided an extensive account of groups overlooked in earlier histories, most notably ethnic groups. Howard Palmer was a historian of ethnicity at the University of Calgary while Tamara Palmer specialized in ethnic literature. Aritha van Herk, an English professor at the University of Calgary, trumped the Palmers' scholarly history with *Mavericks: An Incorrigible History of Alberta* in 2001. It received numerous public accolades, including being chosen by the Calgary Public Library Association as "the book that all Albertans should read" in 2011. She aimed to bring Alberta history to life and relevant to today's sensitivities by telling the stories of the "rebels" in the province's past, implying throughout that these "incorrigibles" were what distinguished Alberta's history from that of other provinces and that gave Alberta its distinct identity.

The debate over popular versus scholarly histories of Alberta has been ongoing. It is evident in the most recent history, a two-volume history entitled *Alberta Formed – Alberta Transformed*, written for Alberta's centennial and published in 2006, only four years after *Mavericks*. The editors of the volumes, Michael Payne, Donald Wetherell, and Catherine Cavanaugh, asked contributors, the majority being professional historians, to choose a date or a limited time period in Alberta's past and to show its importance in the province's history. While acknowledged by professional historians for its incorporation of the most up-to-date research and for displaying recent trends in historical writing, the volumes have not penetrated beyond the walls of academia, while van Herk's *Mavericks* continues to elicit public praise. The remainder of this chapter will look at each of these survey histories in greater depth to show the changing interpretations and approach to the province's history.

History of the Province of Alberta

Archibald MacRae's history is listed as being three volumes in length. In actuality, history only constitutes three-quarters of the first volume. The remaining quarter of volume one, along with volumes two and three, consists of biographical sketches of prominent Albertans. Businessmen and professionals, a significant number of them being Calgarians, make up the majority of entries. These biographical sketches are informative but not of historical value. MacRae does not attempt to set these individuals into a historical context or to show their historical importance.

This caveat aside, MacRae's history is impressive. One would expect a history of the province published in 1912, one of the banner years of Alberta's prosperity, to be Whiggish in approach, with a focus on the current period and a history that records an upward progression to the golden age of the present. MacRae's history is not of this nature. To him, the golden age is in the past, particularly the period when the Native people were dominant. His real interest is to present the "romantic traditions [and] the unique features of Indian tribes and people" (MacRae iv). He notes in his "Preface" what such a history would record:

> What the Red Race said and did, how they loved and won and lost, fevered and fought and died; how this people of philosophic calm, if but of broken expression, viewed 'life's fitful dream.' ... [T]his people of the inscrutable face and lofty mien, had an ancestry as profound, as noble, as extraordinary, as any of the wonderful Orientals. (iv)

He laments and apologizes that too little of his history deals with the Native people. Yet of the first five of the histories reviewed in this chapter, MacRae's is the most extensive in coverage of Native history. As well, MacRae is highly sensitive to the Native view on issues of Native-white relations, and tells the history of these events from the Native perspective.

MacRae devotes three chapters and almost sixty pages to the Indian Tribes of Alberta, discussing their way of life, their beliefs, and their traditions on the eve of the coming of the Europeans. In a chapter on the early explorers and fur traders, he emphasizes their dependence on the Native population for survival and success. He points out that while others look at these Europeans as "the forerunners of civilisation in North America," he sees them as "ahead of that civilisation: they outran it, or ran away from it" (26), and adopted the better way of life of the Native people. He ends his discussion of the fur trade era with a reflection on Lieutenant Governor Morris, one of the sympathetic governors of the North West Territory with regards to Natives.

In referring to the future, the Lieutenant Governor advised the continuance of negotiations with the native tribes, looking to satisfactory regulations whereby the latter might be taught how to prolong their present sources of food and raiment, and at the same time learn of the agricultural methods of the white men. (258)

Even in the post-1870 period, he provides an overview chapter on the "Treaties With the Alberta Indians" along with a separate chapter on Treaty 6 and two chapters on Treaty 7. His chapter on the North West Rebellion of 1885 contains an extensive section on the Native perspective and involvement in that confrontation. MacRae attributes the Native involvement to starvation due to reduced rations on the part of the Canadian government, thus blaming the government rather than First Nations or Métis for their actions. He also sees 1885 as a critical turning point in First Nations history, marking the decline of this "noble race." MacRae reveals his continued admiration for First Nations in the following excerpt:

It is not necessary to hold a brief for all the wild excesses, the bloody cruelty, the monstrous behavior of the Indian tribes, to feel a precious point of contact with their life in its romantic attachment to the beauty and wealth of Nature, untarnished by the machinery of modern industrial conditions. (430-31)

MacRae's discussion of the fur trade era deserves praise beyond its focus on Native history. It also foretold trends in historical writing. He chastises the fur hunters for the "frightful slaughter of fur bearing animals in those days" (38) and provides statistics as to the number of beaver, marten, mink, musquash, and others slaughtered in the latter part of the eighteenth century. He might well have been Alberta's first environmental historian. He might also be considered to be Alberta's first social historian. He has a remarkable chapter on "Life in and about the Forts and Trading Posts," in which he provides detail on the structure of the "typical fort," the daily life of a fur trader, the social hierarchy in the fur trading posts, and the many festivities held at the forts to ward off boredom (141-52).

MacRae devotes a chapter to the Royal North West Mounted Police (NWMP). He describes the Mounties as "a truly magnificent force in its history and traditions" (259). They were responsible for bringing "British Law and Justice … over an immense area" (260). But their real value, in McRae's view, was their positive contribution to Indian-white relations, most evident in the North West Rebellion of 1885. He notes:

> Because he [the Mountie] was pure in intention, because, without alloy, he carried the sense of British justice and a square deal, because his sympathy was unmixed, and he believed the Indian had rights as well as the white man, … the Mounted Police will live in the History of Western Canada. (432)

MacRae's final chapter, "Progress and Development of the Province of Alberta," contains a compilation of statistics that show the remarkable growth in population, but especially in material progress since 1905—"in factories, mines, farms, and transportation" (466). However, in keeping with his romantic approach to history, he is equally intent on noting the "spiritual growth" of the province, "from the history of man subduing the earth to the History of the Church, and the Missionaries subduing man to the Kingdom" (468). He praises the work of the missionaries among the Native population and of the churches for bringing civility to the province. "The Canadian West," he concludes, "has been saved the deterioration and destruction of a crass materialism by the service of the Christian Church" (469). It is an appropriate conclusion to a history that emphasizes the humanizing aspect of Alberta's past, especially with regards to its Native population.

MacRae's history does not adhere to what we today judge history to be. Often it is little more than a compilation of facts and verbatim reports, with limited attempts at analysis or interpretation. As well, he does not acknowledge his sources. Still, the strength of his history lies in the comprehensive treatment of the early fur trade era, and especially of the Native population, albeit from an overly positive perspective. Also, it is valuable to have many of the reports and written accounts of the early "players" in Alberta's history available in one source. Being the first overall history of the province, it is impressive in the topics he covers, and the insights he provides to the people and events that together constituted the history of the province to that point in time.

Alberta's Past and Present

John Blue's three-volume *Alberta's Past and Present* contains similarities to MacRae's in terms of approach, but also differences in interpretation. Only three-quarters of the first volume is historical, the remainder of the volume plus volumes two and three are biographical, with many of the entries being individuals who also appeared in MacRae's volume. Blue also begins with European exploration as did MacRae. Here the similarities end. Blue does not romanticize the past and the Native people. He presents a forward-looking Whiggish approach to history with the golden age in the present not the past. Blue provides an unusual periodization of Alberta's history. He writes: "The first period will cover the early explorations and rule of the Fur Traders. The second period concerns rival fur companies, the Selkirk Purchase, etc.—1811-1821. The third period, which in many ways is the most wonderful of all, deals with the events since 1821—tells the story of the marvelous transformation of the Great Lone Land into the rich and populous Alberta of today" (Blue v). What historians today emphasize as a critical turning point in western Canadian history—the Canadian takeover of the region by the Canadian government in 1870—Blue incorporates into the section dealing with the rule of the Hudson's Bay Company (HBC) after 1821. He does so because he believes that the consolidation of the North West under the HBC and the influx of people into the region during the period 1840 to 1870 prepared the way for its incorporation into Confederation. Blue is clearly most anxious to deal with the third period and sees the first two as only preliminary acts to the final glorious moment when Alberta came into its own. Sections One and Two contain only four chapters (seventy-five pages in total). In Section Three, which covers all of Alberta's history since 1821, he devotes an entire chapter to George Simpson, the governor of HBC, and a chapter on early European explorers and travelers prior to 1870. He sees both Simpson and Lord Selkirk (the founder of the Red River colony) as "visionaries" in preparing the region for a Canadian takeover and large-scale settlement. These two chapters make up an additional twenty pages on the pre-1870 period. Thus all of the history of the region that constitutes Alberta up until the incorporation of the North West into Confederation, Blue tells in less than one hundred pages of a 425-page history. In contrast, MacRae devoted 240 out of 460 pages to the same period.

As noted earlier, Blue's objective in his history was to show ways in which Alberta has always been intricately associated with Canada. He emphasizes how Albertans achieved responsible government, and the importance of that accomplishment for the cultivation of civic citizens. He also dwells at length on how Alberta was integrated into Canadian Confederation, thus making it equal to other provinces as a contributor to the greatness of Canada. Blue discusses the scientific expedition of 1857 headed by Henry Youle Hind and sponsored by the government of the Canadas while overlooking the Palliser expedition sent out by the British government at the same time. Out of the Hind expedition came the vision of a transcontinental nation that would include the North West and be tied together by the Canadian Pacific Railway (CPR). Blue sees this vision as fulfilling the work of the early explorers in the era of the HBC: "The pioneer work of [Alexander] Mackenzie and [David] Thompson was finished, and a new era was breaking over the Great Lone Land" (96).

Blue has a second objective in his history besides integrating Alberta's history with that of Canada as a whole: to chronicle the "wonderful material development" of the Province especially since 1905. In preparation for telling this "story of enthralling interest," he sketches out the contrast of past and present in his "Foreword":

Less than fifty years ago the Blackfeet and the Crees roamed the plains and camped on the sites of the principal cities of the province. They hunted the buffalo and the antelope over the unploughed acres that now comprise the farms and homesteads of half a million people. Elk and deer by thousands found shelter in the foothills and mountain passes where now scores of mining towns and villages prosper and flourish. Less than fifty years ago, there was not a mile of railway between the Red River and the Rocky Mountains. Today there are over six thousand miles of railway in the province of Alberta alone, connected with all the great transcontinental systems of Canada and the United States. The only civilized persons who had penetrated the Great Lone Land were the Hudson's Bay traders, the hunters and trappers, the missionaries and the prospectors on the way to the gold diggings of Yale and Caribou. (v)

By omission, the last sentence speaks volumes about Blue's views of the Native population, and contrasts markedly his views from those of Mac-Rae's. To Blue, the Native people were a dying race whose passing was not only inevitable but also necessary for the "story of this wonderful transformation" to take place. As well, Blue was further removed from the frontier era than MacRae, writing at a time when the Métis and First Nations people had almost become a non-entity in the public psyche.

Blue devotes a chapter to the famed NWMP. However, his approach to the Force is different than that of MacRae's. While MacRae emphasized the role of the Mounties in helping the Natives to adjust to the coming of white settlers and to their new experience at farming, Blue stresses the roles of the Mounties in maintaining a federal and Canadian presence in the region, and in incorporating the West into Confederation. "No institution ever established by the Government of Canada has more fully realised the hopes of the country than the Mounted Police" (172). The other group that Blue identifies as "playing an heroic part in laying the foundations of civilization in the Great Lone Land" and integrating the region into Canadian Confederation is the missionaries. "For the joy of bearing the message of life to the savages and the pioneers of the plains, these sainted messengers," he writes, "endured perils and privations inconceivable" (223-24).

Blue ends his history with a chapter on Alberta women. This reflects the progress women had made in achieving the franchise by 1916. He claims "Alberta women participate in a greater degree in the economic and political life of the Province than in most Provinces of Canada" (419). He attributes their success not to "militant methods, nor denunciation and accusations of men, but by measuring up to the requirements of new surroundings and new duties; and also to the generous appreciation of Alberta men who have placed the women on an absolute equality in all the responsibilities and duties of full citizenship" (419). Blue argues—in a remarkably surprising statement—that "women suffrage was never opposed by any representative body of men in the entire Province" (420); he fails to mention that male representatives in the province never proposed female suffrage until pressured to do so.

A History of Alberta

The long period between Blue's history and James G. MacGregor's *History of Alberta*, published in 1972, was due in part to general trends in the writing of Canadian history, most notably the focus on national history as already noted. It can also be attributed to the lack of research on Alberta's past. Despite the presence of the Historical Society of Alberta, few historians took an interest in the province's history. In fact, MacGregor was instrumental in reviving the fledging Society in the 1950s, while also being involved in the creation of the *Alberta Historical Review* in 1953 (renamed *Alberta History* in 1975). These important developments coincided with a dramatic increase in the number of historians working on Canadian topics as a result of the baby boom generation of the 1960s. The fruit of that productivity would not yield results until the late 1970s and the 1980s. MacGregor's history was both a result of a renewed interest in local history and an impetus for further research on Alberta's past.

MacGregor's *History of Alberta* reflects the strengths and weaknesses of popular history. On the negative side, he does not provide footnotes or a bibliography of sources used. His account is also highly anecdotal. On the positive side, he presents a readable and passionate account of Alberta's past. MacGregor's approach is, like Blue's, Whiggish, an upward projectile towards a near-perfect present. Past individuals were great and worthy of respect, even admiration, in MacGregor's eyes, but their deeds were only preparation for future successes that stand out when compared to those of the past. If, for McRae, the great "heroes" in Alberta's past were the Native people, and for Blue, the NWMP and the missionaries, then for MacGregor, it was the pioneer homesteaders. They were the "enduring settlers" who every year at harvest time continued to contribute to the province's greatness.

MacGregor devotes even less of his book on the fur trade era than his predecessors (only ninety pages compared to 240 pages for MacRae and one hundred pages for Blue). Like MacRae, MacGregor romanticizes the Native peoples in this early period. He describes them as Alberta's first ecologists "content to take [their] place in the pristine ecology without upsetting its equilibrium" (19). He envisions each as "brave, generous, daring, intelligent, and infinitely patient in the chase, ... but rarely would he submit to authority long enough to gain some distant goal" (MacGregor 24).

MacGregor is critical of the NWMP, especially the rank and file. While he notes how fortunate Canadians are to have had in their history "men of the calibre of those who headed the NWMP, selected the recruits, instilled in them their own British ideals of conduct and duties of a police force and disciplined them into the most famous police body in the world" (96-97), he stresses how inexperienced and even incompetent the rank and file members were. Their ultimate success was due not to their innate qualities that they brought from the East, but from the qualities they acquired by being in the West.

MacGregor notes the pros and cons of the Indian Treaties. On the positive side, he points out that the Treaties and the reserves "saved [the Natives] from extinction" (108). On the negative side, he admits that they were duped into signing treaties, unaware of the content. He criticizes the Canadian government for failing to fulfill their treaty obligations and promises. But he concludes that the real cause of the failure of the treaties was that "a stone-age people had no time to adjust to the ruthless new era ahead" (109). (He fails to mention that along with the "ruthless new era" came "ruthless men" intent on obliterating a race that they believed were already destined to die out.) MacGregor had sympathy for the Native people, but ultimately blamed them for their failure to embrace "progress."

The chapter following the one on Indian Treaties is entitled "White Progress to 1881." From this point on, the history of Alberta for MacGregor is the history of material growth and prosperity. Subsequent chapter titles attest to this upward projectile of progress: "Slow But Definite Progress 1885-1900"; "Boom times 1906-1914"; "The Roaring Twenties 1920-1929; "Oil Money 1947-1971." MacGregor intriguingly pinpoints the transition to this new age of progress to "three days, all following within the same week in July 1881."

> On the nineteenth, Sitting Bull surrendered to the American authorities and Canada's Sioux problem ended. The next day, five hundred miles to the northwest on their way to settle on their reserve, Crowfoot and his starving followers straggled into Fort Macleod; Canada's prairie Indians had come to the end of their freedom. Less than a week later the first CPR train to cross the new bridge over the Red River rolled into Winnipeg to initiate the new era. (113)

MacGregor's final chapter, "Abounding Material Riches," continues his upbeat account of the province's material well-being. He begins the chapter with the observation, "Though oil was scarcely the Social Credit of which Aberhart had dreamed, it was nevertheless such a good substitute that his one-time followers lost their old-time fervor" (302). Under Ernest Manning, he notes, "Alberta became a mecca to which businessmen ... could entrust their savings" (304). MacGregor does point out that with the wealth came poverty, especially among First Nations and Métis. He also expresses concern about the quick depletion of the province's resources and the pollution resulting from an overheated economy. But these were "minor" concerns, according to MacGregor, that should not distract from marveling at the province's success over the years. He ends the chapter with a reflection on the province's greatest "resource," youth, and the challenge ahead for them. They will have to choose a path at a time when there is a "perilous fork in the road" (315), MacGregor writes. The easy path is to "the dead end of material success"; the other path, more difficult and even treacherous, "holds forth the promise that along it social values will supersede mercenary motives" (315). It is a strange conclusion to a chapter—and an entire history—that focuses on and celebrates Alberta's history of material progress.

Alberta: A New History

Howard and Tamara Palmer's *Alberta: A New History* is the first authoritative history of the province. It is extensively researched, with an annotated bibliography and endnotes for each chapter, along with being analytical and well written. At the outset, the authors highlight the ways that theirs is a *new* history of Alberta. They point out that it incorporates a wealth of new research done since MacGregor's history. It presents a new perspective on the past, and it focuses on new topics not covered by previous histories, such as coal mining, organized labour, education, sports and leisure, tourism, popular culture, the arts, and women. As well, they note, it "tells the story of the creation of a new society out of the interaction among varied personalities and a myriad of economic, political, and social forces" (Palmer and Palmer x).

In their chapter on the First Nations in the fur trade, they present the current trend in historiography that depicts the First Nations as active agents rather than passive victims of the European fur traders. They point out, for example, that "the fur-trade era was a period of equality between whites and Indians, when the Indians went about their own lives. The two groups met briefly at the posts, and exchanged goods. Each received from the other what it could not produce" (19). They also provide an extensive chapter on the missionaries, a topic overlooked or dealt with only briefly in earlier histories of the province. Instead of devoting a separate chapter to the NWMP, as earlier historians did, they discuss the Force in the context of Canadian expansionism and as a means of ensuring federal government control of the region. They deal extensively with the Indian Treaties, going out of their way to present both Native and white views of the treaties at the time and in recent historiography. They see the North West Rebellion of 1885 as a significant turning point in the province's history: "it marks the end of native power" (49).

The Palmers' history of Alberta really gains momentum in dealing with the period at the turn of the twentieth century. They devote three chapters—close to one hundred pages—to the years 1896 to 1914. They deal in depth with the diverse ethnic groups that came to populate Alberta, and remind their readers that from this point on, Alberta was "an immigrant society" (76). They also see the period as forming a political culture that would prevail throughout the province's history: "one-party dominance, western alienation, agrarian unrest and a strong farmers' protest movement, metropolitan rivalry between Calgary and Edmonton, and a preoccupation with the issues of transportation and resource development" (128). They explain how this unique political culture contributed to the success of the United Farmers of Alberta (UFA) government from 1921 to 1935, and Social Credit from 1935 to 1971. In their chapter on Social Credit, they compare the party to two other "populist" parties of the time, the Co-operative Commonwealth Federation (CCF) and the UFA, in an effort to explain why the latter two parties succumbed to Social Credit (277-80).

In their chapter on "Boom and Bust: The Lougheed Years and After," the authors focus on federal-provincial tensions, particularly while Pierre Trudeau was prime minister. Many Albertans, they point out, saw the actions of the federal government, particularly the National Energy Policy, as an attempt to take control of the province's natural resources. They note that such policies resulted in the rise of western alienation, manifested in the formation of a series of small right-wing separatist parties. They attribute Lougheed's success to being "pragmatic, a good organizer, a team builder, and a tough negotiator" (349).

They end their history on an optimistic note: "Despite the uncertainty of their economic prospects, Albertans face the future with pride in their past achievements. Alberta's relative prosperity, its diverse and enterprising population, vast wilderness and resources, and its natural beauty all combine to suggest much potential for the twenty-first century" (370). While such a conclusion belies the tensions of the time, it does rightly suggest reasons why Albertans could be optimistic about the future.

Mavericks: An Incorrigible History of Alberta

Aritha van Herk's *Mavericks: An Incorrigible History of Alberta* is a highly readable, engaging and informative history of the province. The book title tells a great deal: it is a history of individuals who do not fit the mainstream, who are on the margin, and who are fiercely independent. She argues that Alberta has produced its share of "incorrigible mavericks"; indeed, she sees this as the trademark of the province. Van Herk is her own "incorrigible maverick," going against the mainstream history of the province to find idiosyncratic characteristics or the "dark side" of individuals that do not appear in earlier histories of the province. She reminds readers that "history is about what we keep; its secret story is about what is lost" (van Herk xi). Her objective is to discover "what is lost" and what to her is the more interesting aspect of the province's history.

Given that *Mavericks* is written from her own perspective, she is very much a part of that history. Each chapter begins with a personal experience or reminiscence that sets the stage for the topic she discusses. These evocations link the past to the present and make her account of the past personable. As well, she interjects her own views and opinions throughout the text. One should not, however, get the impression that her history is only of her own making. She has consulted the primary sources and shows a knowledge of the major secondary sources. What she does is to "embellish" the facts and at times to stretch their credibility so as to make her history entertaining.

What has made Albertans mavericks, van Herk argues, is their constant fight against outsiders—"the Centre"—the latter threatening their security, their sense of themselves, and their freedom to be who they are. If there is one weakness in her book, it lies in her nebulous reference to what constitutes "the Centre." It appears at times to refer to the elite in the province of Ontario, but at other times to all Ontarians. In other instances, it refers to what we would call central Canada (Ontario and Quebec). In other contexts, it refers to Ottawa and the politicians and mandarins in the federal government. More generally she uses the term to identify anyone who challenges, criticizes, or simply fails to understand or stands in the way of Albertans doing what they want. In many respects, the term serves as a "scapegoat" for blaming others for unfulfilled hopes or aspirations of Albertans.

She writes an entertaining chapter on the fur traders, which focuses on Anthony Henday, Peter Pond, Alexander Mackenzie, David Thompson, George Simpson, and John Rowland. Her summation of Pond is indicative of her imaginative and lively account of these individuals:

> He never wrote a word about that remote country. What we know about him is mostly second-hand, derived from the journals and writings of his contemporaries, especially his young apprentice, Alexander Mackenzie. And yet it seems a fitting harbinger for Europeans in the area that would become Alberta. An American and a murderer who drew a map that misled more than a few people, he fits right into the tradition of this province, long before anyone could have predicted the maverick place it would become. (42)

She discusses the First Nations in the context of the fur trade as opposed to examining their way of life prior to the coming of the Europeans. She brings her account up to the late nineteenth century, discussing the trials and tribulations they experienced as they were forced to transition from fur trading to farming. She ends the chapter with the reminder: "The Alberta Advantage is advantageous for only a few" (108).

Van Herk romanticizes two groups in her history: the NWMP and ranchers. In regards to the Mounties, she notes how this imperialistic force, created by the Centre, came ironically to be one of the great symbols of pride and joy for western Canadians, including Albertans. As for ranchers, she captures the nostalgia for the ranching era in her conclusion to the chapter in which she deals with ranching:

> The great ranching era lasted only briefly, but that time still sounds ghostly hoof beats in small-town rodeos, in the dust of summer roundups, in the slow loll of grazing cattle scattered over sage-grass hills within sight of the serrated Rockies. Alberta is still, between that old world and this, a wide-open rangeland. (180)

She overlooks the fact that ranching is another Centre-dominated enterprise with many of the owners of western ranches coming from Canada. Senator Matthew Cochrane is a prime example. Both Mounties and ranchers have been designated in contemporary public discourse as essential elements of identity in southern Alberta, thus contributing to the book's popularity.

Van Herk provides an insightful chapter on Alberta's fight to become a province. The great hero is the one who lost: Frederick Haultain, thus reinforcing her image of westerners as those who have consistently had to fight the Centre to get what they wanted and have frequently lost. In the case of Haultain, he wanted Saskatchewan and Alberta to be one big province—big enough to challenge Ontario—but got two. He wanted this province to be called "Buffalo," a more exotic name than Alberta and Saskatchewan; he wanted non-partisan politics, and got party politics with a vengeance; he wanted greater local government control, including control over their own land and resources, but was thwarted by Ottawa; he wanted only non-sectarian schools but got separate schools. In the end, Haultain was not even invited to the ceremonies that brought the two new provinces into existence. Van Herk is right that Haultain has never got his due recognition for the province of Alberta—at least not until she demonstrates his importance in her history.

Her last three chapters consist of freewheeling discussions of prominent Albertans who do not fit into earlier chapters. In Chapter Twelve:

"Bread and Circuses, Culture and Bigotry," she deals with sports and cultural figures who have made a name for themselves inside and outside Alberta. She then offsets these famed people with a discussion of the Centre's image of Alberta as "redneck, intolerant and racist, conservative and neo-Christian, suspicious of anything new, home of white supremacists, gun lovers, and not a few book-banning school boards" (341). While she does not deny that there is some truth to the stereotype, she reminds readers that, "Unstable, eccentric, susceptible to unpredictable fluctuations in opinion and moment, Alberta rides a bucking bronco, sometimes called pluralism, sometimes called grassroots, sometimes called populism, and sometimes called downright mean and ornery" (349).

Chapter Thirteen: Ladies, Women and Broads" is devoted to spirited women in Alberta's history, both "respectable" and "disrespectable." Well researched and well written, the chapter covers Native women, women reformers, and prostitutes. She is especially good at dealing with the "Famous Five"—Nellie McClung, Louise McKinney, Henrietta Muir Edwards, Emily Murphy, and Irene Parlby—who fought to have women recognized as persons, and thus eligible to be appointed to the Senate. But ultimately, she notes, it was a fight for equality. They persevered through three judicial levels to win their case on 18 October 1929. This case fits van Herk's theme of Albertans against Ottawa, except this time Alberta won.

Her final chapter is, as the title "Buffalo and Beaver, Bluster and Blood" indicates, a series of issues of interest that could not be included in earlier chapters. These issues are presented in alphabetical order, and thus in random fashion rather than in a historical continuum. She begins with "Beaver, Buffalo, Bears," all animals associated with the early fur trade era, and ends, appropriately, with "Western Alienation," a theme very much at the heart of *Mavericks*. To show this to be so, she begins her discussion of western alienation with the following reminder: "Just to be repetitious, alienation is a habit we've developed into an art, a sport, a way of making Ottawa nervous." She ends by giving another twist to the popular Alberta government's slogan: The Alberta Advantage. It is, she claims, "that we know more about the rest of Canada than they know about us. And as for what the Centre thinks it knows about Alberta ... well, beware the smoke and mirrors. The emblem of our province is the prickly wild rose, a hardy fenceline thorn, pretty and tough—just like Alberta" (405).

Alberta Formed—Alberta Transformed

Michael Payne, Donald Wetherell, and Catherine Cavanaugh are the editors of, and contributors to, a two-volume collection of historical essays, entitled *Alberta Formed—Alberta Transformed*, published for Alberta's centennial in 2005. Thirteen of the essays (over three hundred and fifty pages) are devoted to the pre-1905 period and sixteen (over four hundred pages) to the post-1905 period, thus giving almost equal treatment to both periods. The editors emphasize this is not a history of Alberta in the conventional sense. Rather, they assigned to each author a year or brief time period in Alberta's history—dating back to pre-historic times— to show its significance in the province's history. Obviously, it is impossible to review all the essays. Instead, I will discuss the two-volume history from a reflective summation article by the three editors, entitled "Looking Back on Alberta History: Reflections in a Rear-View Mirror" (2006), that deals with themes, topics, and reflections in the preceding essays. The subtitle comes from an observation by Marshall McLuhan, the guru of communication technology and a native of Alberta, that "we look at the present through a rear-view mirror. We march backwards into the future" (Payne et al. 770).

The authors note three periods of significant change in the province's history: "a period before the mid-1700s, another from about 1750 to about 1870, and a third from 1870 to the present" (770), a fairly conventional division. The importance and nature of the first period are the least studied and little known, but what is emerging, they point out, is how connected the First Nations were to places and events beyond their own domain. New technologies, for example, "the different ways that stone tools were shaped" (770), were borrowed from other places or brought into the region with new inhabitants; the same was true of cultural practices, as archeologists and ethnologists unveil beliefs inherited from elsewhere but modified for local conditions. In the second period, from the mid-eighteenth century to 1870, fur trading connected Natives in the area of present-day Alberta to other tribes outside their domain, and eventually put them into contact with European fur traders. The authors emphasize that the connections prevailed because they benefitted both parties.

The annexation of the North West by Canada in 1870 began the third major period of change. It was marked by imperial ambitions on the part of the Canadian government to control the region politically, militarily, and economically. The authors note that the very name of the province indicates how English Canada saw the West as its preserve. Here, too, outside events and individuals have shaped the province's history—"two world wars, the economic collapse of the 1930s, the vagaries of world markets for wheat and oil and, among others, the evolution of the Canadian constitution—originated outside of the province" (774). The authors raise the question as to who constitutes an "Albertan" if, from earliest times, all Albertans have come from elsewhere? They note that in the late nineteenth and early twentieth centuries, the dominant Anglo-Canadian male population began to exclude certain individuals from basic rights, such groups as the First Nations, Métis, French Canadians, ethnics, and even women. The authors conclude that the challenge of the future will be to recognize and embrace the province's diversity.

Summing up the Surveys

The six histories of Alberta range in publication dates from 1912 to 2006. Each one is unique in its approach and emphasis. Archibald MacRae's is a romantic account, looking back with admiration on the First Nations. John Blue's is Whiggish in approach, with emphasis on the material progress of the province. He emphasizes the important role that the NWMP and the missionaries played in integrating Alberta into Confederation. James MacGregor sees farmers as the enduring settlers who have been the mainstay of the province. His approach is also Whiggish, focusing on the material prosperity of the post-Second World War period. Howard and Tamara Palmer note the importance of ethnic immigrants who helped create a diversified province. They also shed light on the peculiar political culture of the province. Aritha van Herk unearths the "mavericks" in Alberta's history and brings them to life in her lively and engaging history. Her "hero" is Frederick Haultain, who fought the Centre courageously if unsuccessfully. Michael Payne, Donald Wetherell, and Catherine Cavanaugh's edited volume for the 2005 centennial emphasizes the province's contact to the outside world throughout its history, which has contributed to the province's diversity.

The challenge in writing a provincial history is to emphasize the province's uniqueness while showing how it is part of a larger history, be it regional, national, continental, or global. In the case of Alberta, its history has been intricately tied up with the region of the Prairie West and after 1870, with the Canadian nation-state. In the mid-twentieth century, continental and global forces have also played a significant role. The province's history can only be seen as unique by showing how its response to national, continental, or global forces is different than that of other provinces. While Alberta since 1905 has had its own unique politics, the general nature of its resource economy and its cultural values has not been that different than other provinces. As well, standard themes of "progress" or "diversity" do not set the province apart. These themes can be found in the history of most of the provinces.

The one history that has set the province apart from the others is Aritha van Herk's *Mavericks*. This unique theme, along with her engaging writing style, has made her book a bestseller, at least in Alberta. But she distorts by exaggeration the province's uniqueness, and fails to show how the province has been part of a broader history beyond its own provincial borders. It is a garrison-type of history, looking inward, rejecting outside forces as threats to the province's identity. The implication of her thesis is that Alberta's history has been shaped only from within and only by rejecting all attempts to be part of a larger regional, national, or international history. The challenge ahead for historians of Alberta is to find a theme that both speaks to the uniqueness of the province while being able to be true to the fact that the province's history has been shaped as much by outside forces as from within.

Historiography is a branch of intellectual history. It is an attempt to examine the beliefs and values of earlier periods in history by looking at the view of historians themselves. Historiography in essence turns the historian's role of examining the ideas of individuals, groups, or eras in the past on the historian herself or himself by revealing her or his biases. While historians aspire to be objective and impartial, they are nevertheless a product of their times. With regards to the six histories discussed, all six were written in "good times" in the province's history. Archibald MacRae wrote his history in the "boom period" that lasted from 1896 to 1914. This period saw the largest influx of immigrants of any period in the province's history. This was also the "golden age" when Alberta achieved provincial status, and had a booming economy. John Blue's history was written during the "booming twenties." His history would no doubt have had a different ending if it had been written in the "dirty thirties." James MacGregor's history followed the celebration of Canada's centennial year. Alberta glowed in the glory of the event as much as all the other provinces. The oil boom was on, and the provincial economy looked rosy. Aritha van Herk's *Mavericks* and the collected work, *Alberta Formed - Alberta Transformed* were written around the time of the province's centennial. While the authors admit to trials and tribulations in the past, they celebrate the province's success at not only "surviving," but also thriving.

WORKS CITED

Blue, John. *Alberta: Past and Present: Historical and Biographical.* Pioneer Historical Publishing Co., 1924.

Careless, J.M.S. "'Limited Identities' in Canada." *Canadian Historical Review*, vol. 50, Mar. 1969, pp. 1-10.

Cook, Ramsay. "Canadian Historical Writing." *Scholarship in Canada, 1967: Achievement and Outlook*, edited by R.H. Hubbard, U of Toronto P, 1968, pp. 71-81.

Historical Society of Alberta, www.albertahistory.org/calgary. Accessed 17 Mar. 2013.

MacGregor, James G. *A History of* Alberta. Hurtig Publishers, 1972.

MacRae, Archibald Oswald. *History of the Province of Alberta.* The Western Canada History Co., 1912.

Palmer, Howard, and Tamara Palmer. *Alberta: A New History.* Hurtig Publishers, 1990.

Payne, Michael, et al., editors. "Looking Back on Alberta History: Reflections in a Rear-View Mirror." *Alberta Formed - Alberta Transformed*, edited by Payne et al., U of Alberta P / U of Calgary P, 2006.

Van Herk, Aritha. *Mavericks: An Incorrigible History.* Viking, 2001.

Fin de Siècle Lunacy in Fred Stenson's The Great Karoo

Donna Coates

The Alberta-born-and-raised writer Fred Stenson has produced seventeen works of fiction and non-fiction, numerous magazine articles, and an astonishing 140 scripts for film and video, but it is his recent historical fiction that has garnered the most praise. *The Trade* (2000), set against the backdrop of the fur trade, was nominated for the Giller Prize, and *Lightning* (2003), about the open-range ranch era in late-nineteenth-century Alberta, was also critically acclaimed. *The Great Karoo* (2008), which follows the young men from Alberta towns such as Pincher Creek, Fort Macleod, and High River who enlisted in the 1899-1902 South African War (formerly known as the Second Boer War but renamed to acknowledge that all South Africans, white and black, were affected by the war and that many participated), the only one of his works to combine the genre of war literature with historical fiction, was nominated for both the Governor General's Literary Award for Fiction and the Commonwealth Writers' Prize (Canada and Caribbean region). *Lighting* and The *Great Karoo* are loosely connected: the latter's central character, the Métis cowboy Frank Adams, is the son of *Lightning*'s Alberta rancher Jim Adams and godson and friend of Doc Windham, a Texas friend of his father's whose life lessons Frank occasionally reflects upon during his wartime experiences. Both the first and the last novels share commonalities as well: in *The Trade*, as Stenson tells Herb Wyile, he had "the luxury of creating fiction out of historical materials that had not been heavily fictionalized" (217); to my knowledge, Stenson is the first to fictionalize Canadian participation in the South African War. *The*

Great Karoo signals a departure, however; in spite of Stenson's declaration that he is a "deeply regional" writer ("Fred"), much of the action takes place in faraway South Africa, with brief episodes occurring in Alberta, England, and Ireland. But as Frank puts it, most books about the Boer War "don't contain the feeling of being there. Mostly they're just place names and dates and how many got killed, and who won a DSO or a Victoria Cross" (Stenson, *The Great Karoo* 585). They also omit references to Canadian participation. Stenson's richly detailed descriptions of the ever-changing terrain, which he acquired through a month's journey through South Africa, create for his readers a visceral sense that we are either right in the saddle with the cowboy-soldiers from Alberta, or walking alongside Frank when his horse is stolen or lost and he must serve as a "pedestrian."

When asked about what he was "exploring" in *The Great Karoo*, Stenson replied that his subject was war, which is

> humankind's greatest conundrum. Every day, somewhere, it takes lives and devastates lives. As a species, we keep demonstrating genius in countless ways, but cannot seem to make the slightest headway on this most basic of our problems. We cannot seem to find a different way to negotiate our difference as tribes and nations. With this set of beliefs, it was perhaps inevitable that I would write a novel about war. What causes wars? Why do people accept them in the moment when there is a choice? What is it about being a young man that makes war so attractive? ("Fred")

While these are some of the questions Stenson attempts to answer in his novel, I want to address two other intriguing questions which he posed during an interview with Claire Young: why are Albertans "different" and "in some cases … what right do they have to be different?" (E6).

Regional variation provides a partial response. As historian Carman Miller points out, of the "7,368 young Canadians [who] had served with the British Army in South Africa" ("Heroes" 171), those raised in central and eastern Canada consisted of "a number of university students, teachers, lawyers, engineers, and sons of notables" (172-73), whereas the "contingent from western Canada contained large numbers of cowboys, ranchers, farm labourers, packers, prospectors, and policemen, many of them British born" (173). Stenson's novel reflects Miller's description of the social composition of the troops, as the novel is narrated primarily in third-person by one of his few fictional characters, Pincher Creek's cowboy Frank Adams, who enlists with the Canadian Mounted Rifles (CMR) near the end of 1899. Two others who sign up at the same time and become his friends are also cowboys—the Fort Macleod-born Métis Jeff Davis, who grew up on the Blood Reserve with his siblings and mother Revenge Walker; and Ovide Smith, an enigmatic thirty-nine-year old from St. Flavie, Quebec, who now lives at the South Fork of the Old Man River. Although the class distinctions between those from the West and East are often unfounded, they continue to rankle throughout the war, as the Rifles grumble that British officers regard them as "motley prairie gophers" but consider the eastern Canadian Dragoons "fair-haired boys" (Stenson, *The Great Karoo* 273). Although his manly stance changes as the war grinds on, after his first battle, Frank is gratified to learn that one of the Dragoons has shot himself "rather than face battle" (158), whereas the Rifles he fights with knew "they were not cowards … they could face enemy fire" (161). Age-old rivalry between the West and East has also played a role in recruitment: Pincher Creek's fervently patriotic Fred Morden calls it an "outrage" that the first thousand troops sent to South Africa were "infantrymen from eastern militia" (12) and demands Albertans' right to fight.

Another way of finding answers to these questions in this "great whacking novel" ("Fred"), which spans five decades, three continents, includes references to Rudyard Kipling, Winston Churchill, Cecil Rhodes, the Australians Banjo Paterson and Breaker Morant, and offers cameo roles to John McCrae, Sam Steele, and Robert Baden-Powell, among others, is to pay close attention to the two seemingly unrelated Prologues, both of which are tied to specific historical events. "*Prologue* (I), FORT MACLEOD, *March 16, 1897*," describes the death by hanging of Charcoal,[1] an aboriginal man who murdered Sergeant Wilde, a Mountie (Stenson, *The Great Karoo* 2). Later in the novel, Frank reveals that Charcoal had first killed a member of his tribe for having an affair with his wife. But had Charcoal been caught by the authorities before he killed the Mountie, he would not have been found guilty since adultery "was considered justified" (116). Thus Charcoal dies on the scaffold only because he "had not been caught soon enough" (116). Significantly, as Sidney L. Harring points out, under the type of tribal law enforcement "predominant in intra-Indian affairs" in the late 1800s (245), Charcoal had "substantial support [from his tribe] and successfully evaded capture for months" (245), but the North West Mounted Police (NWMP) had put "massive resources" into lengthy manhunts "to make the point that individual Indians should expect to be dealt with severely by crown authorities if they chose to kill settlers or to defy Canadian law" (245). Harring further observes (although in the context of the alarming numbers of hangings in British Columbia at the time) that "public hangings were symbolic displays of state power. The mode of execution was intended to have maximum impact on the people who watched it. ... [T]hose who were hanged most often died by strangulation, after kicking around on the end of a rope for twenty minutes or more, losing control of bodily functions, bleeding, and making horrible noises" (207). While Charcoal's death comes about through this same disturbing "mode of execution," perhaps equally upsetting (or is to me) is that so many of the local townspeople see fit to attend "the necktie party": they include "Indians" accompanied by children whose "starved bodies" resembled "little cadavers"[2] (Stenson, *The Great Karoo* 2), as well as those from neighbouring communities like Frank and his father. At the end of the prologue, the somewhat ambiguous words of an old man, who remarks that "dey" have hung "da last wild Indian today" (4), and then wonders "what dey'll ever do now" (4), infer that the native population is dwindling.

The text offers additional reasons for that shrinking population. According to Red Crow, "*Chief of the Blood Tribe of the Blackfoot Confederacy of Indians*" (341), his people are "dying steadily, taken off by 'the blood-spitting sickness'" (342). Red Crow (also Revenge Walker's brother) fears that the Bloods "must die out, just like the buffalo" (342), and then expresses his guilt that he is unable to "lead his people away from the source of their death" (342). Every spring, he declares, there are "fewer of us" (26). But Red Crow further adds that the government absolves itself of all responsibility: the new deputy from the Indian office "said its cause was Indians living too close together in their houses and spitting on the floor" (170). Another reason, as Stenson recently pointed out, is that "the buffalo were few; liquor and disease had all but destroyed Blackfoot power" ("Wisdom" 61), a set of circumstances Red Crow has himself contributed to, as for some time he had traded furs/buffalo for whisky (*The Great Karoo* 27-28). Once he became an elder, however, "he invited the mounted police in and assisted them in destroying the whisky trade" ("Wisdom" 61).

Another character in the novel, the American-born Donald Watson Davis (Jeff Davis's father), who left the military in the United States to become a whisky trader in Western Canada, also added to native people's addiction to the white man's liquor and their concomitant loss of power. But unlike Red Crow, Davis remains self-serving: in order to "shake off the competition that was gathering" (*The Great Karoo* 29) in the trade, he married Revenge Walker, who came from a powerful family, but then divorced her and married a school teacher before he ran (twice successfully) for election as a Member of Parliament.

These examples of prejudicial thinking, behaviour, and actions attest to the fact that Western Canada was, at the time, deeply racist. It is Jeff Davis who bears the brunt of the racial slurs, which begin in the text with his attempt to enlist in the war under the command of the British-born Lieutenant-Colonel Herchmer. Herchmer demands that a telegram be sent to Ottawa to ascertain whether or not "halfbreeds" could sign up, and receives the reply, only if "intelligent" (21). Davis's acumen is rarely called into question thereafter, as over the course of the war he proves to be a highly skilled scout who draws upon the warrior techniques Red Crow taught him to outfox his enemies, although some continue to doubt the patriotism of a "Halfbreed" (336). (By contrast, Frank Adams, also Métis, is never the victim of prejudice because he has inherited his father's sand-coloured hair and pale complexion.) Most of the denigrating comments about Jeff come from the CMR's despicable American-born Pete Belton. "Raised to hate Indians" (138), Belton consistently blames Davis for anything that goes wrong and also falsely accuses him of "cowardice" (41). But the extent of the prejudice in Western Canada is nevertheless underscored when even the decent and good Fred Morden, who erroneously blames Davis for the death of his horse, calls him a "stupid Halfbreed bastard" (62). That Jeff reacts "as though he'd been expecting the words" (62) confirms that he has grown accustomed to the frequency of such invectives.

Stenson's second prologue develops another key aspect of the Albertans' difference in attitudes to war by accentuating that even though the Rifles, who stemmed from a non-militaristic (although not non-violent) region of the country, were nonetheless better equipped to defend the British Empire than British soldiers. In spite of the useless training the CMR receive in Regina (these episodes are among the novel's funniest), those from the West prove to be, as Miller notes, "fearless, versatile rough riders"

... "comparable to a Boer Commando, somewhat indifferent to the more conventional rituals of war" ("Crucible" 86). Although the British troops make consistently poor showings, the novel emphasizes that the soldiers are not to blame because, as Stenson underscores from the outset, their efforts were consistently undermined by their leaders' military blunders, many of which he identifies in "*Prologue* (II), COLENSO, NATAL, December 16, 1899" (*The Great Karoo* 5-7). Historian David Steele records that the outcome of that battle was disastrous, with 1,200 British soldiers wounded or missing, whereas the Boers suffered only forty casualties, with eight killed (12). News of this catastrophic event reaches the home front before the Rifles set sail, but it does nothing to diminish their desire to get to South Africa before the fighting ends.

That Stenson should choose to give weight to the ineffectiveness of British command at the outset is fitting, for as military historian Geoffrey Regan asserts, "British generalship in the Second Boer War ranks, along with the Crimean War and the Gallipolli campaign, as a high point in the history of British military incompetence" (50). Similarly, psychologist Norman F. Dixon claims that "the most extraordinary thing about the events of the Boer War was that they could have occurred not only after those of the Crimean War," which he refers to as "the prototype for subsequent ineptitude" (50), "but also after the First Boer War of 1880-81" (52). Dixon expresses incredulity that even though both wars were waged "far from home," in "trying climates," and against "white races" (52), the British learned nothing from either. Stenson's novel records that the British finally won the Second Boer War only by resorting to desperate measures which killed thousands of innocent victims. As Sandra Swart observes, "from 1901 the war entered a new phase, with the Boers resorting to guerrilla tactics. The British response was to remove sources of food and shelter, implementing a devastating scorch earth policy" (*Riding* 106). General Roberts pronounced that "rebels ... should have their farms burned and their families turned out" (Stenson, *The Great Karoo* 315); "Kitchener ... added the gathering of homeless women and children into camps" and contributed to the English language by stating he was "'concentrating them' in 'concentration camps'" (340).[3] Fransjohn Pretorius notes in "The Boer Wars" that the filth and disease within the camps caused severe suffering and numerous deaths, so that "eventually 28,000 Boer women and children and at least 20,000 black people died in the camps." And as Sandra Swart notes,

"Africans' participation was on a substantial scale, with at least 100,000 in military employment on both sides, and the death toll for black combatants and refugees was between 16,000 and 20,000" (*Riding* 104). Or, as Davis divulges in a letter to Red Crow, "black people were made to work for the whites and were treated poorly, as bad or worse than white people treated Indians" (Stenson, *The Great Karoo* 172). Stenson's novel, with its frequent depiction of African blacks taking on back-breaking work in often appalling conditions, underscores that they were exploited by Brits and Boers, both of whom were equally racist and intolerant. Present throughout the text as grave-diggers, horse-handlers, or as spies, their invaluable contribution to the war effort shattered the oft-repeated claim that colonials were volunteering to fight in a "white man's war."[4] It is significant that Frank and Ovide, who are occasionally assigned to both live and work with the blacks, do so without prejudice: they get to know them by name, find them hospitable and generous in their sharing of meager supplies of food and drink, and Frank learns they are more sympathetic to his grief when Ovide dies of "bad arithmetic" than members of the CMR. (While Frank is off scouting with Jeff, Ovide becomes ill: unfortunately, he takes the advice of Eddy Belton, Pete's younger brother, and inadvertently poisons himself. The Belton brothers are thus responsible for Ovide's death.)

The text further suggests that Canadian colonials—here mostly Alberta cowboys and their officers—were largely spared from (and in some instances outright refused) any commitment to the barbarity exercised by both Boers and Brits. According to Colonel Bernd Horn, when the British government was working out the details of how the first Canadian contingent would be deployed, it informed the Canadian government that troops would be, "like all colonial contingents ... absorbed into British units and formations." But the British had failed to anticipate that "Canadians had developed a national identity and pushed for a strong, unified Canadian contingent" (Horn A11). As Miller stresses, the Canadian government's insistence "that their volunteer soldiers be placed into battalions under Canadian officers, rather than in companies and placed in British battalions as the British authorities had initially requested" ("Crucible" 86), proved advantageous: once freed from a "mindless deference to class and social distinction," officers were able to exercise "their own energy, initiative, resourcefulness and freedom from constraints" (96). These colonial officers were not the only ones on the battlefield capable of independent thought, however; the Elgin Commission of 1903 describes "the Canadians and colonial troops as 'half soldiers by their upbringing,' natural horsemen, observant scouts … whose men are trained to think for themselves" (94). Moreover, the American Lieutenant Arthur "Gat" Howard, who forms the notorious Canadian Scouts (many of whom are former CMR) later in the war, also declares that they are the "only soldiers on the British side who were a match for the Boer bitter-enders" (Stenson, *The Great Karoo* 470).[5]

The text includes numerous examples of the Rifles and their leaders' refusals to surrender to imprudent British authority. When, for example, an English Mountie from Fort Macleod informs them they are privileged to be "advance guards" who have the "honour" of "draw[ing] fire so the artillery could spot enemy guns" (150), Albertan cowboy Waldron Hank organizes a meeting where he encourages them to "be damned careful which … orders they obey" and just "try and survive" the war (200). Their survival, which often hinges on starvation, entails a willingness to take risks, though. Disregarding military command, and in full knowledge that they could face court martial or a firing squad if caught, they skillfully rope, kill, bleed, and roast sheep in order to have "full bellies" (110). Captured soon after, they learn they are "damn lucky" to have such a fine man as Pincher Creek's Lieutenant Davidson in charge; his effective pleading of their case means they will escape punishment. While Frank observes that British army officers refuse to give men what they "crave" (67), Davidson is the kind of leader who "like[s] to do what his men want" (138). Although Davidson warns his subordinates that a Tommy had been "court-martialled" (147) for stealing a chicken, he merely "look[s] elsewhere" (147) when, by necessity, the Rifles go rustling again.

Throughout the text, Canadian officers (especially those from the West), prove superior in numerous ways to their British counterparts, in part because they tend to be relatively young in a field crowded with elderly officers who, like Colonel Herchmer, are "tyrant[s]," often found "staggering; cursing wildly; and forgetting what [they were] about to say" (178), and so bound by adherence to decades of military rule that they lack judgment. As Regan argues, the failure of the sixty-eight-year-old Lord Frederick S. Roberts to defeat farmer-enemies he outnumbered by a hundred to one could also be blamed on age, because "It is a problem of any system which depends on promotion by seniority rather than merit that men can achieve positions of considerable power and responsibility at an age when their faculties are no longer as effective as they once were" (38).[6] Another aspect of military conduct which underscores the westerners' common-sense approach lies in their disdain for unyielding military discipline. Unlike the British, who insist upon stringent punishment for slight misdemeanour, the Albertans readily dismiss minor infractions. When the British threaten to shoot a Rifle who has fallen asleep during battle, the Fort Macleod officer in charge of his sentencing simply says, "Don't waste [my] time" (Stenson, *The Great Karoo* 199). Under their Canadian leaders, the Rifles are freed from the British officers' absurd imposition of military ritual which forces men to attend daily drills when seasick (56); to move equipment about needlessly (77); to attend church parades in the blazing sun while suffering sunstroke (94); or to spit-and-polish boots that within minutes are filthy from marching in the mud (441). Similarly, at the Canadian Scouts' camp under Howard's command, when there is no fighting to be done, idleness prevails (441).

Davidson further demonstrates his strengths as a leader either by disregarding British officers' foolish orders which threaten to place his men in jeopardy or, on occasion, in typical Canadian fashion, striking a compromise. He also adopts the unusual tactic (by British standards) of informing his men how various combat tactics have worked (or not) on the battlefield. Unlike his British counterparts, whose worst shortcoming some historians regard "an underestimation, sometimes bordering on the arrogant, of the enemy" (Dixon 67), Davidson admires the Boers' skills and attempts to formulate his own adroit deceptions which emulate their skills and determination (Stenson, *The Great Karoo* 239). Colonel Evans, another capable Canadian officer assigned to lead the CMR, also acknowledges the Boers are as smart and "by no means defeated" (153-54) as consistently rumoured to be and, like Davidson, apprises his men of his plan to win the next skirmish (153). Evans also takes the hitherto unheard-of approach of notifying the CMR about the nature of their missions and destinations, a practice so unfamiliar to the men that it takes them completely by surprise. Davidson is also the rare leader who utilizes his men's strengths (particularly Davis' scouting abilities) and, aware of Ovide's and Frank's competence with horses, often assigns them horse detail. Unlike many British commanders, Davidson is neither vindictive nor malicious (262).

Davidson's greatest strength as leader, however, lies in his deep concern for the well-being of his subalterns, which again runs counter to British command. As Dixon writes, one of the great failings of British officers was their "apparent imperviousness ... to loss of life and human suffering amongst their rank and file" (67) or, as Frank cynically puts it after being ordered to play his part in what he knows will be more bureaucratic bungling, "Throw some soldiers on the fire. Show these Boer farmers what mad bravery Britain could summon from the ends of the earth" (Stenson, *The Great Karoo* 194). By contrast, Davidson is utterly overcome with grief when Albertans Fred Morden and Robert Kerr are both killed in action and so wracked with guilt over having convinced them to enlist by claiming "Britain's interests were their own" (244), that he makes a passionate speech to the CMR praising Morden's bravery and writes letters to General Hutton and the people of Pincher Creek demanding they not ignore "the dead men's heroism" (254). By describing in detail the proficiency and consideration of officers Davidson and Evans in his novel, Stenson draws comparison to Joseph Boyden's depiction of the Canadian officers Sergeant McCann and Lieutenant Thompson in his Great War novel *Three Day Road* (2005). Both stress that young and inexperienced Canadian officers not bound by high regard for military tradition are obliged to figure out the way *this* war works, and do; both novels argue that these untested leaders ultimately put up a better fight than the senior British military commanders unable to learn from past mistakes or adapt to changing conditions, but continue to repeat practices which had never worked.

Arguably, serving under men like Davidson proves instructive to Frank. Although he reflects early in the novel that neither he nor Ovide are leaders, whereas Davis and Morden clearly are (114), he proves himself wrong when Davidson promotes him to the rank of Acting Corporal in charge of three men. Although the four initially joke about Frank's new role, seconds after Frank realizes his men are in danger, his "acting rank suddenly meant something," and he immediately issues clear, direct orders that help secure his men's survival on the battlefield (236). Months later, while serving with the Canadian Scouts, he is again promoted, this time to Corporal, with Danny from Regina and two Australians under his command. Prior to this latest advancement, Frank has often felt, like many other war-weary, disillusioned soldiers, that he has no reason to live. But when he has men who depend on him for their safety and well-being (550), he foregoes his customary heavy drinking because he is "enjoying the men under him and almost enjoying the war, and d[oes] not care to have a rum-cloudy head in the morning" (516). He also warns Davis, whose sudden inexplicably reckless behaviour often places Frank and his men in danger, that he will no longer tolerate it. In a manner reminiscent of the constructive teaching methods of Boyden's Sergeant McCann and Lieutenant Thompson, Frank patiently instructs his subordinates how to perfect the "hoolihan throw, the overhand toss where you didn't swing the rope and scare the horses" (513); how to snub and saddle horses; and how to choose suitable mounts (513). Like Davidson, Frank acquiesces to his subordinates' wishes to fight in perhaps the last battle of the war (530) because they argue he has trained them well; and redolent of Davidson's passionate concern for his men, Frank feels "sick" when he hears that a young Canadian Scout has been killed, but relieved that "this dead boy" had not been "one of his" (515). While I have argued elsewhere that Boyden's *Three Day Road* should be considered a kind of "military conduct manual" which provides an analysis of how positive interactions between superiors and their subalterns might be actuated in the context of a hierarchical relationship,[7] here, I assert that *The Great Karoo* should also be required reading for all those contemplating how men in command should behave under the appalling stresses of war.

Not long after Frank arrives in South Africa, he begins to "think" (96, 159, 197, 216) about how badly the war is organized, and about the irrational, even foolhardy way the war is being conducted. Like Boyden's Xavier, who also begins to "think" early in the war, Frank becomes critical of British army practice, particularly Lords Roberts' and Kitchener's failures to provide their men (and horses) with an adequate food and water supply. Ironically, Frank realizes that when the British should have maintained "the old way of supply—with each battalion looking after itself," a system which *had* worked well in the past, they deemed it "outmoded" and "replaced it with one big system: the smooth-functioning one that kept their army sick and hungry, and in one place" (146). This pathetically inefficient and seriously defective system leaves the men suffering through freezing nights without the aid of tents or blankets (154, 197), and hence often insures that many were often "too sick to go on. They were left coughing and with fevers for the Red Cross ambulances to find" (197). Miller's assertion that medical care was often dispensed "according to rank and title rather than need" ("Crucible" 86), also occurs in the text; Frank is sickened when he learns that Dakomi, a black African labourer he has befriended, has died because a British doctor has given priority to a major's superficial wound (Stenson, *The Great Karoo* 304). Ultimately, Frank's precise observation—that the number of men "who had died of enteric fever and dysentery" was a "much bigger number than those killed in action" (337)—leads him to conclude that there was no point in the Boers bothering to attack them because "the Field Force was taking itself apart so efficiently" (96). Frank's assessment is correct, as Thomas Pakenham documents that of the "twenty-two thousand imperial and colonial soldiers who died during the Boer War, 5,774 were killed by enemy action (or accident) and shoveled into the veld, often where they fell; 16,168 died of wounds or were killed by the action of disease (or the inaction of army doctors)" (572). Frank's increasingly assiduous study of the war also brings him to recognize, like Davidson and Evans, how truly innovative, enterprising, and creative the Boers were, particularly in terms of their use of modern weaponry when the British continued to rely on antiquated equipment.

Several Albertans prove as resourceful and inventive as the Boers, however: they are Davis, Young Sam, a Nez Perce horse wrangler from Pincher Creek whose forefathers had fought the US Cavalry, and James Whitford who is, like Frank's mother, a Montana Halfbreed. But while she had moved from Manitoba's Red River to Montana and then to the District of Alberta, Whitford's "Indian half was Crow and the rest American" (208). Frank knows that Whitford is a legend, "said to have been in the U.S. Cavalry" and rumoured to have "survived the Custer massacre" (208), though it was "broadly known that no one had" (208). Both Young Sam and Whitford scout and track for Lionel Brooke, a British remittance man turned rancher from Pincher Creek who volunteers to fight with Lord Strathcona's Horse, a private army under the command of Sam Steele, but has defected to try to hunt down (unsuccessfully) the South African Boer general, rebel leader, and politician Christiian de Wet. The exceptional abilities of Davis and Whitford in particular negate Davidson's comment earlier in the novel that "being Indian doesn't add anything" (252): it does, as even the accomplished scout Casey Callaghan, an Irish teamster from Maple Creek, Saskatchewan, consults Jeff when he requires an "expert" opinion on scouting (451). Moreover, Red Crow has trained Jeff so well to be a "good and ... useful warrior" (26), that the British General Francis William Butler is moved to remark how "remarkable" it is that "a Halfbreed in a white man's war" (340) should have achieved the rank of regimental sergeant-major.

Like Boyden's aboriginal soldiers Xavier Bird and Elijah Weesageechak, Davis and Whitford readily adapt to the harsh conditions of war. While members of the Rifles appear gaunt-faced and years older after only one month in South Africa, Jeff remains vigorous and healthy; the middle-aged Whitford is so fit that he can "run forever" (491). In spite of their lack of familiarity with the South African landscape, both Davis and Whitford are able to find food when none of the others can spot wildlife in the barren landscape; Davis also cleverly imitates the sounds of the local birds and animals. Most significantly, Davis ceases doing any "war work" during the winter because, unlike his superiors, he has studied the Boers' routines and realizes that they remain idle while waiting for spring to arrive (503). Although Davis's commanding officers often assume that his languor stems from either boredom or disinterest in their war plans, they fail to comprehend that he has simply figured out their strategies in advance (517). Jeff also proves to be an astute judge of human character. He devises a clever plan which outmanoeuvres Colonel Herchmer and forces him to rethink his foolish scheme to shoot the battalion's most valuable horses (88-89). Moreover, aware of Ovide's devotion to horses, Davis pries him from his sick bed by informing him of the horses' desperate conditions on the voyage to South Africa (56-58): both horse and human heal quickly. Like Davis, Whitford and Young Sam have carefully studied their "white masters" and cleverly mimic Brooke's snooty British accent while maligning his irrational notion that the Brits treat the Boers fairly. Both Davis and Whitford concoct brilliant—in Whitford's case humorous (496)—fictional narratives which help Frank locate Alma Kleff, the young Boer he has (foolishly) fallen in love with (315).[8] But because Frank is often a poor judge of character, he convinces himself that Jimmy is his foe and hence never acknowledges his discretion, quick-wittedness, loyalty, or intelligence. Years later, after he has been back in Pincher Creek for some time, he learns that it was Jimmy who saved not only his life, but the lives of Jeff and Danny by killing the sniper who had drawn a bead on them.

Another important aspect of the Albertans' primacy lies in their knowledge of, and passion for, horses and their corresponding revulsion for the appalling conditions they are forced to endure. As Swart observes, horses imported to foreign soil had to contend with numerous problems, such as "eating unusual fodder, drinking too much water after hard work, a spell out in very hot or very cold weather, unfamiliar pathogens and alien plants, [that] can all lead to incapacitation and death" (*Riding* 104), and in Stenson's novel, they do. Those who brought horses from overseas were also disadvantaged because Boer mounts "had more immunity to local diseases and were usually more robust because they had not suffered the rigours of maritime transportation, which weakened these imported horses' immune systems" (Swart, "Horses" 354), and, moreover, they were ridden by "adaptable, experienced horsemen fighting in familiar environs" who thus had "greater mobility" (*Riding* 105). But Swart further acknowledges that both Boer and British sides "relied heavily on mounted troops, and the casualties suffered by these animals were on a massive scale" ("Horses" 349). On the British side, "326,073 horses ... died over the course of the war, at the rate of 66.88% of the total headcount," a figure "widely regarded as proportionally the most devastating waste of horseflesh in military history up until that time. The slaughter was actually described as a 'holocaust' by an eye-witness, Frederick Smith" (348-49). Swart further adds that "the theatre of war carried a heavy cost, with the scorched earth policy shattering the rural economy of the two Boer Republics and transforming the landscape itself" (*Riding* 104).

But whereas the British sent to the front "large, unwieldy animals" (Stenson, *The Great Karoo* 35), some, but not all, of the Albertan cowboys chose horses capable of withstanding the rigours of combat in a strange new territory. These would be, of course, Davis, Adams, Whitford, and Callaghan, who ride into war on *cayuses*, "descendants of old-time Spanish horses ... that had run wild for centuries before becoming saddle stock again" (43). Frank observes these horses "tended to do better at picking their way over rough ground. Their eyes were set better for seeing in every direction, and that kept them from falling into badger and gopher holes" (43). Frank's Dunny also sees better in the dark than Frank (460). Because their cayuses can swim, both Frank and Jeff are able to escape a "sickly camp" by offering to go scouting across a flooded river (479). Throughout the novel, Frank frequently acknowledges how strong Dunny is: while other horses quickly grow sick and weak even in the early stages of war, "she still had her flesh and her clarity and still responded to every flicker in the bush, quick ears snapping" (96). Later he observes that although other horses were "still thin and weary" (248), Dunny "was sparky and insisted on pushing ahead" (248). Frank further acknowledges that Dunny's "freakish vitality" (107) and "intelligence" (451) have more than once saved his life. Stenson's textual statistics further confirm the superiority of cayuses: "by December 1900, [only] fifty of the eight-hundred horses brought from Canada had survived" (336), and by July 1900, only six remain (253). Among them are Frank's Dunny, Jeff's Blue, and Casey's General. (The text infers that had Dunny not been stolen but remained under Frank's care for the duration of the war, she might have, like Jeff's Blue, arrived back in Halifax at war's end "fatter and sassier than ever" [587].)

But while the Albertans know their way around horses, the Canadian government has no idea how to transport them safely to Halifax by train or to Cape Town by boat. British horses transported to South Africa fared no better, however, because according to Swart, the military did not know how to convey them to South Africa effectively and efficiently, either. While Swart suggests that no one on the British ships "had any veterinary experience" (*Riding* 109) and adds that the Army Veterinary Department (AVD) was "widely damned as inadequate in dealing with equine casualties" ("Horses" 349), both veterinarian Staff Sergeant Tracey and Ovide conceive imaginative ploys to help horses not only survive the journey, but to heal upon arrival: for example, they allow the horses to exercise in the sea after disembarkation so their tender feet can then be shod quickly (Stenson, *The Great Karoo* 75). But Frank, who "thinks on behalf of the horses" (90), wonders what the point of pampering them has been if, having arrived, like their British counterparts "incapacitated—dehydrated, malnourished, and their immune systems severely compromised" (Swart, "Horses" 351), they were given so little time to acclimatize or revive but were pressed into duty almost immediately.

In suggesting that Frank "thinks on behalf of the horses," Stenson leaves himself open to the accusation that, according to David Brooks, critics often raise—that it is "unwise to extend ... our feelings to the things and creatures around us, because this is to colonise them, to appropriate them for our own purposes, and so to some extent to relegate or deny them their unique essence" (52). Brooks argues, however, that if we do not ascribe human feelings to non-human animals, we then make an exclusion which "is a *violent* isolation and effacement of the very creature we are supposedly respecting" (52). Brooks further stresses that "the extension of our feelings to the things and creatures around us is the basis of empathy, and the only kind of empathy we can feel, since the actual nature of 'feelings' … of these things and creatures cannot be known to us" (52). He concludes that it would be instructive if "we saw their pain as our own" (54). Stenson's Ovide clearly feels that pain: after his mare has to be shot (when he knows she could have survived with proper rest and care), Frank observes that "Ovide's face was hard to look at. The emotions all boiled over there, and the sunken eyes were deep and glaring" (105). Moreover, "in Ovide's way of thinking, there were certain things you could not forgive. Deliberately killing a horse was chief among them" (105). But while Frank "thinks for the horses," Ovide thinks *like* a horse; he has the "ability to fool a horse's mind, to wake it from its nightmare and help it remember there was something about living that it liked" (58). To further comfort sea-sick horses on board ship, he talks, sings, gently strokes ears, lips, and noses (59). So acute is his empathy for horses that he "lacks any self at all" (52), and on occasion even "mutters" like a horse (257). When he encounters men from Lord Strathcona's Horse in Cape Town, he asks after the well-being of the Albertan horses, not the local inhabitants (211), and later, once released from a sick bed, rushes straight to the horses (176). Although the text offers no reasons for Ovide's enlistment, it seems likely that while he might have wanted to see lots of horses and does, he has doubtlessly anticipated that war will be harder on horses than humans, and wants to help care for them, not see them die. But he is helpless to offer aid on more than one occasion. For example, one of the problems the horses encounter on the boat that transports them to war is that while they become seasick in the same way as the men, "they can't puke" (58): according to Swart, "simple indigestion [for horses] can mean death" (*Riding* 103). As they watch the horses' agony, the men suddenly consider puking "a gift from God" (Stenson, *The Great Karoo* 58). John Sorenson concurs that animals suffer differently, noting that while war is a "nightmarish" experience for humans, it is truly hell for horses:

> Horses are sensitive animals, well known for their flight reflexes, and in combat the noise, smells and explosions must have been indescribably frightening. Obviously, humans suffered greatly in these conditions but they could at least understand what was happening around them and some were able to console themselves with thoughts of patriotism, heroism, glory

and sacrifice for their nation. Horses had no such consolations but, prevented from escaping, simply had to endure the incomprehensible terrors inflicted upon them. In wartime, those animals we have forced to work for us as beasts of burden are threatened by even greater dangers than those they normally face. In all wars, animals' lives are cut short by direct violence, overwork, exhaustion, disease and starvation. (27)

As Sorenson concludes, "our assertion that nonhuman animals exist only as property has allowed us to exploit them in countless ways" (27).

Like Swart, who observes that "the war and contemporary writings helped propagate the idea of seeing and talking about the horse as an individual, with a personality and agency of its own" ("Horses" 357), Stenson, too, insists that "horses ... are characters of considerable importance" ("Fred"), their significance perhaps made more comprehensible once imbued with human characteristics. While Swart argues that "horses mattered as individuals in a way that other animals did not" (*Riding* 125), Stenson stresses that horses "are important parts of the emotional landscape" ("Fred"). Accordingly, after the deaths of Fred Morden and Robert Kerr, the Rifles seek comfort not from each other, but from their horses (*The Great Karoo* 246). Swart also attests that "the value of horses was such that their loss brought combatants to utter despair" ("Horses" 360), and for some, amounted to "their worse experience of the war" (360), a statement borne out when the theft of Dunny brings Frank to his lowest ebb. Although some of the men felt that "time would make him forget," if anything, "Frank's sense of loss was increasing and ascending into a right twist of obsession" (Stenton, *The Great Karoo* 275). When Davis eventually finds Dunny, Frank is disappointed to learn that she and The Blue have "buddied up" (447), but soon laughs when he realizes that the two mares had "planned a rendezvous" (461). Frank notes that The Blue is a jealous lover, as he gives a gelding accompanying Dunny and Frank a "warning look" (494), which leads Frank to "marvel at the unerring constancy of buddied horses. Compared to it, human relationships were fickle and qualified" (461). But the bond between horse and man is, for the Albertans, also one of absolute fidelity: some Rifles signed on for another tour of duty rather than give up their horses that "had carried them through a year of war" (336), whereas others remained to find "missing horses" or to "avenge a friend" (468). It is noteworthy that neither the despicable Pete Belton nor his slightly nicer but dumber brother Eddy ever express any genuine concern for the health or safety of horses, perhaps because, as Swart observes, "the treatment of horses was increasingly … a hallmark of civility" (*Riding* 130). Equally important is that after Ovide's death, Frank goes about his work with horses "carefully, trying to mimic Ovide" (Stenson, *The Great Karoo* 301), and vows thereafter to act out "what Ovide would have heard and done" (301).

As Swart also observes, "some Boers granted their horses almost mystical powers, feeling that they would warn them of danger ahead" (*Riding* 127), an attribute Stenson applies to his horses. On one occasion, Frank notes that "Dunny did not like the look of the bridge" ahead, and she is right because when Frank "forces her on," he sees they are in danger, as the Boers "loved what they saw: the enemy laid out like a buffet meal" (*The Great Karoo* 187). When Eddy Belton steals Dunny, Frank is offered a "ridgling," defined as "a colt whose nuts, one or both, stayed inside his body. … [R]idglings were sterile because their bodies were too hot inside to make living jism" (279). Although at first unimpressed by the ridgling, who looks "pissed off, then bored, then calm, then asleep" (281), Frank sets out to train him carefully: he talks constantly, informs the ridgling what comes next, and then once saddled, tells him stories (281). The ridgling, like Dunny, is also impressively "mystical": he anticipates an explosion which finds Frank the only survivor by "staggering around in his knee-halter, wittering" (332) and shortly after gives Frank a look which says "'Let's get the hell out of here'" (314). But in part, the ridgling remains an angry horse nonetheless: after he and Frank find shelter with a Boer family, the ridgling escapes from their barn: once returned, he looks "tired" but "pleased with himself" (370). But then, finding himself stuck back in the barn, he signals his displeasure by "kick[ing] the wall for an hour" (370). Although he clearly resents the reprimand, he remains loyal to Frank; when separated, he refuses to go north because that is not the direction Frank would take (417). (The ridgling also becomes bilingual when Jimmy Whitford, an even-better trainer than Frank, speaks to him in Cree.) That equine agency is significant becomes evident later in the novel: after the now-lame Dunny is returned to Frank, he invites her to "have her say" about the gelding he finds to replace her, but notes that Dunny seems "more disinterested than disgusted" (495); by contrast, the gelding, anxious to please, pretends "to have energy like a man applying for a job" (495). Horses also appear to be shrewd judges of character—Dunny flattens her ears whenever the reprehensible American Pete Belton passes by (265)—but they are also, like children, susceptible to affection. Dunny falls prey to Eddy Belton's "petting and nuzzling" (268), which makes it easy for him to steal Dunny away from Frank.

Stenson's suggestion that "horses are generators of the story" ("Fred") partially explains Frank's reasons for going to war. Having learned that "they could take their own horses" to South Africa (Stenson, *The Great Karoo* 12), Frank jumps at the opportunity. Like many cowboys, he does not want to be "fenced in," but to ride in "a big and fenceless prairie" the way "Alberta used to be when it was wide open and innocent of the plow. … [He] had wanted to ride on Dunny in such a place, so he could talk about it when he was old" (107). But before he confronts the harsh realities of battle, he imagines himself and the intrepid Dunny as heroes:

> On the ocean, Frank had spent many hours staring at the line that divided water from sky. In his head, he was watching himself in battle. Across the sweeps of imaginary landscape, he and Dunny galloped. They scared up fantastic birds. A herd of giraffes tall as storefronts raced away. Dunny had never been braver, or more sure-footed. Neither of them so much as flinched when Boer bullets floated by. (72)

It does not take long before he realizes that he had "outfoxed himself. Like a moose to a horse, the Great Karoo was open all right, but was nothing like Alberta would have been in that condition. Thinking that it would be like home, but a purer version, had been a dangerous mistake" (107). Years later, back in Alberta, Frank admits to his children and grandchildren that he was no "war hero" who would ever "take much of a risk to shoot a Boer" (587); during the later stages of the war he carries a pistol, but without any bullets, and does not know if he killed *one* or not. During the war, he begins to regard any act of violence, even cudgeling a sheep, abhorrent. He also admits to being frightened in battle, terrified of flooded rivers, and hence in no way resembles, as Andrea Petitt puts it, "the archetype of macho culture. The epithet 'cowboy' is often used to describe a rough, careless, daring and macho person" (67). Frank is none of the above: an often lonesome cowboy, Frank is devastated when Dunny is stolen; moved to tears when Morden treats him as a friend; feels "pangs of loss" when Davis rides away without him; and cries over the death of Ovide and the loss of Dunny.

Frank is also not the only Albertan to enlist with the concept of heroism in mind, although Davis's motives for enlistment have more to do with making love than war: as he tells Frank, he has "a girlfriend on the Blood. Her father doesn't want [him] to have her. If [he] kill[s] enough Boers, he'll change his mind" (290). But when he learns that both Red Crow and Ran After have died, he engages in "bursts of heroism" and occasionally becomes "dangerously brave" (533) by "skylining" (535) and singlehandedly engaging ten Boers in a fight. Neither Frank nor Callaghan understand Jeff's behaviour because they have failed to comprehend that Jeff's war has always been far more perilous than their own. As surrendered "white men" in Boer hands, Frank and Casey would risk losing their "tunic[s] and [their] boot[s]" (464), but Jeff would be murdered for being "black," a "nigger" (464).[9] Hence he chooses "not to be executed" (465), but "to die in some way he could accept" (533). Another of the Albertan recruits, Fred Morden has been convinced by his patriotic parents that the British Empire is a force worth dying for; having memorized Tennyson's poem, "The Charge of the Light Brigade," about the imperialist notion of heroism, Morden goes to war believing "the dream of glory (or duty) still existed" (132). Accordingly, he makes a foolish "heroic sacrifice" which, knowing he could have surrendered, angers Frank. Morden also fails to understand that gallant acts of heroism are rendered less possible as wars become increasingly mechanized and technological. Morden's sacrifice does serve a purpose, however, as it deters Morden's cherished young friend Tommy Killam from enlisting in the Second World War; instead, he declares that he wants "to live his life right here in Alberta" (584). His response, Stenson infers, should apply to all others who believe they will find honour and glory in the trenches, or who volunteer to fight in wars against enemies they know nothing about.[10]

These references to motivation for enlistment, including the notion of heroism,[11] indicate that few, if any, of the CMR or those Albertans who fought with the Canadian Scouts deserved their reputations as the "very tough desperados" (587) as the British newspapers describe them after the war. Surprisingly, Frank and Jeff, both in England at the time, are pleased with the description, perhaps because, as Amy Shaw points out, there was an "interesting focus" on recruits' "physical bodies. These men served as representatives of prescriptive [even idealized] manliness to Canadians reading about their exploits, and as foils for the images of the Boers against whom they were fighting" (97). Those who might be designated as "tough desperados" were two hard-riding, death-defying cowboys—the Australian-born Charlie Ross and the American Gat Howard—neither of whom ever saw a war they didn't like. Fighting, the thrill of adventure, the constant need to put themselves in risky situations, form the sum of their lives: significantly, neither has a home to return to. While Frank knows that "with their histories of derring-do and their Distinguished Service Orders," some soldiers "would follow them to hell and back" (Stenson, *The Great Karoo* 469), he is not one of them, in part because both had fought at the 1885 Northwest Rebellion which dispossessed his mother's family from their land. (Sam Steele had also rejected Ross's desire to fight with the CMR.) Ross, who was interrogated but never charged with encouraging the men under him to swear an oath to take no Boer prisoners (and then when captured reputedly made them dig their own graves [502]), is particularly disgraceful. While Ross is a "fanatical" Boer hatred, Frank notes that the many of the Rifles found it "hard ... to get a proper hatred going for the Boers" (102). Frank believes that Jeff has refused to burn the Kleff farm; and both he and Davis refuse to round up women and children, even though they had been warned that "fugitive women were forming laagers as they went east, well-armed and every bit as dangerous as their menfolk" (456). But in spite of these Albertan men's efforts to save lives, not destroy them, and in what are perhaps the novel's most poignant lines, Frank comprehends that "war was a kind of arithmetic that worked only by subtraction. Even in the moments of glory and achievement, there was always less than there had been before. Horses that had been alive were dead or ruined. Men who had been perfect in their young bodies were gone or reduced in some way" (527).

At war's end, both Frank and Jeff return to Alberta and use their "Boer War Scrip" (579) to purchase ranches and farms. Yet, although Jeff is known to be a highly ranked soldier, the local townspeople—one a writer named Kelly—consider him a "shiftless, unmoral, and whisky sodden Halfbreed" (588). Similarly, Whitford receives no rewards, financial or otherwise, from the Canadian government. The Americans also refuse to offer him pension monies for his service as a US Calvary Scout, it being more convenient to believe that he had been killed "*at the Battle of Little Bighorn*" (581). All that is known of Whitford is that he lives with the Cree in Hobbema, Alberta. Like the thousands of other "blacks" who devoted years of their lives to fighting in "a white man's war," he has nothing to show for it. This is what Frank notes in the brief memoir he writes in 1942 at the behest of his grandchildren on the fortieth anniversary of the ending of the Boer War, but then he promptly destroys the memoir in large part because he knows "it was a stupid war from start to finish and benefited no one but the rich. The proof is that the black people of South Africa never did get the vote, just like Indians here in Canada don't have the vote to this day" (587). Frank is right to be angry, since at the time of the Boer War, Amy Shaw records that only male British subjects in Canada could vote; excluded were women, Aboriginals, Japanese, and Chinese Canadians (99). Although women were enfranchised federally in 1918, Aboriginals did not get the vote until 1960. South African blacks did not get the vote until 1994. Stenson has remarked, however, that it is his hope both Ovide Smith and Jeff Davis "will be known and remembered now that they are part of a present-day narrative, and that southern Albertans and other Canadians will find them interesting and be proud of them" ("Fred"). We do, and we are. My hope, however, is that this is only Stenson's initial foray into the writing of war literature, not his last.

NOTES

1   For more information on Charcoal's history, see Dempsey.

2   Harring comments that the Northwest Rebellion, "which looms large in western Canadian history" (245), led to a change in NWMP/Indian relations under policies that were "cruel and unworkable" and resulted in starvation (244). The arrest and punishment of Indian offenders also rose to far higher levels by the 1880s; imprisonment became "an enormously powerful symbol of the meaning of police power" (244). Stenson's novel also hints at high rates of aboriginal incarceration.

3   This was not the first appearance of internment camps, however: both Spain and the United States had used them earlier. But as Stenson's novel indicates, the Boer War camps were the first time that entire regions were depopulated. For further information, see Tone.

4   While Frank provides the "ant's eye view" (Stenson, *The Great Karoo* 152) of the war, the Irish-born General Francis William Butler, a former Lieutenant-General of the British army who served in some of the most important British colonial wars of the

nineteenth century, offers an experienced insider's view. Butler, who traveled several times to Northwestern Canada—once to serve as intelligence officer at the 1870 Red River expedition—frequently voices in separately titled sections his increasing disillusionment with British imperialism and his condemnation of the attempts to coerce "the rebel forces to accept British democracy," when it is questionable whether "Britain had been a democracy herself" (440).

5   Howard's nickname came from his having demonstrated the effectiveness of the Gatling gun as a killing machine. Howard is one of Frank's mother's "least favourite humans" because he had fired on her relatives with a machine gun at Batoche during the "1885 Halfbreed rebellion" (Stenson, *The Great Karoo* 167).

6   Stenson strikes a balance here, however, as not all the aged are incompetent. Both Butler and Red Crow, who both view war as pointless and futile, are thus logical and wise, whereas the younger Kitchener is clearly unbalanced (65, 477); moreover, the bizarre behaviour of three other leaders—only one of whom is old—should have seen them removed from office (327-28).

7   See my "Killer Canucks."

8   Boyden's Xavier also makes a disastrous, ill-fated romantic liaison. While both soldiers expend a lot of fictional time searching for the women they have fallen in love with, Stenson's Frank offers a brief depiction of the devastating conditions of the camps, which remind him of the terrible treatment of aboriginal children in Alberta. Glimpsing a wire cage "full of Boer prisoners," Frank reflects that "not one child played in that enclosure, something Frank had seen before during a starvation spring on the Blood Reserve" (488).

9   Earlier in the novel, the Boers have killed Young Sam for being a "nigger" (464), even though Lionel Brooke, whose stupidity and selfishness are responsible for the death of Young Sam, tells them that he is "an American Indian, a Nez Perce" (464). Sadly, neither Frank nor Brooke knows how to pay their respects for Young Sam's death, since he is not a Christian (394).

10 Stenson has indicated that he finds numerous comparisons between the wars in Iraq and Afghanistan to the Boer War. Both the United States and the British Empire purported to be bringing democracy to these countries, whereas the control of resources—oil in the Middle East and gold and diamonds in South Africa—were the real reasons behind the wars ("Fred").

11 Stenson complicates the notion of heroism by including in his text the story of an officer, Colonel Hannay, who is a paragon of moral distinction. At the battle of Paardeberg, Hannay finds Kitchener's orders so absurd that he sends his men on errands rather than ordering them to face certain death. He then rides heroically into battle himself, but is shot instantly (124).

Works Cited

Boyden, Joseph. *Three Day Road*. Penguin, 2005.

Brooks, David. "The Fallacies: Theory, Saturation Capitalism and the Animal." *Southerly*, vol. 73, no. 2, 2013, pp. 47-61.

Coates, Donna. "'Killer Canucks': The Role of Aboriginal Epistemology in Joseph Boyden's Great War Novel *Three Day Road.*" *(Re-)Connecting Through Diversity: Canadian Perspectives*, edited by Jelena Novakova et al., Megatrend University / Serbian Association for Canadian Studies, 2011, pp. 23-41.

Dempsey, Hugh A. *Charcoal's World*. Prairie Books, 1978.

Dixon, Norman F. *On the Psychology of Military Incompetence*. 1976. Jonathan Cape, 1979.

"Fred Stenson on *The Great Karoo*," http://www.bookclubbuddy.com/2010/fred-stenson-on-the-great-karoo/.

Harring, Sidney L. *White Man's Law: Native People in Nineteenth-Century Canadian Jurisprudence*. U of Toronto P, 1998.

Horn, Colonel Bernd. "Into Africa." Excerpt from "Doing Canada Proud." *National Post*, 1 Feb. 2013, p. A11.

Miller, Carman. "Bringing Our Heroes Home: Resistance, Disorder, Riot, and 'Mutiny' Among Canada's South Africa Warriors." *The Apathetic and the Defiant: Case Studies of Canadian Mutiny and Disobedience, 1812-1919*, edited by Craig Leslie Mantle, Canadian Defence Academy Press / Dundurn, 2007, pp. 171-91.

———. "The Crucible of War: Canadian and British Troops During the Boer War." *The Boer War: Army, Nation, and Empire*, edited by Peter Dennis and Jeffrey Grey, Canberra, A.C.T., Army History Unit, Department of Defence, 2000, pp. 84-98.

Pakenham, Thomas. *The Boer War*. Random House, 1979.

Petitt, Andrea. "Cowboy Masculinities in Human-Animal Relations on a Cattle Ranch." *Elore*, vol. 20, no.1, 2013, pp. 67-82.

Pretorius, Franzjohan. "The Boer Wars." www.bbc.co.uk/history/british/victorians/boer_wars.01.shtml.

Regan, Geoffrey. *Someone Had Blundered. ... A Historical Survey of Military Incompetence*. Batsford, 1987.

Shaw, Amy. "The Boer War, Masculinity, and Citizenship in Canada, 1899-1902." *Contesting Bodies and Nation in Canadian History*, edited by Patrizia Gentile and Jane Nicholas, U of Toronto P, 2012, pp. 97-114.

Sorenson, John. "Animals as Vehicles of War." *Animals and War: Confronting the Military-Animal Industrial Complex*, edited by Anthony J. Nocella II et al., Lexington Books, 2014, pp. 19-31.

Steele, David. "Salisbury and the Soldiers." *The Boer War*, edited by John Gooch and Frank Cass, 2000, pp. 3-20.

Stenson, Fred. *The Great Karoo*. Anchor Canada, 2008.

———. *Lighting*. Douglas & McIntyre, 2003.

———. *The Trade*. Douglas & McIntyre, 2000.

———. "Wisdom." *Alberta Views*, May 2014, vol. 7, no. 5, p. 61.

Swart, Sandra. "Horses in the South African War, c. 1899-1902." *Society and Animals*, vol. 18, 2010, pp. 348-66.

———. *Riding High: Horses, Humans and History in South Africa*. Johannesburg, Wits UP, 2010.

Tone, John Lawrence. *War and Genocide in Cuba, 1985-1898*. U of North Carolina P, 2008.

Wyile, Herb. "History 'from the Workingman's End of the Telescope.'" Interview with Fred Stenson. *Speaking in the Past Tense: Canadian Novelists on Writing Historical Fiction*, edited by Herb Wylie, Wilfrid Laurier UP, 2006, pp. 189-217.

Young, Claire. "From Ranch to War: Novelist Stenson Explores the Motivations for Early Albertans Fighting Foreign Wars." *Calgary Herald*, 28 Sept. 2008, pp. E1, E6.

The "Father" of Ukrainian-language Fiction and Non-fiction in Alberta: Rev. Nestor Dmytrow, 1863-1925

Jars Balan

In 1897 Canada's federal Department of the Interior hired a Greek Catholic Ukrainian priest from the United States named Nestor Dmytrow[1] to tour the settlements that had been established across the Canadian West over the previous five years by Galician and Bukovynian farmers from the Austro-Hungarian Empire. His job was to report on the conditions that he found there, and to document the material progress that was being made by the settlers. At the same time, it was understood that he could provide some spiritual comfort to the immigrants, who were living in a harsh and unfamiliar environment far from their homeland without the benefit of the clerical leadership that they had been accustomed to in their native villages. Father Dmytrow began his fact-finding mission in April, starting out from Winnipeg, Manitoba, after which he visited colonies in the Dauphin and Stuartburn areas of that province. He next travelled by train to Edmonton so as to inspect the districts being homesteaded by Ukrainians outside the city, in the vicinity of the Edna (subsequently renamed Star) post office some eighty kilometres to the northeast, and around Rabbit Hill, just west of Edmonton's modern-day international airport.

As he was making these preliminary rounds, Dmytrow was penning a running account of his experiences that he was mailing back to Mount Carmel, Pennsylvania, for publication in the newspaper *Svoboda* (*Liberty*), whose editor he had been before leaving for Canada. His articles appeared in the Ukrainian-language weekly roughly three weeks after they were written, providing detailed despatches about his adventures and the situation of Western Canada's earliest Ukrainian pioneers. A month after the final installment of his travelogue appeared in *Svoboda*, it was also published in booklet form under its series title, *Kanadiis'ka Rus': Podorzhni spomyny* (*Canadian Ruthenia: Travel Memoirs*), and by early July 1897 it was already being advertised as being available from the newspaper for ten cents to readers in North America.[2] Even more importantly, the fifty-six-page imprint was distributed in western Ukraine, educating potential immigrants about what they could expect to find if they were to settle on the Canadian prairies. Thus, in one fell swoop Fr. Dmytrow broke ground for Ukrainian-language journalism in Canada, as well as being responsible for the publication of the second work of non-fiction documenting the Ukrainian-Canadian experience.

While churning out his weekly installments for his *Kanadiis'ka Rus'* series, Dmytrow also found time on the road to produce an equally historic piece of literary prose that creatively blended fictional with non-fictional elements. It was based on an event that Dmytrow had learned of, or heard about, from people he met along the way, and was later followed by other works of short fiction written in a similar vein. The very first of these hybrid works was authored or completed in Calgary, where in 1897 rail passengers going to Edmonton had to transfer to the northern C & E line. Titled "Ruska paskha—i frantsuzkii ks'ondz. Obrazok z zhytia emigrantiv" ("Ruthenian Easter—and a French Catholic Priest: A Scene from Emigrant Life"), it begins with an account of an immigrant couple from Galicia travelling by train across southern Alberta on the eve of Easter celebrations.

"Ruthenian Easter—and a French Catholic Priest" tells the story of Stepan and Maryna and their two small children as they contemplate their imminent arrival in Calgary. Stepan hopefully asks Maryna if they would be eating *paska* that Easter, only to have her snap at him and complain derisively about having been brought "somewhere to the ends of the earth, where it wasn't the way it should be among people ..." (Dmytrow, "A Ruthenian" 56).[3] Stepan avoids antagonizing her further and instead retreats into a daydream about how Easter was celebrated in his native village, recalling the extreme fasting of the older people and the hi-jinks of the boys, who would steal gates and mischievously burn them along with wagon wheels and stamp mills. He especially relishes his memories about assisting the priest and taking part in all of the rituals associated with the Easter service, while also recollecting how as a child he had once sinfully "pinched raisins from the *paska*" (56) and broken the meatless fast by gulping down some *kovbasa* (sausage) behind a barn on the Saturday before the Holy Resurrection Liturgy.

Upon reaching Calgary the family immediately proceeds to the Immigration hall, where they meet up with other fellow Ruthenians who have temporarily decamped there. Determined to commemorate Easter in the traditional manner, the newcomers have already begun baking Easter bread, or *paska*, and obtaining the eggs and meat that are essential ingredients of the traditional paschal meal. While Maryna scrambles to catch up with the other women making preparations for the Easter feast, Stepan and the men discuss the problem of finding a clergyman who would come and bless their special dishes as custom required. The only problem is that at this time there were as yet no Ukrainian priests in Canada, and Roman Catholic clergymen were totally unfamiliar with the Easter rituals as practised by the Slavic settlers from eastern Europe.[4]

The men decide that since there is a nearby Roman Catholic church, two of them would go to it and summon its pastor to perform the blessing. They deduce that even "though it's not quite like our faith … our reverends wouldn't always be going there on church holidays to give confession, because if it were a sin, then our reverends wouldn't go there, of that you can be sure" (57). Their comments are incongruously drawn from the Ukrainian experience in the United States, where Greek Catholic clerics had been residing since the 1880s, while Dmytrow was the first Ukrainian priest to visit Canada.

Be that as it may, Stepan is one of the men delegated to the task because he had been a sexton in the old country, and therefore knew how to properly conduct himself with men of the cloth. The utter naivety of the peasant immigrants is conveyed by Dmytrow in his observation that "along the way they debated whether the priest knew Ruthenian or not, but they came to the conclusion that anyone with an educated mind like that of a priest, would have to speak Ruthenian" (57). After coming to the door, listening to the request of the two men, and failing to make any sense of their babbling before vainly trying to speak to them in French, English, and German, the Reverend Father nevertheless takes his hat and goes with them to the Immigration Hall although he has no idea of what was being asked of him.

The immigrants are next confronted with the challenge of how to explain to the priest that they want him to bless the foods that they have laid out before him. As hard as they might try using mimed gestures, they are unable to successfully convey what they want the French Canadian *pater* to do. Eventually, he determines that his hosts are obviously devout Christians, and decides that they must have generously invited him to come and share in their feast. When he reaches out to help himself to some of the food, the immigrants react with alarm because they believe he is simply raiding their Easter provisions without first performing the appropriate blessing with holy water. The story ends on a somewhat comic note of mutual misunderstanding, with Stepan scratching himself "once more on the nape of his neck as if to say, 'It's not the same here, the way our reverends bless paska!'" (57). This theme of cultures colliding due to a lack of understanding is one that Dmytrow would return to in several of his other later works with New World settings.

"Ruthenian Easter" appeared in the 20 May 1897 issue of *Svoboda*, but at the bottom it was datelined "Calgary 8 May 1897." It was the first piece of literary prose to be written and published by a Ukrainian in Canada, and thus has a special place in the history of Ukrainian-Canadian literature. It seems obvious that it must have been inspired by a real event, which Dmytrow undoubtedly learned about during his visit to Alberta. That this was the case is confirmed by a short news item carried in the *Edmonton Bulletin* on the front page of its weekly edition on 20 April 1897. The brief report read as follows:

> Some of the Ruthenian ladies and gentlemen who are being imported to populate the district—the parents of "future Canada"—when passing through Calgary on their way to Edmonton, took some of their bread, butter and eggs to one of the Catholic priests to have it blessed in accordance with a rite of the Greek church, of which they were members, and which rite is generally observed at Easter. The ceremony being one which is not observed in this part of the world was unknown to the priest and he erroneously supposed that the "necessities of life" brought to him were in the way of donations and not

wishing to take any of their much needed supplies and also not wishing to offend the foreigners, took a little of each. The wearers of the sheepskin coats with the fur inside, thereupon saw that something was wrong and when they realized the situation hurriedly retired, evidently believing that "a half loaf (even though unblessed) was better than no bread."

Since the *Bulletin* story was published on the very day that Dmytrow left Winnipeg for Alberta, it seems almost certain that he read it following his arrival in Edmonton, or perhaps saw a copy of the paper while travelling on the train from Calgary. Then again, he may not have ever read the article at all, but merely learned of the incident that formed the kernel of "Ruthenian Easter" from the immigrants he encountered en route. Whatever the source, it can be stated unequivocally that Dmytrow's first literary sketch written in Canada was based on an actual occurrence, to which Dmytrow added his own creative touches. It is somewhat curious, however, that the *Bulletin* article describing the Calgary encounter appeared in print immediately after Latin Easter on 18 April 1897, but several days before Easter fell according to the eastern Rite calendar, on 25 April. One suspects that the newcomers at the Calgary Immigration Hall simply celebrated Easter according to the western Church calendar along with other Christians in Canada, a decision they made either consciously or possibly out of ignorance of the different dates. Whatever the case may be, as the story was dated on the same day that Dmytrow departed from Calgary on his return to the east, having spent a total of seventeen days in Alberta, it seems likely that the story was written while he was in the Edmonton area or on the train south, and then mailed while making the connection to Winnipeg.

Nestor Dmytrow's mission to Canada had its origin in an earlier visit made to the first Ukrainian colonies in the West by a friend and fellow immigration activist, Dr. Josef Oleskow (Iosyf Oles'kiv, 1860-1903). An agronomist from the city of Lviv (Lemberg) in Austro-Hungarian Ukraine, Oleskow made a six-week trip across Canada financed by the federal Department of the Interior in the fall of 1895 to assess how the Ruthenian settlers from Galicia were faring, learn about the areas suitable for agricultural settlement, and investigate other economic opportunities that might be available to immigrants in frontier industries needing unskilled labour. Upon completing his tour of Western Canada, Oleskow travelled to Pennsylvania to meet with Dmytrow and his circle of fellow priests and activists with a view to encouraging both the re-immigration of some American Ruthenians to the Canadian prairies, while at the same time working together to redirect the flow of immigrants from Galicia away from South America in favour of Canada. Oleskow visited the United States from 21-30 September 1895 on the invitation of Frs. Ivan Konstankevych and Nestor Dmytrow, spending time in Shamokin and Mount Carmel before returning to Ottawa for follow-up meetings at the Department of the Interior to discuss immigration issues.[5] He then made his way back to Galicia, where he wrote up a thorough overview of his findings, published in Lviv that December under the title *O emigratsii* (*About emigration*) by the M. Kachkovsky Educational Society. Written as a practical handbook and guide, it included the earliest descriptions of Alberta and the Austro-Hungarian immigrants settled in Canada's West to be published in Ukrainian. It was thanks to Oleskow's recommendation and his connections with Canadian officials in Ottawa, that Fr. Dmytrow was contracted to produce a first-hand report on the Ukrainian colonies in the Canadian West and subsequently to serve as a field immigration agent.[6]

Nestor Dmytrow was born in 1862 in the village of Utishkiv, located fifty-seven kilometers northeast of the city of Lviv in the Zolochiv region, in what is now in Busk raion of Lviv oblast. The son of farmers, he completed his secondary education at Lviv's Ruthenian Academic Gymnasium No. 13. In the fall of 1890, shortly before his twenty-eighth birthday, he entered the seminary of the Lviv Greek Catholic Archeparchy. It was as a student activist that Dmytrow got interested in the plight of the Galician peasantry that had emigrated abroad, and with like-minded friends urged young priests to minister to the settlers overseas. After finishing his theological studies and pastoral training, he was consecrated into the priesthood by the head of the Ukrainian Greek Catholic Church, Metropolitan Sylvester Sembratovych, in April 1894. A year later he immigrated to the United States, settling initially in Shamokin, Pennsylvania, in an area that had attracted a considerable number of Ukrainian immigrants from Austria-Hungary.

The thirty-four-year old Fr. Dmytrow immediately threw himself into community work, and at the second convention of the Ruthenian National Association, held in May 1895, he moved that the association purchase the newspaper *Svoboda*, which had been established by another Greek Catholic priest in September of 1893. Although the Ruthenian National Association had voted the previous February to make *Svoboda* its official organ, the paper's founder, Fr. Hryhorii Hrushka, continued to finance and legally own it. Fr. Hrushka subsequently tried to sell the newspaper when he needed money for another venture, but an attempt to assemble a co-operative formed of other clerics proved unsuccessful. Consequently, the newspaper was bought by Nestor Dmytrow and Fr. Ivan Konstankevych with their own money, the two men becoming the joint editors and publishers of the influential weekly periodical, which was also beginning to develop a readership among settlers in the fledgling Ukrainian agricultural colonies of Western Canada.

In July 1896 *Svoboda* moved its operations to Mount Carmel, west of Shamokin, where Nestor Dmytrow had relocated. Although Rev. Konstankevych assisted with the publication, Dmytrow was a leading contributor and the de facto chief editor prior to his departure for Canada.[7] His proximity to the press appears to have been responsible for initially stimulating his journalistic and literary productivity, though it has not yet been possible to determine whether or not he had ever tried his hand at writing, editing, or publishing before coming to America.

Dmytrow's account of his visits to the Ukrainian colonies in Western Canada appeared in *Svoboda* in eight installments between 22 April and 10 June 1897. His initial report from Alberta was published in the same issue as "Ruthenian Easter" on 27 May as the fifth installment of *Kanadiiska Rus*, his final submission from Alberta being printed as the seventh installment on 3 June. His commentary about his experiences chiefly focussed on the time he spent in the Edna-Star (also known as Limestone Lake and Beaver Creek) and Rabbit Hill districts outside of Edmonton. It also included some observations of a more general nature, such as the following remarks conveying his impressions of the prairie countryside, as he travelled by train between Calgary and Strathcona:

> I will not force myself to describe those boundless domains
> that stretched out on both sides of the railway tracks, because
> that would be a pointless exercise. Whoever has not seen those
> limitless, uninhabited, deserted prairies in Assiniboia[8] won't
> have the capacity to imagine them. The grass was already

greening—and hundreds of head of cattle were idly cropping the grass. I asked an Englishman where the stables for the cattle were, and he in reply waved his hand in the air, with this gesture making it known that the horizon—that was the enclosure for this steppe livestock. (Dmytrow, *Kanadiis'ka Rus'* 30-31)

Dmytrow continues his report from Alberta by relating details of his first encounter with fellow Galicians upon arriving at the end of the rail in Strathcona, or South Edmonton:

Just before the train station in Edmonton, I spotted several of our grimy women in the doorway of a building, who, upon noticing me waved their hands—they had seen me in Winnipeg and now were staying, as if quarantined, in the Immigration Hall. I subsequently went into that shelter for our people and witnessed a horrible sight. In two large rooms, strewn about the floor, amid filthy rags and gigantic Galician chests, there lay women and children of various ages. Several dirty, sleepy, and unattractive women wandered around the kitchen, where a stove smoked as if it were a locomotive. There was a murderous stench, it was simply impossible to breathe. I announced that I would come at 9 o'clock to bless the *pasky*, and quickly fled outside. At the appointed hour I returned to them, and found everything in a state of readiness. On a long table there lay gigantic *pasky* and all kinds of Easter breakfast food. The women had by now dressed up a little, and with children in their arms—were waiting for me. Following the blessing of the Easter breads, during which they loudly wept, I said a few words, presented the cross for veneration, and after I had removed my vestments strongly rebuked the women for having such untidy living quarters. The wicked women nodded their heads and blamed one another for the disarray. There were fifteen families there, generally from Yaroslav County. The men had gone off to find farms outside the city.

On Easter Friday in the afternoon, because English people don't move from their houses before noontime, I drove out in the company of a Presbyterian preacher to Edna. (31-32)

Dmytrow's harsh remarks about the women and the state of things in the Immigration Hall are classic examples of why his writings make such insightful and entertaining reading even today. Blunt to the point of being tactless, he expressed himself freely about what he saw and what he thought, often in ways that today would be considered to be politically incorrect. Indeed, his candour sometimes created problems for him, as happened in the wake of his trip to Edna-Star. That was because a few of the settlers were already subscribers to *Svoboda*, and when he described them on a couple of occasions in an unflattering light, they understandably took offense.[9]

It is possible from his descriptions of the homesteads he visited around Edna-Star to literally track quarter-section by quarter-section much of his itinerary during the week he spent northeast of Edmonton. He provides detailed information about the buildings that had been erected by each of the farmers he looked in on, the livestock they possessed, and the amount of land that had been cleared by them, so as to give an accurate picture of their relative wealth and progress. While this was clearly done for his report to Ottawa, he also includes passages about his other activities, such as this intimate description of the first eastern Rite liturgy to be celebrated in the province of Alberta:

On the very same day I also inspected the farms of all of the more established farmers and dropped into the school, which was in the process of being constructed, to prepare everything that was necessary for the Divine Service. The entire gallery wailed like little children when "Christ is Risen" was sung. After the D[ivine] S[ervice], following the blessing of the *pasky*, everyone went to their homes, and subsequently all gathered for Vespers and a cheerful discussion took place in front of the school on the celebration of Easter in the Old Country, and in Canada. The people gathered around me with genuine, heart-felt gratitude and with tears in their eyes thanked me—saying, 'Reverend-Father, for two years now we've sat like wild beasts in our shacks on Easter and sprinkled our un-blessed *paska* with tears.' I had to flee into the school to do the Vesper service, because I myself could not keep from crying. On Easter Monday I again conducted a service at the school as well as Vespers, while on Tuesday, [I did the same] in the eastern end of the colony, in the home of the honourable Ivan Halkow, from Horozhanna Mala, county of Horodok. In the course of those three days 159 people gave confession and I baptized and anointed with oil twenty-five children for them. On Wednesday and Thursday I visited farmers on the western section not far from the [North] Saskatchewan River, while on Friday [I toured] the western parts—beginning with the hon-ourable Ivan Danchuk from Borshchiv county. On Sunday, af-ter the Divine Service, there took place with great solemnity the blessing of the first Ruthenian cemetery in Canada, and at the same time we erected a cross in commemoration of free-dom. A committee was also elected which after the harvest was to undertake the building of a church and a residence for a future priest. (Dmytrow, *Kanadiis'ka Rus'* 34-35)

Dmytrow's account of his time in Alberta concludes with some fascinating observations that he made about his trip back to Winnipeg from Edmon-ton, several of his anecdotes providing glimpses into what train travel was like in Canada at the end of the nineteenth century.

In the meantime, Nestor Dmytrow's presence in the Edmonton area had been noted in a front page announcement in the *Edmonton Bulletin* on 26 April 1897, six days after the item appeared about the Calgary incident which served as the basis of "Ruthenian Easter". The notice read:

REV. LESTOR DYMYTRIW, of Mount Carmel, Pa., a dele-gate sent out by the Russian National Union arrived on the last train and drove out on Friday to Edna, to interview the German and Russian settlers located there, and to inspect the country and its advantages for immigration. Rev. Mr. Dymy-triw [sic] is here for the primal purpose of securing locations for fifty families from Mount Carmel, where there is a Ruthe-nian colony settled, and as the colony is becoming crowded some of these are forced to emigrate. From what the reverend gentlemen has seen of the country he is highly pleased with its prospects and the field for immigration which it offers. He intends to stay in the district about two weeks.

The misspelling of his name is just one of several variants found in English-language references to him in period sources which, besides providing additional information about his endeavours, sometimes contain factual inaccuracies or details which contradict those in Dmytrow's own reports. At this time, Ukrainians (i.e., Ruthenians, Galicians, or "Bukowinians") were still often identified as Russians, hence the mention of "Russian" settlers here and elsewhere, though Ukrainians were also frequently referred to as "Austrians".

Following his return to Manitoba, Dmytrow travelled to Ottawa and made a brief side-trip to Pennsylvania before coming back to Canada in July. During the next two and half months he visited settlements in Stuartburn, Dauphin, and the rural districts around Yorkton, Saskatchewan. He was back in Alberta from 25 September to 4 October 1897, in an effort to counter the impact of a mission earlier in July by two clergymen sent by the Russian Orthodox Church in San Francisco. Although he did not write or publish anything about this second visit, his activities were described in an article published on 28 October 1897 in *Svoboda*, titled *Svoboda* "Visty z ruskykh' kolonii v Kanadi" ("News from the Ruthenian Colonies in Canada," 2-3) and written by a correspondent who was accompanying him. He also received coverage in three news items that appeared in the *Edmonton Bulletin*, one of which (on 11 October 1897) reported on the fact that he had been to Edna with Bishop Emile-Joseph Legal of the Roman Catholic Diocese of St. Albert to choose a site for a church to be constructed there in the fall.

Meanwhile, probably sometime during the summer months when he was mostly based in Winnipeg, Dmytrow began work on a longer piece of prose fiction. A novel titled *Timko Harvryliuk: Opovidanie z emihratsiinoho zhytia* (*A Story from Immigrant Life*) described the experiences of a peasant who quits Galicia for Canada. The opening chapter was carried in *Svoboda* on 2 September 1897, the eighth and last appearing on 21 October. As with *Kanadiis'ka Rus'*, the series was later issued by the Svoboda press as a seventy-nine-page booklet,[10] first advertised for the price of fifteen cents on 16 March 1899.

Each chapter of the novel relates a different phase of the immigration process, beginning with Timko making the difficult decision to leave his native village with his family for a fresh start in the New World. The chapter headings then perfectly summarize the narrative line of the novel: "Timko in Lviv"; "Timko Sells His Land"; "Timko Goes to Get His Passport"; "Timko En Route to Canada"; "Timko at Sea"; "Timko in Canada"; and "Timko on the Farm". Once again, Dmytrow distinguishes himself with some of his graphic descriptions, among them this portrayal of the effects of a storm that the immigrants suffered through during their Atlantic crossing:

> It began to grow light out. The storm subsided, the high seas grew smaller, the roaring dimmed, and afterwards only the echoes of that terrible night could be heard. The clamour still resounded in the ears of the people—[but] the sun shone brightly, and the weather outside turned beautiful. People began poking their heads out, like corpses from a grave, and looked to see if death, that angry witch, had finally withdrawn to a distance. Slowly, some of them could be seen on deck, and they were frightful looking, as if they had risen from a grave. Others, especially the women were throwing up on the middle deck, almost barfing their guts up. The unfortunate people threw up non-stop—they were heaving the whole day. They were even up-chucking last year's *paska*, not just potatoes and cabbage. Where does all of that vomit come from?!—Gradually, people showed up for breakfast. Looking like cadavers, they groaned and rued that moment, when the idea came to them to travel on that cursed ship. (*Svoboda* 1)

Needless to say, Dmytrow was obviously trying to paint as realistic a picture as possible of some of the hardships that immigrants might expect to be faced with coming to Canada so as to prepare them for their journey. His journalistic pieces contain some equally explicit depictions, often dealing with the dirty and dishevelled appearance of Galician and Bukovynian peasants, and their unfamiliarity with elementary sanitary practises.

The final chapter of the novel is devoted to the long train trip to Edmonton and to Timko's settlement on a homestead in the Ukrainian colony northeast of the city. The account of the former clearly draws in part on the impressions that Dmytrow first wrote up in "Ruthenian Easter" and *Kanadiis'ka Rus'*:

> By the morning of the second day the train had already reached Assiniboia. Timko looked outside and was seized by fear. It was a wasteland, a boundless wasteland. Wherever you cast your eye, there was stunted, dry grass. There wasn't so much as a patch of cultivated land, nor was there a single shrub to be seen. Everything was uninhabited and mute, except that far, far away you might see a herd of livestock and a pack of horses. All day long the train rolled through that wasteland, all day long Timko looked through the window. (*Svoboda* 2)

The sense of the expansiveness, emptiness, and seeming desolation of the southern prairies was acutely felt by the pioneers from the Austro-Hungarian provinces of western Ukraine, who were used to living in crowded villages that dotted a typically more verdant and less monotonous landscape. Fortunately, the situation brightened the closer one got to Edmonton, as is evident in this passage about approaching the city from the much drier south:

> on the following day Timko transferred to a different train and again spent a full day travelling, right until evening. From the afternoon of that day the countryside finally gave way to fields and forests. It was an undulating land, covered with forests, amongst which there were fields of wheat. Our muzhik breathed easier and spontaneously began to whisper a prayer. Before nightfall the train finally came to a stop and everyone went to the local immigration hall. (2)

The story then continues with a description of the two-day trip by wagon to the Ukrainian settlement and some details about how the Havryliuks established themselves on a homestead in the pioneering community. The novel ends with Timko's optimistic prediction for the future—appropriate considering the author's priestly vocation—as he digs in the family garden with his initially skeptical wife, Paraska:

> "There will be churches, and it will be like it is among peo-
> ple, if only God grants us good health," Timko concluded and
> tossed out a gigantic potato with his shovel. (3)

Therefore, despite depicting the many challenges and fears that needed to be overcome by emigrants to Canada, Dmytrow's ultimate goal was to encourage others to follow in Timko's footsteps.

After spending the winter in Buffalo, New York,[11] where his wife Konstance Konstankevych gave birth to their first child (a son they named after his father), Dmytrow returned to Canada to work as an immigration agent for the federal government.[12] Although he planned to make an another trip to Alberta in the summer of 1898, he did not get further west than Saskatchewan—probably because he had been successful in helping to recruit another Greek Catholic priest and fellow Ukrainian activist from Galicia, Rev. Paul Tymkiewich, who arrived in Edmonton in May 1898. Nor did Dmytrow ever come back to Canada once he had returned to the United States in the fall of that year.

Given the rigours of travel at the end of the nineteenth century, the demands of his schedule, and the purpose of his mission, Dmytrow's literary achievements are in retrospect quite remarkable. Besides his travelogue, his novel, and additional journalistic articles, he also authored four other literary prose pieces in a series called "Scenes from Canada," complementing similar works that he wrote for *Svoboda* in a sequence titled "Scenes from America." Two of the other Canadian short stories by Dmytrow, like "Ruthenian Easter," were inspired by actual events. "Vyishla za Menonita" ("She Married a Mennonite"), printed in *Svoboda* in installments on 24 February and 3 March 1898, described the courtship and marriage of a daughter of a Ukrainian homesteader with the son a neighbouring Mennonite farmer. It was clearly inspired by a *Svoboda* correspondent's 13 January 1898 report of a wedding that took place two months earlier near Stuartburn, Manitoba, conducted by a priest with the Russian Orthodox Mission. The second story or literary sketch, published in *Svoboda* on 24 March 1898 under the English-language heading "ASSIMILATION," was an account of another early intermarriage, this time between a Ukrainian girl and an Englishman in the Dauphin area in mid-October 1897. Documented in a *Svoboda* item on 4 November 1897, it is noteworthy that Dmytrow chose to transpose the event into a third person account—without mentioning himself by name—even though he personally officiated at the nuptials. Why he chose to fictionalize the event is open to question, but he may have done so to feel freer in commenting on the wedding, or to remove himself as a pivotal character in the proceedings.

Besides his other Canadian works, which include a tale about an aged father searching for a lost son and a satirical story about a naïve teacher who immigrates in the hope of finding an easy life in the New World, Dmytrow published a variety of articles, some American fiction, a little poetry as well as a couple of translations in *Svoboda* in the late 1890s and early 1900s. However, in terms of his overall output as a writer it is his Canadian oeuvre that holds the greatest interest, not only for its historical significance but for its unique content and literary qualities. Although his literary ambitions were modest, Dmytrow possessed a keen eye for detail and recognized material that would make a good story, or at least one that would be interesting to readers of *Svoboda* in the Americas and in the Old Country. He understood that the Canadian West would appear exotic and enticing to the Ukrainian peasants he wanted to coax in the direction of Canada instead of South America, and he set out to educate them by means of journalism and fiction to better prepare them for immigration overseas.

In terms of non-fiction, Josef Oleskow's *O emigratsii* (*About Emigration*, 1985) provides a useful contrast to Dmytrow's travelogue, *Kanadiis'ka Rus.'* Both works cover much of the same ground literally and figuratively, describing trips made across some of the same parts of Canada, and being motivated by the same concerns—namely, they were written primarily as informational reports and intended to offer practical guidance for potential settlers. The two authors, who knew each other, also had similar attitudes towards the Ukrainian peasantry, most notable in the frustration that they repeatedly expressed about the low level of culture typical of the vast majority of *muzhiks*. Each could not resist editorializing about their fellow countrymen in moralizing and rather patronizing ways, but they were at the same time equally optimistic about the long-term prospects of the settlers that they encountered in Canada. And, of course, the objective of the two works was to encourage western

Ukrainian immigrants to choose Canada over Brazil, a goal that they fulfilled in related, yet different ways.

Whereas *O emigratsii* reads in large part like the study and handbook that it is, having been written by an author with a scientific background, *Kanadiis'ka Rus'* has qualities that are more akin to an adventure story, as its narrative is infused with Dmytrow's distinct personality. Certainly, the fact that the latter had a worldview that was grounded in pastoral work ministering to a wide range of people, naturally gave him a less clinical outlook and made him more visceral in his responses. Oleskow's detailed discussions of the geography, climate, soil, flora, and agricultural suitability of the terrain he passed through inevitably have the character of a textbook, which befits a man of his training and professional disposition, but makes for drier reading. Dmytrow, on the other hand, conveys similar information—admittedly, without the same depth, breadth, or expertise—in a concise and colloquial manner, making his travelogue much more engaging, if not as thorough or itemized in its presentation.

While both authors provide inventories of the situation of individual farmers they visited, Dmytrow also includes sketches of some of the unusual people he met along the way, giving a strong anecdotal quality to his chronicle. And because Dmytrow wrote his travelogue in a series of despatches that were published while he was still on the road, there is an immediacy about them that is missing from Oleskow's summary of his Canadian tour, which he undoubtedly organized and polished after his return to Galicia. Thus, Dmytrow's impressions of "Canadian Ruthenia" are documented in a chronological narrative in which each installment picks up where the previous one left off, while Oleskow structures his material more thematically, and only broadly corresponding to his itinerary. The latter approach enables the Lviv professor to go into greater detail on specific subjects that he believes are important to address, but it disrupts the overall flow and lacks the spontaneity that are the attractive features of Dmytrow's prose.

The difference between the two authors is especially evident in their commentaries about train travel, with Dmytrow distinguishing himself with his vivid vignettes of fellow passengers, and Oleskow conveying a lot of well-researched facts and observations about fares, the landholdings of Canadian railway companies, and the expanses traversed in getting to the settlement areas. Dmytrow essentially takes his readers along with him on his journey, dramatically describing how he stumbled through dense bush at dusk when trying to reach a remote colony outside of Dauphin, Manitoba, or how he rode two days on a wagon from Edmonton to the Edna-Star colony in the company of a disagreeable Presbyterian preacher and a free-spirited youth who was their driver.

In short, although the objectives of the two men were the same and there are many parallels in the stories they tell about Canada, they informed readers using different, if complementary strategies—*Kanadiis'ka Rus'* having a more literary feel to it, by virtue of its conversational style and serial structure. Not only that, but by also utilizing fiction as a vehicle for discussing the immigrant experience, Dmytrow showed a canny understanding of how to wrap some of the lessons he sought to impart in the form of compelling and artistically rendered tales. For instance, in *Timko Havryliuk*, he portrays Josef Oleskow (without specifically naming him) as a stuffy Lviv professor and implicitly criticizes him for the fact that *O emigratsii* was published by the conservative and Russophile Kachkovsky Society, and not the rival Ukrainophile Prosvita Society, which had a politically progressive orientation. Nevertheless, Dmytrow at the same time acknowledges that Oleskow was the leading authority on immigration to Canada, and encourages aspiring immigrants to look to him for advice.

As for Dmytrow's fictional writings, they somewhat resemble works by two other authors who made their reputations writing about the Canadian West around the turn of the century: Ralph Connor and Emily Murphy. Like them, he was a promoter of settlement on the prairies, which all three depicted as an exciting, if occasionally daunting frontier offering both great opportunity and adventure. However, Dmytrow's works certainly did not enjoy the commercial success of his Canadian counterparts, due in large part to the fact that his audience was circumscribed by issues of language and limited literacy. However, he also had a more utilitarian attitude towards fiction, which is especially apparent in *Timko Harvryliuk*. Rather than developing a contrived plot or exploring different characters in his novella, he remains chiefly focussed on using his hero's travails in making his way to Canada so as to explain all of the steps required, and the pitfalls to be avoided, in successfully reaching a homestead on the prairies. Many of the descriptions are vividly drawn and Timko is convincing in his role as a typical Galician peasant, and there are also nice touches such as the exaggerated remarks about the seasickness experienced on the ocean crossing. While hardly an epic rivalling other works in the extensive body of literature comprising the New World immigrant genre, *Timko Havryliuk* (along with *Kanadiis'ka Rus'*, i.e., *Scenes from Canada*) effectively served its ultimate purpose, which was to encourage, guide, and reassure at least some of the settlers seeking a better life in a strange and distant land.

Some nine decades after his death, and more than a hundred and fifteen years after he visited Canada, Nestor Dmytrow's Canadian stories still make for captivating reading, and not just for historical reasons. That is because they memorably capture a time, people, and places that while far removed from our present day and age, remain fresh and vibrant thanks to his efforts as a pioneering writer in Canada's West.

NOTES

1   Although pronounced "Dmytreev" in Ukrainian (with the stress on the first syllable) and commonly spelled "Dmytriw" in many English-language Canadian sources, letters signed by the Reverend and contemporaneous references to him in English (including legal documents) almost always rendered his last name with an "o," the spelling used by his family and found on his death certificate and tombstone. The source of the two variants is the orthography used by late nineteenth-century Ukrainian, in which the printed accented "ó" was pronounced "ee". It is also worth noting that for his published works, Dmytrow often simply used his name without his clerical title, most likely to underscore his progressive views.

2   Ruthenia is a Latinized form of Rus,' the medieval principality ruled from the city of Kyiv between the tenth and the thirteen centuries, before being dismembered under the impact of the Mongol invasion. "Rusyn" (sometimes spelled Rusin, or rendered as Ruthenian) was the name that most Ukrainians used to identify themselves until the end of the nineteenth century, after which it was displaced by the modern term "Ukrainian" from the designation "Ukraine," first popularized on maps from the Cossack era. In the eighteenth century Muscovite tsars adopted and adapted the name "Russia" from "Rus'," so as to symbolically lay claim to the inheritance of Kyivan Rus' hundreds of years after its demise.

3   All excerpts from Dmytrow's works cited in this essay are translated from Ukrainian by me. The translation of "Ruthenian Easter" by Myroslav Shkandrij contains some slight differences with my own rendering in English.

4   In 1596 a section of the Orthodox Church in Ukraine and Belarus entered an agreement that created a Byzantine-Rite Catholic Church recognizing the authority of the Holy See in Rome, in exchange for being allowed to retain most of the ecclesiastical practises and customs of the eastern Church, which included keeping the Julian calendar.

5   For details about Oleskow's mission to Canada, see Kaye. A scan of the original of *O emigratsii* [*About Emigration*] can be accessed electronically through Peel's Prairie Provinces, the online bibliography of the Bruce, Peel Special Collections Library at the University of Alberta.

6   Like Dmytrow, Oleskow should be pronounced "Oleskeev" and is therefore written as "Oleskiw" in some English-language sources.

7   *Svoboda* continued to be published in Mount Carmel until 12 July 1900, after which the paper was produced out of Olyphant, Pennsylvania, just north of Scranton. See Mushuha (45) and Kravcheniuk (6). This Ukrainian-language newspaper currently published in Jersey City, New Jersey, hosts a complete digital archive of its newspapers from 1893 to the present, and is the most convenient place to look up issues cited in this paper.

8   Assiniboia was the name given to southern Saskatchewan and a part of southeastern Alberta before the 1905 creation of the three prairie provinces. In 1897, Calgary and Edmonton were technically within that part of the Northwest Territories which was administratively known as the District of Alberta.

9   As was fairly common among clergy and many others of his generation, Dmytrow had very negative and stereotypically anti-Semitic opinions concerning Jews, also holding Orthodox Bukovynians in low regard, albeit for different reasons. On more than one occasion, he praised Native Canadians as being more dignified than the Ukrainian immigrants to Canada, and unfavourably contrasted settlers from Galicia and Bukovyna with those who had migrated to the United States from the Lemko region of Carpathian Ukraine. At the same time, he disparaged the often submissive attitude of his peasant countrymen and Galician women in general, and was especially critical of their uncouth behavior and indifference to matters of personal hygiene. However, he greatly esteemed the values of English civilization and liked "American women" for their assertive self-confidence.

10 Published versions of the novella are extremely rare, though a microfilm of it is available at the New York Public Library, where its title is transliterated as *Timko Gavriilukw: opoviedanie zw emigratiinogo zita* [sic].

11 Interestingly, the only mention made of Dmytrow in the Calgary press was a short news item on page four of the *Calgary Herald* on 11 November 1897 announcing that: "Rev. Nestor Dimitrov, the Greek Catholic priest who recently visited the Galician settlement at Edmonton, has returned to Philadelphia. He will return in May, bringing a priest of his church for Edmonton."

12 As part of the agreement that created the Greek Catholic Church in Ukraine and Belarus, Rome allowed for parish priests to be married, as has always been customary in the Orthodox Church. However, there are questions surrounding Dmytrow's marital status when he arrived in North America, since Roman Catholic bishops in the United States and Canada fiercely opposed the immigration of any non-celibate Greek Catholic clergy. The possibility exists that Dmytrow might have wed in Pennsylvania, after his ordination, which technically would be in violation of canonical procedure.

Works Cited

Dmytrow, Nestor. *Kanadiis'ka Rus.' Podorozhni spomyny*. [Canadian Ruthenian: Travel Memoirs]. Mt. Carmel, Pa, Vydavnytsvo chasopys "Svoboda," 1897, pp. 30-2, 34-5.

———. *Kanadiis'ka Rus'. Podorozhni spomyny* [Canadian Ruthenia: Travelers Memoirs]. Winnipeg, Ukrainian Free Academy of Sciences, 1972. Sources for the History of Ukrainians in Canada 1. Originally published in 1898, edited and introduced by Michael Marunchak.

———. "A Ruthenian Easter—and a French Catholic Priest. A Scene from Emigrant Life." Translated by Jars Balan. *Alberta Views*, Mar.-Apr. 2004, pp. 56-7.

———. "Ruthenian Easter—and a French Catholic Priest. A Scene from Emigrant Life." Translated by Jars Balan. *Logos: A Journal of Eastern Christian Studies*, vol. 46, nos. 3–4, 2005, pp. 477-82.

———. "Ruthenian Easter and the French Catholic Priest: A Scene from the Life of Emigrants (1897)." Translated by Myroslav Shkandrij, www.umanitoba.ca/faculties/arts/world_literature/uk/dmytriw.shtml. Accessed 29 Nov. 2016.

———. *Timko Havryliuk. Opovidanie z emihratsiinoho zhytia.* [Timko Havryliuk: A Story From Emigrant Life] Mt. Carmel, Pa., Z drukarni "Svobody," 1899, catalog.nypl.org/search~S1?/tTimko+Gavriliuk/ttimko+gavriliuk/1,1,1,B/frameset&FF=ttimko+gavriliuk&1,1,?save=b16806118. Accessed 29 Nov. 2016. Excerpts translated by Jars Balan.

Kaye, Vladimir J. *Early Ukrainian Settlements in Canada 1895-1900. Dr. Josef Oleskow's Role in the Settlement of the Canadian Northwest.* U of Toronto P, 1964.

Kravcheniuk, Dr. Osyp. "Holvni redaktory" (The Main Editors). *Svoboda*, 15 Sept. 1993, p. 6.

Mushuha, Dr. Luka, editor. *Propamiatna Knyha vydana z nahody soroklitn'oho iuvileiu Ukrains'koho Narodnoho Soiuzu* (Memorial Book Published on the Occasion of the Fortieth Anniversary of the Ukrainian National Association). Ukrainian National Association, 1936, p. 45.

"Local," *Edmonton Bulletin*, 20 Apr. 1897, p. 1.

———. *Edmonton Bulletin*, 26 Apr. 1897, p. 1.

———. *Edmonton Bulletin*, 11 Oct. 1897, p. 1.

Olesk'ov, Iosif. *O emigratsii* [About Emigration]. Lviv, M. Kachkovsky Society, 1895, peel.library.ualberta.ca/www/peelbib/2229/pages/4/Pg004.png. Accessed 29 Nov. 2016.

Svoboda [Liberty]. 1893-2016, www.svoboda-news.com/arxiv.htm. Accessed 29 Nov. 2016.

Contributors

JARS BALAN is an Edmonton author, poet, editor, and literary translator. Since 2000 he has served as Coordinator of the Kule Ukrainian Canadian Studies Centre for the Canadian Institute of Ukrainian Studies at the University of Alberta. A specialist in the history of Ukrainians in Canada, he has written and published extensively on Ukrainian Canadian literature and drama. Another of his interests is the inauguration of organized religious life among Ukrainian immigrants to Canada.

DONNA COATES is an Associate Professor in the English Department at the University of Calgary. She has published dozens of articles and book chapters on women's literary responses in fiction and drama to the First and Second World Wars, to the Vietnam War, and to contemporary warfare. With Sherrill Grace, she has selected and co-edited *Canada and the Theatre of War, Volume One: Eight First and Second World War Plays* (2008), and *Volume Two: Six Contemporary Plays* (2010). With George Melnyk, she has edited *Wild Words: Essays on Alberta Literature* (2009). Her edited collection of essays, *Sharon Pollock: First Woman of Canadian Theatre*, appeared in 2015. She is currently completing a manuscript on Australian women's fictional responses to twentieth-century wars and is compiling an eight-volume anthology set on women and war for Routledge Press' History of Feminism series.

MOIRA DAY is a Professor of Drama, Adjunct Professor in the Women's and Gender Studies program and associate of the Classical, Medieval and Renaissance Studies unit at the University of Saskatchewan. She has published and edited extensively in the area of Canadian theatre. A former co-editor of *Theatre Research in Canada* (1998-2001), she has also edited two scholarly play anthologies featuring the work of pioneering and contemporary western Canadian playwrights, and a book of essays on contemporary western Canadian theatre and playwriting. She has also co-edited two special issues of *Theatre Research in Canada*: Canadian Theatre Within the Context of World (with Don Perkins, University of Alberta) and Theatre and Religion in Canada (with Mary Ann Beavis, St. Thomas More College). She also recently co-edited a special issue of *Canadian Theatre Review*, titled "The New Saskatchewan."

R. DOUGLAS FRANCIS is Professor Emeritus of History at the University of Calgary, where he specializes in Canadian intellectual history and western Canadian history. He is the author of *Frank H. Underhill: Intellectual Provocateur* (1986), *Images of the West: Changing Perceptions of the Prairies, 1690-1960* (1989), and *The Technological Imperative in Canada: An Intellectual History* (2009). He is a co-author of a two-volume history of Canada: *Origins: Canadian History to Confederation*, 7th ed. (2012), and *Destinies: Canadian History since Confederation*, 7th ed. (2012). He has co-edited a number of volumes, including *Canada and the British World: Culture, Migration and Identity* (2006) and *The Prairie West as Promised Land* (2007), and has published numerous articles in his areas of specialty.

KATHERINE GOVIER is an Edmonton-born novelist, whose first novel, *Random Descent*, described the lives of Alberta townspeople. Her next Alberta novel, *Between Men*, was set in late nineteenth-century Calgary. She has published a total of ten novels, three short story collections, and several works of non-fiction. She spends her summers in Canmore, Alberta. She has received both the Marian Engel Award and the Toronto Book Award for her writing. Her latest novel, *The Three Sisters Bar and Hotel*, was published in 2016. It is set in Canmore.

TASHA HUBBARD (Nêhiyaw/Nakota/Metis) is a filmmaker and writer, and the mother of a nine-year-old son. Her first solo writing/directing project Two Worlds Colliding, about Saskatoon's infamous Starlight Tours, premiered at ImagineNATIVE in 2004, was broadcast on CBC's documentary program Roughcuts in 2004, and won the Canada Award at the 2005 Geminis. Her recent animated short film, Buffalo Calling, screened as part of the Ga Ni Tha exhibit held on the occasion of the 2015 Venice Biennale.

She is in post-production on an NFB-produced documentary about a 1960s Scoop family. As part of her academic career at the University of Saskatchewan, Tasha does research in Indigenous digital media, the buffalo and Indigenous ecologies, and Indigenous women and children's experiences.

GEORGE MELNYK is Professor Emeritus of Communication, Media and Film Studies at the University of Calgary. He began his research into Alberta literature in the 1990s. The result was the two-volume *Literary History of Alberta* (1998-99). In 2003 he co-edited *The Wild Rose Anthology of Alberta Prose* with Tamara Seiler. This collection was followed in 2009 with *Wild Words: Essays on Alberta Literature*, which he co-edited with Donna Coates. Professor Melnyk is the author or editor of over twenty-five books relating to Canada. He is also an essayist, whose latest collection, *First Person Plural*, was published in 2015.

JOSEPH PIVATO is Professor of Literary Studies at Athabasca University, Edmonton. His research is focused on ethnic minority writing and Canadian literature. His publications include several books, such as *Africadian Atlantic: Essays on George Elliott Clarke* (2012), *Mary di Michele: Essays on Her Works* (2007), *Echo: Essays on Other Literatures* (1994), *F.G. Paci: Essays on His Works* (2003), *Contrasts: Comparative Essays on Italian-Canadian Writing* (1985 and 1991), *Caterina Edwards: Essays on Her Works* (2000), *The Anthology of Italian-Canadian Writing* (1998), *Pier Giorgio Di Cicco* (2011), and articles in academic journals and book chapters. He has been a Visiting Professor at Macquarie University and the University of Wollongong in Australia, at the University of Udine in Italy, and the University of Toronto, and an invited speaker at international conferences. After a B.A. (English and French) from York University, Toronto, he earned an M.A. and Ph.D. (Comparative Literature) from the University of Alberta.

NEIL QUERENGESSER is Dean of Arts at Concordia University of Edmonton. He is a Professor of English literature specializing in Canadian poetry and its intersections with the discourses of science and theology. His recent publications include articles on the poetry of Tim Lilburn, Margaret Avison, and Susan McCaslin. He is also co-editor of the authoritative edition of Robert Stead's *Dry Water* (University of Ottawa Press, 2008).

Tamara Palmer Seiler is Professor Emeritus (Canadian Studies) in the Department of Communication, Media and Film, at the University of Calgary. Her research and teaching interests have included Canadian and American literature, rhetoric, Canadian immigration history, narratives about immigrant and ethnic minority experience, multiculturalism, North American cultural history, and the West in North America. She has published a number of articles and book chapters on the representation of immigrant and ethnic minority experience in Canadian literature, and is the co-author/editor of several books and articles on Alberta history and culture. Her latest book (co-authored with Robert M. Seiler) is *Reel Time: Movie Exhibitors and Movie Audiences in Prairie Canada, 1896-1986* (Athabasca University Press, 2013).

Geo Takach is Associate Professor, School of Communication and Culture, Royal Roads University. He is a veteran writer, filmmaker, and instructor who has taught diverse aspects of communication at four Albertan universities and beyond. His efforts as a professional communicator and/or artist span hundreds of publications in speeches, print, film, radio, television, and cyberspace. His epic exploration of essences of Alberta's soul led to the production of a documentary film for television (*Will the Real Alberta Please Stand Up?*), an award-winning book bearing the same title, and an award-winning Ph.D. dissertation (University of Calgary) in the area of environmental communication. His research has been profiled in national, provincial, and local media, where he has also been quoted as an expert on issues around Alberta, identity, and the bituminous sands. His most recent books are *Tar Wars* (University of Alberta Press, 2016) and *Scripting Environmental Communication* (Palgrave Macmillan, 2016).

Harry Vandervlist is an Associate Professor in the Department of English, University of Calgary. He writes on modernist fiction, in particular Samuel Beckett's early work, and on Canadian literature, focusing on the Banff poet Jon Whyte (whose collected poems he edited in 2000) and literary representations of the Rocky Mountains. He has published numerous reviews and author profiles of Canadian poets (*Quill and Quire, Alberta Views Magazine*, and *Fast Forward Weekly*), and has served on the editorial boards of the University of Calgary Press and NeWest Press. Recent publications include "The Challenge of Writing Bioregionally: Performing the

Bow River in Jon Whyte's Minisniwapta: Voices of the River" (*The Biore-gional Imagination*, edited by Thomas Lynch, Cheryll Glotfelty, and Karla Armbruster, University of Georgia Press, 2012) and "Re-Envisioning Epic in Jon Whyte's Rocky Mountain Poem 'The Fells of brightness'" (*Sustaining the West*, edited by L. Piper and L. Szabo, Wilfrid Laurier University Press, 2015).

CYNTHIA ZIMMERMAN has been a commentator on Canadian playwriting and on the voice of women on the Canadian stage for her whole career at Glendon College, York University. Now Professor Emerita, she continues to publish and teach in her research specialty areas, Canadian theatre and contemporary women playwrights. Previously book review editor of *Modern Drama* and omnibus reviewer of drama for "Letters in Canada," the *University of Toronto Quarterly* annual survey of publications, she has authored or co-authored a number of books and produced numerous articles, chapters, and public papers. She is the editor of the three-volume *Sharon Pollock: Collected Plays* (2008), *The Betty Lambert Reader* (2007), and *Reading Carol Bolt* (2010), published by Playwrights Canada Press.

a PROUD PARTNER in

Campus Alberta

A book in the Campus Alberta Collection, a collaboration of Athabasca University Press, the University of Alberta Press and the University of Calgary Press.

AU PRESS
Athabasca University

Athabasca University Press | aupress.ca

Public Deliberation on Climate Change
Lessons from Alberta Climate Dialogue
Edited by Lorelei L. Hanson
978-1-77199-215-2 (paperback)

Visiting with the Ancestors
Blackfoot Shirts in Museum Spaces
Laura Peers and Alison K. Brown
978-1-77199-037-0 (paperback)

Alberta Oil and the Decline of Democracy in Canada
Edited by Meenal Shrivastava and Lorna Stefanick
978-1-77199-029-5 (paperback)

THE UNIVERSITY
of ALBERTA PRESS

University of Alberta Press | uap.ualberta.ca

Trudeau's Tango
Alberta Meets Pierre Elliott Trudeau, 1968–1972
Darryl Raymaker
978-1-77212-265-7 (paperback)

Seeking Order in Anarchy
Multilateralism as State Strategy
Robert W. Murray, Editor
978-1-77212-139-1 (paperback)

Upgrading Oilsands Bitumen and Heavy Oil
Murray R. Gray
978-1-77212-035-6 (hardcover)

UNIVERSITY OF CALGARY
Press

University of Calgary Press | ucalgary.ca/ucpress

Writing Alberta
Building on a Literary Identity
Edited by George Melnyk and Donna Coates
978-1-55238-890-7 (paperback)

The Frontier of Patriotism
Alberta and the First World War
Edited by Adriana A. Davies and Jeff Keshen
978-1-55238-834-1 (paperback)

So Far and Yet So Close
Frontier Cattle Ranching in Western Prairie Canada and the Northern Territory of Australia
Warren M. Elofson
978-1-55238-794-8 (paperback)